WALKING THE OLD WAYS
OF SOUTH SHROPSHIRE

Mitchell's Fold stone circle, walk 7

WALKING THE OLD WAYS OF SOUTH SHROPSHIRE

The history in the landscape explored through 26 circular walks

Andy & Karen Johnson

LOGASTON PRESS

LOGASTON PRESS
The Holme, Church Road, Eardisley, Herefordshire HR3 6NJ
An imprint of Fircone Books Ltd.
www.logastonpress.co.uk

First published by Logaston Press 2019, reprinted 2021

ISBN 978-1-910839-34-8

Text and photographs copyright © Andy and Karen Johnson

All rights reserved. The moral right of the author has been asserted
Without limiting the rights under copyright reserved above, no part of this publication may be reproduced, stored in or introduced into a retrieval system, or transmitted, in any form or by any means (electronic, mechanical, photocopying, recording or otherwise), without prior written permission of the copyright owner and the above publisher of this book

Printed and bound in Poland

Logaston Press is committed to a sustainable future for our business, our readers and our planet. This book is made from paper certified by the Forest Stewardship Council

British Library Catalogue in Publishing Data
A CIP catalogue record for this book is available from the British Library

Contents

Walk Location Map   vi

Introduction   vii

Walk 1	Ludlow, Stanton Lacy & Bromfield	1
Walk 2	Craven Arms, Stokesay Castle & Norton Camp	17
Walk 3	Clungunford, Clunbury & Hopton Castle	28
Walk 4	Offa's Dyke west of Clun	40
Walk 5	Clun & Bury Ditches	45
Walk 6	Bishop's Castle	54
Walk 7	Mitchell's Fold, Ladywell & Grit Mines	62
Walk 8	Stiperstones, Tankerville & Bog Mines	70
Walk 9	Bridges & Ratlinghope	78
Walk 10	Church Pulverbatch	84
Walk 11	Picklescott, Woolstaston & Smethcott	89
Walk 12	Church Stretton & Caer Caradoc	97
Walk 13	Acton Burnell & Langley Chapel	108
Walk 14	Holdgate, Shipton & Wilderhope Manor	117
Walk 15	Much Wenlock	127
Walk 16	Morville, Upton Cressett & Aston Eyre	137
Walk 17	Bridgnorth and south	148
Walk 18	Worfield	162
Walk 19	Claverley	170
Walk 20	Highley	179
Walk 21	Cleobury Mortimer, Mawley Hall & Reaside Manor	187
Walk 22	Stottesdon & Sidbury	197
Walk 23	Bitterley & Titterstone Clee	204
Walk 24	Burwarton, Aston Botterell & Brown Clee	217
Walk 25	Bouldon, Clee St Margaret, Nordy Bank, Tugford & Broncroft	230
Walk 26	Diddlebury	242

Index   253

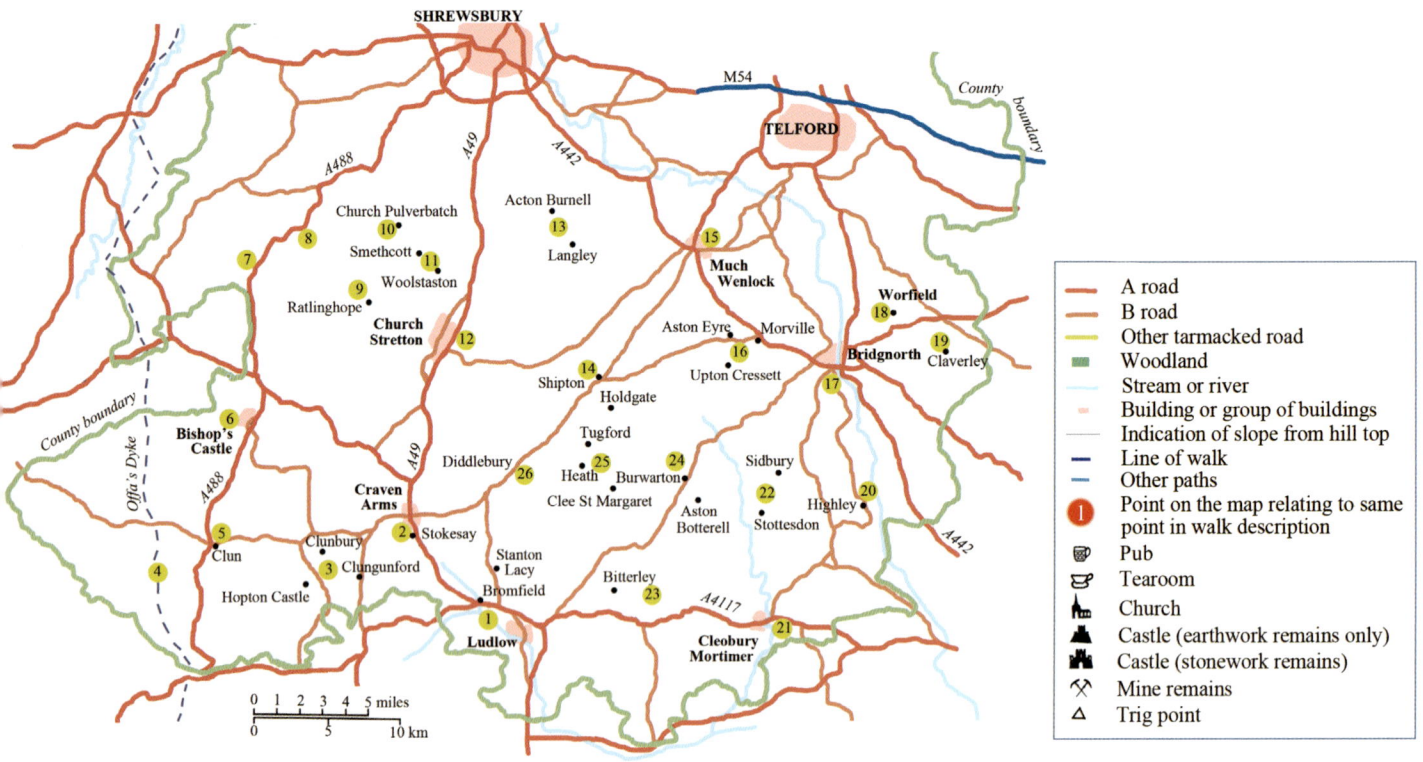

Map of south Shropshire showing the locations of the walks

vi

Introduction

The walks in this book have been designed to take you by paths, tracks and minor roads to a cross-section of the area's history. Each walk includes a sketch map (at a rough scale of 1.75 inches to 1 mile), the numbers on the map relating to the number of the appropriate stage of the text describing the walk. The description should be enough to guide you round the route, the maps essentially giving a bit of extra help as well as indicating how far you've gone, and how much further you have to go! We have walked each walk at least twice, once in summer and once in winter, to check that our directions can be followed at all times of the year. However, you might wish to take the relevant OS Explorer map with you so that, for example, you can identify distant hills or villages seen from viewpoints reached.

Boxed information provides the background to castles, churches, mines, prehistoric sites, stately homes, parks, mills, almshouses, deserted villages and other places of historic interest passed en route. For towns such as Ludlow, Church Stretton and Bridgnorth we have been selective about the information included, so that the book stayed portable! For sites with information boards and

A view above Coston Farm on walk 3

Goats near the walled garden of Mawley Hall, walk 21

Remains of prehistoric cairn on Stapeley Hill, walk 7

churches where there is a leaflet available we have aimed to indicate the main features and sometimes provide additional information to that given at the site.

As for when to do the walks, each season has its advantages. In summer the paths are firm underfoot, but foliage can obscure what there is to see; winter may give you clearer views but you may find yourself slithering around in mud at field gateways. In the preambles to the walks we mention obstacles that may crop up in one season or another, such as a ford, or a narrow path that can get tangled by nettles or brambles, and we indicate where it may be a good idea to wear Wellingtons.

The walks range from 3.5 to 9.5 miles in length. Given the terrain of south Shropshire it is not surprising that most are set in rolling countryside, but the occasional walk is pretty flat while some involve respectable hills. The preamble to each walk indicates the type of terrain and the nature of the paths or tracks, and also the number of stiles to be encountered, though none of the walks have too many of these.

The preamble also gives an idea of the historical features that the walk includes. If you read through the walk before you set out, that will give you a good idea of what there is to see, and also of the countryside en route. All the photographs have been taken from the walks themselves, except two aerial views (courtesy of Clwyd Powys Archaeological Trust) that help show the features of a couple of the hillforts, and one painting from a few centuries ago to show how landscaped parkland once looked.

In the months between the first and second times we walked these routes we were surprised to notice how many changes had occurred, many of them for the better: a dilapidated bridge replaced, a faulty stile renewed or even replaced by a kissing gate. Changes will continue to happen, so keep your wits about you. Some changes will be big: woods felled, a path turned into a muddy route by heavy machinery, new fences erected to sub-divide fields. Always remember that you are legally allowed to seek an alternative route around an obstruction if you find one on a public path. Of course, make sure you close any gates you open, see that if you're walking with a dog, you keep him or her under control when you're walking amongst cattle, horses or sheep, and follow all the other aspects of the Countryside Code.

We've mentioned a few pubs and tea rooms that feature on some of the rural walks, and included information current at the time of going to print. However such establishments tend to open and close depending upon trade, so it would be a good idea to check that the relevant place is going to be open before you plan a walk in which refreshment will play a key part. We haven't mentioned any such places in the larger towns, as these will always have a number of options.

We've imagined that you'll be driving to the start of the walks, so have suggested where to park. Point 1 on each map marks where each walk starts and is usually adjacent to where we've suggested you park, apart from in the towns.

Descending Caer Caradoc, walk 12

Sunken way out of Cleobury Mortimer, walk 21

Heading towards Offa's Dyke, walk 4

When we checked walks 16 and 22 in 2021 for this reprint, the problems noted in the first edition had not yet been resolved. We have notified Shropshire County Council, and trust that the issues will be sorted out soon.

We'd like to thank those of our friends who have come and tested walks with us, notably David Styan, Kathy Leong, John Rogers and Rafael Cruz. And then there are the authors we worked with when running Logaston Press, whose knowledge provided much of the information given about the history of the area: Michael Shaw and his book *The Lead, Copper & Barytes Mines of Shropshire*; Kathryn Davies and *Artisan Art, Vernacular wall paintings in the Welsh Marches, 1550-1650*; Sylvia Watts and *Shropshire Almshouses*; Barrie Trinder and *The Industrial Archaeology of Shropshire*; Roy Palmer and *The Folklore of Shropshire* and John Barratt and *Cavalier Stronghold, Ludlow in the English Civil Wars, 1642-1660*. In addition, Pevsner's *Buildings of Shropshire*, pieces by Di Bryan on Titterstone Clee, information alongside aerial photographs taken by Chris Musson, discussions with Keith Ray, Herefordshire's recent county archaeologist regarding Offa's Dyke, and the excellent Shropshire History online compiled by Shropshire Archives, together with a knowledge and feel for the south-western part of the area covered by this book over more than 30 years, have all contributed to the decisions of which possible routes to include and information provided. And of course our heartfelt thanks go to Richard and Su Wheeler of Logaston Press for publishing the book.

Andy & Karen Johnson
July 2021

View between Sidbury and Stottesdon, walk 22

Nordy Bank looking towards Brown Clee, walk 25

View of Ludlow Castle towards the end of walk 1

Walk 1
Ludlow, Stanton Lacy & Bromfield

9 Miles. A largely flat walk on a mixture of tracks, lanes and field paths with some road. It explores some of Ludlow, passes through the area of an extensive Bronze Age cemetery, visits Stanton Lacy Church, which is part Saxon, and the gatehouse of Bromfield Priory and its church, unusual for its ceiling and the fact that it was incorporated into a house, and returns with views of Oakly Park and Ludlow Castle. You can accomplish the walk without needing to cross a stile.

The walk starts at Ludlow Castle. With a town so full of history at every step, this book can only give a brief

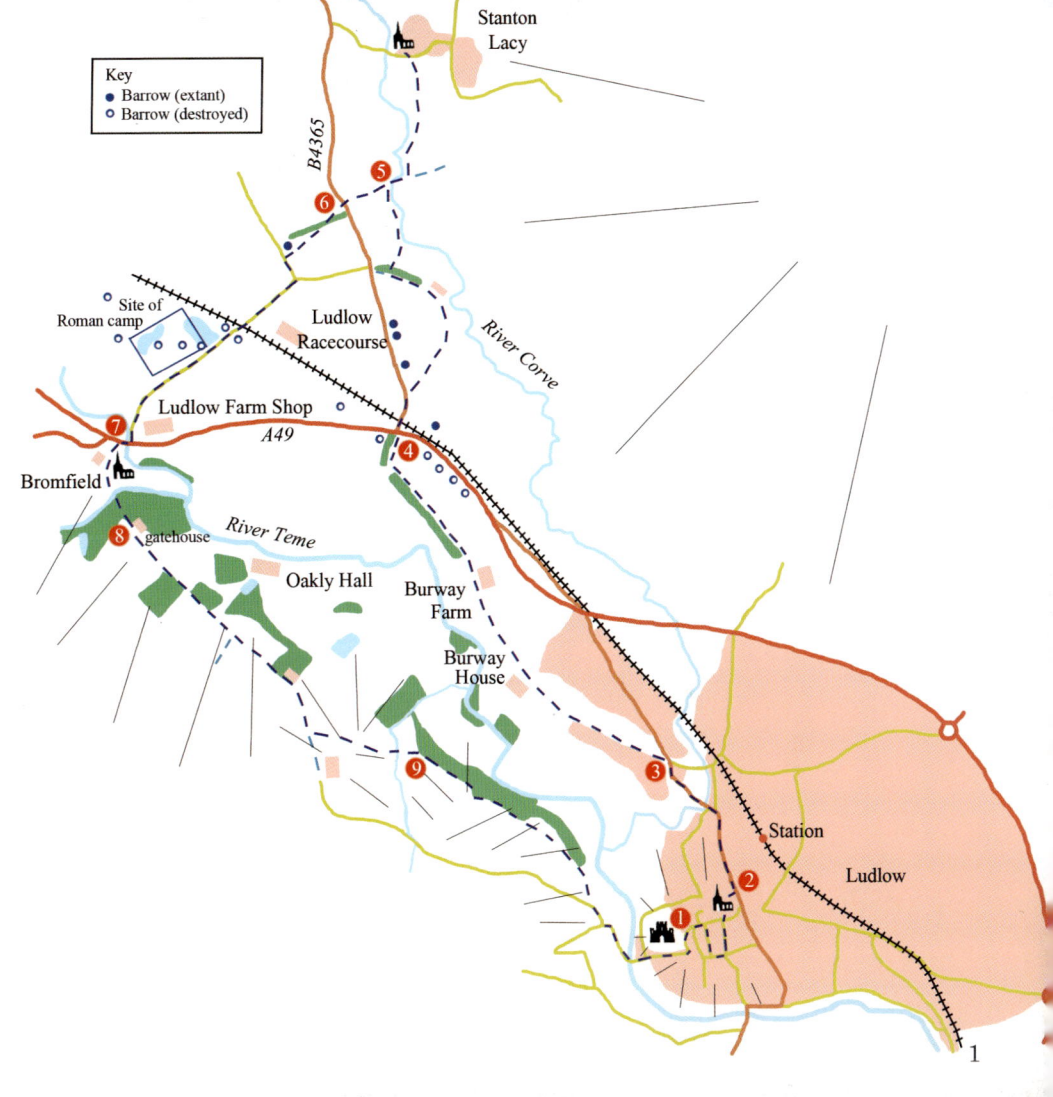

TOWN AND CASTLE

The town owes its existence to two factors: the junction of a north-south route that followed the course of what is now Corve Street and Old Street to a ford across the Teme with the Clun-Clee Ridgeway, and the siting of what became a major Norman castle. The walk will take you through an early burial cemetery at Bromfield, but there was also a tumulus where St Laurence's Church now stands: the Saxon word *hlau* or low often refers to a tumulus (though it can just refer to a hill) and it is from this that it is thought Ludlow takes part of its name, a tumulus having been reported to have been levelled on the site of the present church in 1199. 'Lud' might refer to the name of a local tribal leader, though more likely to the rapids on the River Teme, having the same derivation as 'loud' as in the noise made by the water cascading down the river. The castle was begun, probably in the late 1080s, by the Lacy family. What was the gatehouse was converted into a keep c.1130, the other significant Norman building within the complex being the unusual Round Chapel that stands in the inner ward. Town and castle had a torrid time during the Anarchy, (the civil war between Stephen and Matilda), but at the end of the 1100s the church was rebuilt, and it was probably around this time that the regimented burgage plots were laid out on the south side of the town running down to the Teme. Those boundaries near the castle were readjusted when this was extended to include an outer bailey, as were others when the town walls with their seven gates were built in the 1230s and 1260s.

The castle passed to the Mortimers by marriage in 1307, when Roger de Mortimer added extravagant new quarters fit for a queen, the queen being Isabella, wife of Edward II, with whom Mortimer consorted and ruled the kingdom for three years after Edward II's murder. By 1328, at the peak of Mortimer's power, the town had a weekly market and three annual fairs. The town prospered through the collection and marketing of wool, a trade that developed into actual cloth manufacture in the 1400s. In the early 1300s a north aisle and porch were added to the church, followed by a south transept c.1340 and a north transept after the Black Death. The church was then partially rebuilt in 1433 in the Perpendicular style, with its soaring tower.

The present centre of Ludlow owes much to the town and castle becoming the base of the Council in the Marches. This began under Edward IV, heir to the Mortimers, as the Prince's Council – a court for his sons. It was revived under Henry VII when, along with the Council in the North and the short-lived Council of the West, the Council in the Marches formed part of a Tudor system of regional government, that in Ludlow having responsibility for Wales and the Marches. The council consisted of bishops, judges, lawyers and landowning gentry and also had a permanent staff. Having meetings in Ludlow created a need for a town home for many of those involved, together with offices and accommodation for visitors. Thus much of the centre of Ludlow consists of houses built or rebuilt from the mid 1500s to the late 1600s, the council being abolished in 1689. The town continued to thrive thereafter as a 'genteel' place to visit, with, for example, a promenade laid out around the outside of the castle in 1771, whilst gloving became an important trade. The arrival of the railway, a boon for many towns, made it easy for people to visit places other than Ludlow and the town gently subsided into the role of a market town with just a handful of Victorian suburbs and no great Victorian rebuilding of the centre.

introduction to what there is to see. Books specifically on the castle and the church can be bought in each, and a range of books on local history is available at the Castle Bookshop in the market square.

❶ With your back to the castle entrance gateway, first look half-right at Castle Lodge, the large and largely stone-built house topped by a timber-framed storey. In the late 1500s this was the home of the porter and then the governor of the castle. The lodge was probably rebuilt in stone in the 1570s by Thomas Stackford, who served Sir Henry Sydney when he was President of the Council in the Marches (see the box on Ludlow Town and Castle on page 2), the timber-framed top storey being a later addition.

Now walk down the market square to its end and turn right down Raven Lane. Look out for numbers 14/15 with their carvings on the timber-framing and also number 9 with its modern carvings. At the junction at the bottom, turn left and walk along to the next junction, then turn left up Broad Street. Before you do so, look to the right to see the Broad Gate, (see photograph above), one of the remaining gateways in the old town walls. Look closely at the houses in Broad

ST LAURENCE'S CHURCH

One of the largest parish churches in the country, it is full of interest. The present building largely dates to the Perpendicular period, with elements of Decorated (notably in the rare hexagonal porch) and earlier construction. There is a wealth of stained glass that includes images and coats of arms of those associated with the castle, of the Annunciation, the legend of St Laurence, the Tree of Jesse and the Palmers' Guild. (A Palmer was a pilgrim who had been to the Holy land and brought back a palm branch as proof of their journey. Most members of the Guild weren't pilgrims, but wished to be associated with what was the chief organisation in Ludlow for some 300 years from 1250. A largely mutual organisation supporting its members, money was also given to priests to say masses for their souls.) The church also contains several ornate tombs and a memorial tablet commemorating the burial of the heart of Prince Arthur, Henry VIII's eldest son, who died in Ludlow aged 15. There is also one of the best collections of misericords (the small 'bum rests' on the underside of the choir-stall seats which helped support members of the choir when standing for long periods) carved with historical and fantastical designs. Then there are the choir stalls themselves, the carvings on the chancel roof, the vaulting of the crossing ... and to cap it all you can climb the tower for sweeping views of the castle, town and surrounding countryside.

Street as you walk up to the Butter Cross at the top. Some are classic timber-framed buildings, while others are examples of buildings that have been refaced in Georgian brick, some are true Georgian buildings, and others are a hotchpotch of old below and new above.

The Butter Cross was built in 1744, with an extension later added to its western side. Keep to the right-hand side of the Butter Cross and then walk up the narrow lane to the church, which you may wish to look at. The walk continues by turning to the right in front of the church (or to the left as you emerge from the church), following the footpath round the outside of the church past the recently opened Jubilee Garden and so to the Reader's House. (The photograph on the left shows both.) The house is named after the reader who would have read the Bible out loud in English at a time when reading was not a widespread skill, and so help the parish clergy. The house was probably built in the mid 1500s, though parts might be even earlier, and the timber-framed porch was added in 1616.

Continue past the Reader's House, then turn right down a narrow passageway and head down some steps to enter the courtyard of the Bull Inn and so into Corve Street. Almost opposite is the Feathers Hotel.

THE BULL INN
This building may date back to the 12th century, but the first note of its existence is in 1319, when it was recorded as a tenement. It became an inn in the mid 1400s when the jettied timber-framed range was built. In the 1500s it was extended towards the church, and a stables added. It is first known by the name of the Bull in a will of 1580. A fire destroyed the façade in 1794, resulting in this being rebuilt in the Georgian style.

THE FEATHERS HOTEL

The core of the building was certainly in existence in 1544 when it was owned by Thomas Hakluyt, Clerk of the Council in the Marches. In 1619 it was sold to Reese Jones, an attorney at the Council, who hailed from Pembrokeshire. It was he who commissioned the refronting and enlargement of the house. Carved on the collars of the three gables are ostrich feathers, the symbol of the Prince of Wales which are also shown on the coat of arms for Ludlow, and after which the building is named, so referring to the various princes who were based at Ludlow Castle. By 1670 the building had become an inn.

❷ Turn left down Corve Street. Beyond the traffic lights at the junction near Tesco's you reach an area of the town that contained an important leather-working industry in the past. The Great House, the timber-framed building on the right-hand side shortly after the junction, was erected in the early to mid 1500s and was owned first by wealthy cloth manufacturers and then by tanners. It was all but derelict by the 1970s and was then restored. Further on, the timber-framed house on the right with bright yellow painted panels was until fairly recently one of those buildings which had been refaced with lath and plaster which hid the timber framing. Continue down Corve Street and follow it round to the left and over the river.

❸ Opposite the next road off to the right, just past the petrol station, turn left up Burway Lane. Keep on along the lane which will eventually become a (possibly muddy) track. It passes to the right of Burway House, crosses a tarmac lane, then after a little way passes to the left of most of the buildings of Burway Farm. It then heads through a small paddock to enter a large field by a small gate. Follow the edge of the field on your left above a wooded bank, and at the far end of the field follow the field boundary round to the right to leave the field by a gate onto the A49.

④ Cross the A49 (take care) and take the road opposite (signposted to Much Wenlock). Cross the railway line, then turn right on the track that runs alongside the racecourse. Beyond the line of the race course and amongst the tees and bunkers of the golf course is a Bronze Age cemetery, though without playing a round of golf it is difficult to see which of the mounds are the sites of tombs; a much larger tumulus will be passed later on in the walk.

RACECOURSE

The first recorded horse race on this course took place on 27 August 1729. At that time the course was longer and solely used for racing on the flat. During the 1800s hurdles began to be added for some of the races and gradually the course moved to hosting only races with jumps. The course is known for its speed, with low jumps and tight cornering. It hosts some 16-18 events each year between October and May.

BROMFIELD BRONZE AGE CEMETERY

This cemetery consists of at least 20 barrows and three flat cremation cemeteries spanning the period c.2000 to 900BC. The walk map shows the approximate location of the five remaining barrows and 13 of those ploughed out, some of which can still be seen as cropmarks from the air under the right conditions. Near the most north-western ploughed-out barrow marked on the map was also found a level cemetery consisting of some 130 shallow pits used for burials over about an 800-year span commencing around 1800BC and showing a variety of burial practices.

Two small bowl barrows can be made out, with a little difficulty, from the path past the racecourse. The northernmost barrow is roughly 12m in diameter and stands up to 1.5m high, the other lies some 23m to its south and is smaller, at c.7m in diameter and 0.5m high. The larger barrow was partially excavated in 1884, when evidence of a cremation burial was found together with a small piece of bronze. It is thought that the other barrow was excavated too, but it is not known if anything was found. Both barrows are surrounded by a c.1m wide ditch, excavated during the construction of the monument to provide material for the mound. Both ditches have become infilled over subsequent years. In another barrow were found two cremation burials, one in a stone-lined cist. Evidence has been found to suggest that the site was in use, but not necessarily for burials, from at least 2560BC.

The cemetery complex has also been found, from aerial photographs, to contain two parallel lines of pits, one 160m long, the other 190m long, some 35-40m apart. It is thought that these pits would have once held wooden posts and so formed a cursus that was probably used as a form of processionary route. It has been suggested that as the site lies at a point where Corvedale meets the valleys of the Teme and the Onny, the different burial practices might suggest that it was a shared space utilised by groups of people with differing traditions living in each valley.

Keep following the track, and it will bend to the left and then pass a few houses on the right. Beyond the last house there is a barn and then a stretch of woodland. Initially this woodland masks a deep bank, but keep an eye out for where the bank ends, for here you want to take a slightly indistinct footpath (indicated by a waymarker) that leads through a level area of woodland to a kissing gate on its far side. Go through the gate and into a field. Head straight on, crossing the line of a channel in the field, to reach the River Corve. Head left along the river, keeping it to your right. At the far end of this field you will reach a bridge across the river.

5 Here you have a choice: the circular walk continues to the left, and a detour over the bridge takes you to the church in Stanton Lacy with its Saxon remains, and then brings you back to this bridge.

The Detour: Cross the bridge, and turn left to follow the river, now on your left. Pass through a gate into the next field and again follow the left-hand boundary to a gate and stile that lead onto a track. Continue along the track and you'll reach a road, on the far

STANTON LACY CHURCH

The Domesday Survey makes it clear that this was a wealthy area, and was home to a substantial Saxon church, elements of which still survive. (Before the Norman Conquest the large parish included the area of Ludlow.) Saxon pilasters can be seen on the outside of the west and north walls of the nave and on the north transept. The north wall of the nave also has a blocked Saxon doorway, above which is a stone carved with a plain cross. Saxon long and short work remains on the west wall to the right of the pilaster strips, which mark the boundary between Saxon and later work. That later work dates largely to the 13th and 14th centuries.

side of which is Stanton Lacy Church. Having visited the church, return to the footbridge back across the Corve.

Continuing the circular walk: When you reach the bridge, turn left (so with your back to it) (or if re-crossing the bridge, keep straight ahead) and shadow the field boundary on your right to reach a small gate on the far side that leads out onto the B4365.

❻ Cross this and head up the bank and through another small gate into a field. Here the path turns slightly left to cross a corner of the field (look out for the direction arrow by the gate) to another small gate that leads into a strip of woodland. (It might prove easier, depending on the time of year, to walk round the field's headland to reach this gate.) Once through this next gate, continue through the woodland, where, if you have emerged in the right place, you will find a short post with a waymarking arrow on it. From here turn right and head up this next field, aiming for the top left-hand corner,

ROBIN HOOD'S BUTT

This barrow stands c.4.5m high with a diameter of 7m at its top. Along with the barrows in the racecourse this barrow was partially excavated in 1884 by C. Fortey, who recorded finds of cremated human bones and a small piece of bronze spear or arrowhead 10ft below the top of the mound. The mound would once have been surrounded by a ditch, from which some of the material to create the mound would have come, but this has infilled over the years.

where you will join a track that passes between the racecourse on your left and the aforementioned large tumulus on your right. This is known as Robin Hood's Butt. Quickly you will reach a tarmacked lane on which you turn left – keep an eye out for golfers as you'll be crossing some fairways.

Follow the road down to meet a larger road within the racecourse, on which you turn right. Keep on the road across the level crossing and on down to meet the A49. Shortly beyond the station you will start to pass a quarry on your right – this was the site of a Roman marching camp.

ROMAN MARCHING CAMP

In 1991 a length of the camp's ditch was excavated and shown to cut into a ring ditch which marked the outline of a burial barrow. The section of the ditch was found to be well preserved, indicating that the rampart (measuring between 3 and 3.5m wide) may have been pushed back into the ditch soon after the abandonment of the camp, perhaps to deny its use by others. Evidence for cooking ovens were also found, their alignment running parallel with the ditch and presumably cut into the back of the rampart. There was evidence of several episodes of firing, suggesting that the camp may have been more than just a marching camp occupied on a temporary basis. In 2002 a hearth was seen nearby, and with iron fragments found in the 1991 excavation this suggests that smithing was also carried on here. Within the area of the barrow marked by the ring ditch it was found that an enigmatic boat-shaped feature 14m long, up to 4m wide and up to 1m deep had been cut, void of any artefacts. A small circular cremation pit was later dug into the area surrounded by the ring ditch, which contained cremated human bone and charcoal.

RAILWAY STATION

The railway station opened in 1852. There was originally just one platform, with a second added in the 1860s when the line was expanded from one track to two. The platforms were later extended to serve Ludlow Racecourse. The station continued to serve passengers till 1958 and goods till 1964, since when the station buildings have been converted to residential use.

As you near the A49 you might want to visit the Ludlow Farm Shop on the left; there's a café and there are toilets just behind the Post Office.

🔴 The walk continues by crossing the A49 and turning right over the Teme. Follow the pavement and turn left onto a small lane, near its junction with the A4113. The lane will quickly bring you to the remains of Bromfield Priory and its gatehouse.

BROMFIELD GATEHOUSE

This is the gatehouse to the priory precinct, but only the northern two-thirds of the lower storey (the side that faces the road) date from this use. The upper timber-framed part dates to after the Dissolution (probably when Charles Foxe built a house on the site of the claustral buildings [see box on opposite page] though details of its construction are unusual for such a date), whilst the southern third and the oriel window over the arch were added for the parish school established in 1836. The building was remodelled and the timber-framing limewashed in 1992 for the Landmark Trust in readiness for letting as holiday accommodation.

BROMFIELD PRIORY AND CHURCH

In the mid 11th century the church here was a royal minster served by 12 canons who were gradually replaced by monks. Shortly after the ending of the Anarchy, the period of civil war between the supporters of King Stephen and those of the Empress Maud, Henry II's foundation of a Benedictine priory subject to Gloucester Abbey seems to have regularised the changed position. Henry might also have created this foundation to help rectify depredations during the Anarchy, when written sources suggest that Bromfield was the site of a temporary castle utilised during the conflict, not that any evidence on the ground has yet come to light for such a castle. The present church incorporates parts of the nave, crossing and north transept of an early Norman church built before the foundation of the priory, the nave probably always being used by the parishioners. During the 13th century the north-west tower and north aisle were added for the further use of parishioners. The priory gradually went into decline and shortly after the Dissolution was acquired by Charles Foxe, who built a house out of the claustral buildings, the south transept and the crossing. The house subsequently burned down (some remains can be seen adjoining the south side of the church) and in 1658 the crossing was refitted as the chancel, to which a painted ceiling in the Baroque style was added in 1672, painted by the Cheshire artist Thomas Francis. The church was restored in 1889-90 by Hodgson Fowler, who also designed the triptych behind the altar. Windows in the Decorated style were inserted in the nave and chancel during the restoration.

Having visited the church, continue along the lane, with the gatehouse on your left. Over to the right, before the lane swings left and drops down to a bridge, there is a wooded area across a field to your right; this is the site of a moated grange.

> **MOATED GRANGE**
> The moat is 50m square, the ditch still some 2m deep and the 'island' raised about 1m above the external ground level. There are the remains of a stone building on the island, probably dating to the 13th or 14th century. The building is believed by some to have been a grange or farm belonging to the priory, but by others, due to its probable high status, to be that of a wealthy local landowner or lord, or even the priors of Bromfield.

As you drop down to the bridge, you may get a good view (depending upon the time of year) of the remains of the house that Charles Foxe built on the side of the church, and at the bridge you can see a currently derelict 18th-century sawmill standing on the bank of the Teme. The bridge has earlier origins, though its arches were restored *c.*1989. Across the bridge and a little further up the lane you reach the gatehouse to Oakly Park. The gatehouse was designed by Charles Cockerell in 1826, its one-bay façade dominated by a full-height arch. On the recessed wall within the arch is a head in relief.

OAKLY PARK

The original house on the site was timber-framed; this was extended in brick to the north and south. In 1772 Clive of India, 1st Earl of Powis, pulled down much of the house, rebuilding it 'to a better plan', apparently using William Haycock as his architect. In c.1784-90 the Clives employed J.H. Haycock to make further substantial changes. In 1819 the Hon. Henry Clive, a fan of neoclassical architecture, asked his friend the architect Charles Cockerell to remodel the house. Little was done at first but in 1836 Henry Clive decided that his growing family needed a larger dining room and more bedrooms, and a neoclassical transformation ensued.

❽ Continue along the lane to the right of the gatehouse, and this will take you past and above Oakly Park, of which glimpses may be had, especially in winter. Keep straight on, passing another lane on the right, and you will drop down through some woodland to cross a small stream, rise up the other side and then pass through a gate near a lodge. Not long past this lodge you will reach a pair of tracks to the left separated by a hedge. Take the second of these, which will lead you between hedges into a field. The path through the field may have been kept clear by the farmer, but if not, cross the corner of the field, aiming just to the left of a large oak that stands just beyond the hedge on the far side of the field. Here you will find a gate into the next field. The path heads diagonally down this next field between two telegraph poles, aiming to the left of a large oak that stands on the far field boundary. As you walk across the field you will see that you are heading for its opposite corner, where you will find a metal kissing gate into the next field. Having crossed the stream on the far side of the kissing gate, the path heads uphill to another kissing gate, and then straight across a narrow field to the edge of woodland on the far side.

❾ Turn right here and walk all the way along the edge of this very long field. At the end, go through the kissing gate. In the next field the path shadows the woodland on your left, rather than sticking close to its edge, and at the far side drops down to a gate in the corner of the field, crosses a stream by a bridge, enters the next field by a kissing gate, then rises up a steep bank. The path then follows the edge of the bank on your left, then crosses the field to its far right-hand corner to leave it by a kissing gate and join a tarmacked lane. Turn left on this and left again (essentially keeping straight ahead) when it meets another road. Follow this along and over Dinham Bridge and so back up into town.

You will pass, on the right, the remains of a chapel built soon after the death of Thomas à Becket in 1170 and then, on the left, the large Dinham House (see photograph on right). The central part of this house was built in the early 1700s and the wings were added in 1748/49. It later became the town house of the Earl of Powis (the current earl still owns Ludlow Castle) and one of its 'guests' for six months was Lucien Bonaparte, brother of Napoleon, who was captured by the Royal Navy in 1811 when en route to America.

Walk 2
Craven Arms, Stokesay Castle & Norton Camp

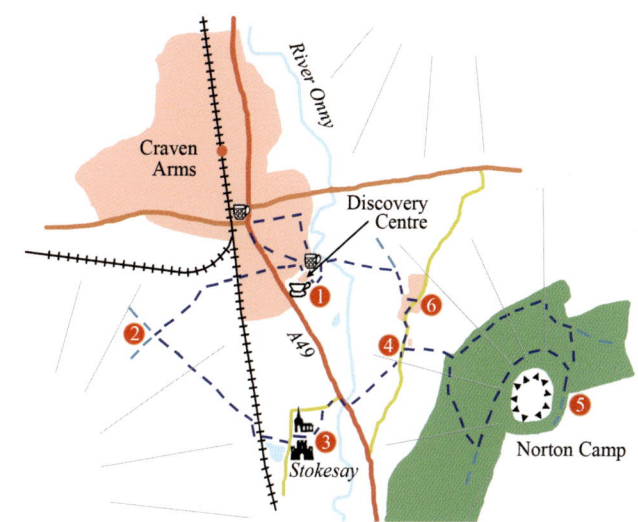

5.25 miles in rolling countryside (the climb up to Norton Camp is a reasonable pull) on a mixture of tracks and paths mostly in good condition though that round the edge of one field could be awkward depending upon the time of year and crop. The walk passes Stokesay Church and Castle (you may wish to include a visit to the castle, which is in the care of English Heritage), passes round some of the ramparts of Norton Camp, and you may also wish to visit the Land of Lost Content (see boxed text on page 27 for opening times). There are some stiles.

Park at the Secret Hills Discovery Centre on the southern edge of Craven Arms (or somewhere nearby if you don't feel like making the suggested small contribution to help keep the centre going).

❶ The walk starts by turning left out of the Discovery Centre's car park and walking up to the A49. Cross this and take the footpath along Dodds Lane, keeping ahead when you meet the road proper. This will lead you onto

CRAVEN ARMS
The town grew as a Victorian market centre due to its becoming the junction of various railways. The Shrewsbury & Hereford Railway passed through in 1852, being joined by lines from Knighton, Bishop's Castle and Much Wenlock over the following 15 years.

SHROPSHIRE HILLS DISCOVERY CENTRE
Designed by Niall Phillips, this was built between 1999 and 2001 and has a grass roof. It contains exhibitions, has much information on the area, a café, and the grounds include 30 acres of meadow alongside the Onny with several paths. It is open daily between 10am and 5pm.

a track at its end which then passes under the railway line. Keep on the track to a stile at its end. Once over this stile, follow the field boundary on your left uphill to the far left-hand corner of the field, where you will find a stile into the next field.

❷ Cross the stile and turn left (you are now on the Shropshire Way) and follow the field boundary down to a stile into the next field. Once over this, keep following what is now an ex-field boundary back down to the railway line. Here the path bears right, then passes through a gate and back under the railway line to enter a field with Stokesay Castle ahead of you. Follow the track between hedge and small lake to join a lane beside the castle. Turn left on the lane and then right through a gate into the churchyard to visit the church (and castle, if you wish).

STOKESAY CASTLE

The castle may have begun its life as a moated site with a single tower – the present north tower, entered by an external stairway at first-floor level – sometime in the late 1100s or early 1200s. The wealthy Ludlow wool merchant Laurence of Ludlow bought the tenancy of the site in 1281 and began transforming the building, receiving permission to crenellate his home in 1291 as work was nearing completion. The north tower was essentially retained, with some modifications, whilst any freestanding timber hall was replaced by a new open-hearthed great hall (which has a complex roof structure), now joined to the north tower and with a solar block to the south reached by an external staircase, as was then the fashion. The hall and solar are ascribed to a date of c.1260-80, the south tower to after the licence to crenellate was given. Tree-ring dating suggests that the whole rebuild was complete soon after that licence was given, and analysis of the timberwork suggests that the same team of carpenters worked throughout the building period. The castle has been altered very little since, with the exception of the building of the gatehouse and the demolition of the kitchen, service range and any ancillary buildings which would have stood in the courtyard.

Laurence drowned in 1294 on a business trip to the Low Countries but his descendants remained in ownership of Stokesay for more than 200 years until the castle passed to the Vernon family. Henry Vernon carried out repairs c.1577 but, falling into financial difficulties, in 1598 sold the castle to Sir George Mainwaring. He in turn sold it in 1620, the buyer being Dame Elizabeth Craven and her son William, the 1st Earl of Craven. It was William who built the Elizabethan gatehouse, which probably replaced an earlier one built of stone, his accounts showing that he spent more than £468 in 1640 'about the building at Stokesay', and further money 'for finishing the work' in 1641; tree-ring dating of the gatehouse timbers has confirmed it was constructed in 1639-41, and the elaborately carved brackets and lozenge patterns of the timberwork bear comparison with houses erected in Ludlow around this date. The north tower first-floor jettying was begun shortly after 1578, with further work carried out by William, who also remodelled the rooms in the solar, adding panelling. He also replaced the first-floor ceiling in the South Tower with moulded beams.

During the 18th century the buildings fell into decay, becoming an agricultural store and workshop with a smithy in the south tower. In 1853 Frances Stackhouse Acton, a local landowner as well as being a noted antiquarian and artist, became concerned at the state of the castle and organised the clearing of much rubbish and the carrying out of a series of repairs. In 1869 the glovemaker John Derby Allcroft bought the castle and carried out extensive restoration work, building a new home for his family nearby. The castle subsequently passed into the guardianship of English Heritage.

20

STOKESAY CHURCH

Skirmishing around the church during the Civil War caused it severe damage. In 1654 the tower and nave were largely rebuilt, sufficient remaining of the chancel for it simply to be repaired and re-roofed. The Norman south doorway has survived, but the church's most interesting feature is the range of 17th-century fittings and decoration – a west gallery, oaken box pews, a pulpit complete with sounding-board and reading pew, a canopied squire's pew and wall paintings of Biblical texts.

❸ To continue the walk, with your back to the church entrance door, turn left and walk down to the gate out onto the lane. Turn right on the lane and follow it down to the A49. Turn right on the A49 along the footpath and cross the bridge over the River Onny. At the end of the bridge you can then either cross the A49 and step over the crash barrier on the far side and head down the little path (and so see the weir that dates back to the 1700s and was extended by Thomas Telford in 1822 that lies partly under the bridge), or continue for about 100 yards along the A49 and then cross it, to take a lane back alongside the A49. Whichever route you take, you'll come to a footpath sign at the top of some stone steps that you need to descend and so come to a kissing gate into a field.

Cross the corner of the field (or follow the headland around) to another kissing gate above the Onny. There are two paths at this point, one alongside the Onny which you don't take, and the one you do want, which leads initially to the right of the line of an ancient meander, now a sunken line in the field or a pond (depending upon the time of year), and then up the bank on the right to a stile into another field. Here the path technically crosses the field straight to its top left-hand corner, but the farmer may not have reinstated the line of the path and you may need to take to tramlines or whatever sensible route suggests itself.

❹ Once at the corner of the field, head out through the gateway onto a road on which you turn left. You'll quickly come to a footpath sign off to the right for the Three Woods walk, just this side of a house, and you take this path. It leads uphill and into some woodland, where the path forks. Take a good look at this area, for you will be returning to it from the left and will need to recognize it! For the moment, take the right-hand fork and follow the path along the edge of the woodland. After a while the path rises slightly uphill and forks. You want to take the left-hand path which slants up and across the hillside to eventually meet a gravelled track, on which you turn left.

Follow this track along and gradually the banks of Norton Camp will come into view on your right, more so in winter, but especially where in *circa* 2017/18 the banks were largely cleared of trees and undergrowth. The track eventually comes right up against the banks, shortly after

which there is a gateway into the corner of a field on your left. Stop a moment to take in the view (on a clear day), with Brown Clee and Titterstone Clee hills over to the left.

🔴 From this point you need to retrace your steps along the track for about 100 yards. Where the track

NORTON CAMP

Norton Camp is D-shaped in plan and measures some 360m by 350m, enclosing *c.* seven hectares. Most of the perimeter is marked out by two ramparts with an external ditch to each, the inner rampart being steeper and with a narrower top. Rock-cut faces are still visible in places in the ditch between the two ramparts. The south-western side has two further outer banks, whilst there is just a single rampart on the north-western side surmounted by the remains of a low stone wall. The hillfort had two entrances, one on the eastern side and another at the south-east, both with entrance corridors. Subsequent quarrying for stone in the north-western part has left several depressions and breaches in the ramparts, whilst cultivation and the growth of trees has obscured some of the rest of the interior of the hillfort. Nevertheless, seven hut circles were noted in the north-western area in 1908. The size of the hillfort suggests it acted as a central location for a large community that lived and farmed in the surrounding valleys, where food may have been stored and guarded and where communal festivities and ceremonies took place.

THE BATTLE OF WHETTLETON

In June 1645 the small Royalist force that garrisoned Stokesay Castle surrendered to Lt Colonel Reinking. Reinking, a professional Dutch soldier, was at the head of Parliamentary forces that had been gathered at Shrewsbury and sent south to harass the Royalist forces operating in the Corvedale area from their bases at Bridgnorth and Ludlow. To counteract this threat Sir Michael Woodhouse, the Royalist commander at Ludlow (for whom also see page 36) drew together contingents from a number of garrisons and a small Royalist field army in Worcestershire, giving him a force of some 2,000 men to oppose a Parliamentarian force roughly half that size. Reinking left a garrison at Stokesay, but withdrew the bulk of his forces to the north to await reinforcements. The Royalists decided to attack and Reinking was persuaded to stand and fight. Details are sketchy, but the Royalists were probably hampered by having a bevy of commanders each with a small contingent of troops, making coordinated action difficult. An advance by their cavalry was beaten back by the Parliamentarian horse, an action followed by an advance of Parliamentarian infantry which gradually beat the Royalist infantry from their positions behind hedgerows. In the event some 100 Royalists were slain along with some of their leaders and several officers were taken prisoner, along with field guns, horses, bags and baggage.

bends to the left, you want to take a narrow path that leads off to the right. (It is marked by a post with waymarking signs just to its right, but this might be buried in tall nettles and assorted undergrowth depending upon the time of year). Within a short time the path follows a length of tall metal mesh fencing on your left and soon after that turns away from the line of the fence to reach a fork. Take the left-hand path which now more sharply descends the hill, sometimes as a narrow path, sometimes as a wide track. Ignore paths off to the right until you return to the junction of paths where you entered this wood and which we suggested you memorise! Here you turn right and return down the path that you walked up. When you reach the minor road, turn right. Follow this along to the soon-reached hamlet of Whettleton.

🔴 **6** Here you take the footpath off to the left signposted to Secret Hills. This passes over a grassy area between some houses and a single storey stone-built barn but soon becomes a farm track and swings right. Keep on this track to its end, where you cross a stile into a field. Here your path turns left, shadowing, but slightly diverging from, the field boundary on your left to pass over the crest of the field and drop down to a path just to the left of a little stream, and so over a footbridge. Keep walking ahead across the next field and this will bring you to a footbridge across the River Onny. Once over the bridge, follow the

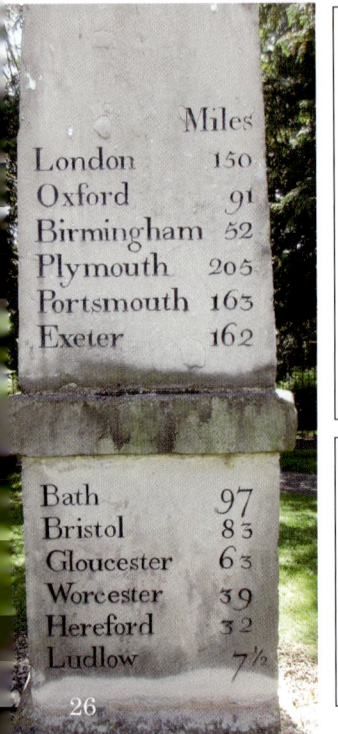

CRAVEN ARMS HOTEL
This was built as a coaching inn c.1830 at the junctions of the Hereford to Shrewsbury road and the road that then led to central Wales and thence Holyhead. A stable court was built behind the inn, which is named after the Earls of Craven, local landowners (see under Stokesay Castle on page 19) from whom Craven Arms takes its name.

MILESTONE
The large sandstone milestone lists the distances from the Earl of Craven's inn to 36 towns and cities before the construction of Telford's more direct and improved London to Holyhead road (now the A5).

lane and at its end go through a small gate to enter the grounds of the Secret Hills Discovery Centre, turning right after a few yards to return to the Centre itself.

For the short circuit through part of Craven Arms, turn right out of the Discovery Centre's car park and then

	Miles
London	150
Oxford	91
Birmingham	52
Plymouth	205
Portsmouth	163
Exeter	162
Bath	97
Bristol	83
Gloucester	63
Worcester	39
Hereford	32
Ludlow	7½

almost immediately take the tarmacked path off to the left. This will lead you to the A49. Turn right and walk up to the roundabout by the Craven Arms Hotel.

Turn right at the roundabout and walk along till you reach Market Street, where you will find the Land of Lost Content museum.

Turn right down Market Street and this will lead you past the Stokesay Arms pub and so back to the Secret Hills Discovery Centre.

LAND OF LOST CONTENT
This describes itself as 'Britain's foremost collection of pop culture ephemera, obscure and ordinary objects from the pre-digital era' and includes 33 displays over three floors. It currently advertises itself as being open between 1 February and 30 November between 11am and 5pm every day except Wednesday and Sunday (though it is open on the latter day in July and August). You may want to check opening times at www.lolc.co.uk. There is a self service café with honesty box.

Walk 3 Clungunford, Clunbury & Hopton Castle

7.75 miles on a mixture of minor roads, tracks and footpaths, most of which are in good condition, with about eight stiles all told. There is one short section of B road, but it has a pavement. The walk is set in hilly countryside, with the steepest gradient being the descent into Clunbury; the ascents are relatively gentle. The walk includes the churches at Clungunford, where there is also a motte, and Clunbury, together with the recently restored Hopton Castle. It also passes manor houses and the site of an earlier manor house.

If you do this walk at a weekend, you could stop at the Bird on the Rock tearooms near the end of your walk (they're open between 10 and 4pm), though it would be worth checking in advance that they'll be open.

Park near the church in Clungunford.

❶ Standing on the B4367 (the road by the church) with your back to the church, turn right, cross the River Clun, and walk up to the road junction with the Bird on the Rock tearooms. (As you walk along the B road, keep an eye out for Abcott Manor away to your right.) Turn right by the tearooms (the road is signposted to Abcott and Twitchen), and then right at the next road junction soon reached. This lane will take you above Abcott Manor on the right, of which only some chimneys and the roof can easily be glimpsed from this angle.

Follow the lane till it ends, continuing along on the track for a short way and then turning left under the railway line and then immediately right on a track that follows the railway line, which is now on your right. The track eventually leads into a field. For the next mile or so the paths have in places been slightly diverted from the course shown on OS maps (should you also be using

ABCOTT MANOR

Dates of 1541 have been obtained for the felling of the timber for construction of the main hall and later in the 1540s for the cross wing. A parlour wing was added *c*.1620-30. Abcott was initially in the possession of the Prynce family of Whitehall in Shrewsbury. At the Dissolution Richard Prynce, born *c*.1523, obtained a considerable portion of the lands of Shrewsbury Abbey, using stone from some of the buildings to construct a house now called Whitehall in Abbey Foregate. He was a lawyer working for the Council in the Marches of Wales based at Ludlow, a town he represented in Parliament in 1558, subsequently being elected for Bridgnorth.

those) according to the remnants of some signs that linger and from information supplied by the owners of Coston Manor.

> **COSTON MANOR MOAT**
> The almost rectangular moated site marked by poplars is now partly overlain by the railway embankment. It is approached by a causeway in the part of the site that survives on the near side of the embankment. The ditch is 10m wide and 2m deep and is surrounded by a low outer embankment on all sides except that parallel to the line of the walk. It is thought, as with most such sites, that the raised island was once the site of a house, such sites being constructed in the 1400s and 1500s by the well-off who were not able to obtain a licence to crenellate their houses but wanted to show off their status.

Thus, once in this field, the path diagonally crosses a corner of the field (aiming for a farm on the ridge beyond) to turn right in front of the hedgerow to follow it along to a gate in the far left-hand corner of the field. Go through this gate and go straight across the next field to a gate on the far side, noticing the area marked out by poplars to your right – these mark the remnants of a moated house site.

② Through this next gateway, the path then follows the embanked wall on your left round the grounds of Coston Manor, turns right by a nest of gateways in a corner of the field and passes in front of another house to leave the field by a gateway just beyond this house. You then follow the track through the farm buildings, with all the houses to your left. When you reach the lane on the far side of the buildings, turn right and walk along it till you reach the first gate on the left which carries a sign 'Bridleway to Clunbury'. Go through this gate and follow the hedgerow on your right up to the initial crest of the hillside where you come to Upper Coston farm.

③ The bridleway heads down through the farmyard, and jinks left then right to leave it by the left-hand of two gates and so enter a field. The path once again follows hedgerows and field boundaries on your right, rising through fields towards the next crest of the hillside. Shortly before you reach the final crest (with its line of trees on the right), you come to a small metal gate in the field boundary on your right (where there may also be a post that includes yellow waymarking signs, though both gate and post have been somewhat 'freestanding' in recent times). Here the path turns half left across the hillside, to pass to the left of a single tree that stands in the field, and heads towards the far corner of the field. Here you will find a small metal gate leading out onto a track on the far side.

Cross this track and head steeply down the hillside. Clunbury is laid out below you. You go through a small gate just below the crest of the hill and turn left on the path to slant down the hillside. The path almost immediately forks, and you take the right-hand path. This will lead you down, via a gate near the bottom, to a road.

❹ Turn right on the road to enter Clunbury, where the walk makes a small loop. Carry on down the road, ignoring turnings to first right and then left and then turn right for the entrance to the churchyard.

Having looked at the church, carry on through the churchyard, passing the stone-built Clunbury Hall on the left, and turn right on the track on the far side to walk under the spreading branches of a line of tall beech trees. Turn right on the road at the far end of the track, then right and left when you reach the road junction ahead (so completing the loop). Follow this road all the way till you reach its end at a junction with the B4385.

CLUNBURY CHURCH AND HALL

'Bury' often signifies that a settlement was once a place fortified by the Saxons, but no evidence of any fortifications has come to light and in this instance 'bury' probably simply suggests it was once the site of a Saxon manor. It was certainly held by a man called Swein in 1066, but by 1086 had been granted to the Norman Picot de Say, a descendant of whom granted it to Much Wenlock Priory c.1190. Medieval open fields probably lay to the south of the village. The church is essentially of Norman construction, though windows in the nave were replaced with ones in the Decorated style in the early to mid 1300s, the upper parts of the tower rebuilt probably in the 17th century, a Victorian porch added (the lower part of the west jamb of another south doorway remains visible to the east of the porch), and the chancel largely rebuilt in 1848. The roof, perhaps the finest feature of the building, has been dendrochronologically dated to 1495-96. Outside there is a 13th-century tomb recess which is probably related to a piscina on the inside of the nave wall at this point: the piscina would have been related to an altar and it is probable that the tomb recess is that of the altar's donor.

Clunbury Hall would have originated as a farmstead but now comprises a late 18th- or early 19th-century house built of roughly coursed limestone.

5 Turn left on the B road and almost immediately right through a metal kissing gate onto a footpath. The path heads down the bank and across the narrow field to a 'bridge' across a stream, and then heads just to the right of a barn on the far side of the field. Here there is a post marking a junction of paths: the one you'll be following to Hopton is marked with yellow waymark signs that depict a viaduct. Turn left in front of the barn and once past it turn half right to cross a part of the field, aiming for a gate that leads into the next field; en route you'll cross a bridge across a ditch. The farmer of this next field doesn't always reinstate footpaths after agricultural operations, but the path technically crosses this field to the far right-hand corner, where you should see a stile at the junction of the far hedgerow with the line of the wood higher up the slope. If this route looks too difficult, then you could follow the field edge on your right and then alongside the wood to reach the stile; a reasonable headland has been left here each time we have used this path.

Across the stile, the path initially follows the edge of the wood on your right. When the wood makes a turn to the right, the path carries on across a corner of the field to a stile on its far side to enter woodland. Cross this stile and follow the path through some old coppiced woodland for a few tens of yards till it emerges onto a wide gravelled forestry track (it's a bit of a scramble up the bank). Turn left on the forestry track and follow it to the crest of the hill, where the path turns off to the right and passes through woodland till it reaches a gate through which you go to emerge onto a road.

6 Cross the road and go over the stile on the far side into a large field, to then follow the hedgerow on your right along to the far side of this field. Here you will find a stile into the next field from where the path should head to the left-hand side of the remains of a small red brick building on the far side of the field, but you may need to choose the best tractor tramline down the field to reach this point. As you descend, look out for Hopton Castle almost straight ahead of you in the valley bottom below. Near the remains of the red brick building you will find a stile that you cross to then follow a path down to a road on which you turn right. When you reach a T-junction, turn left and then right at the next road junction to reach Hopton Castle.

7 Turn left out of the castle entranceway to retrace your steps to the last road junction, where you turn right. Follow this along till the road makes a sharp turn to the right, where you go through the gate on the left and take the footpath that slants uphill, initially following the line of a track. Keep on the track past an old quarry on the right, but where the track swings right, you carry on ahead to a stile just to the right of a block of woodland. Cross this stile and follow the edge of the wood on your left to the gateway into the next field.

HOPTON CASTLE

The castle was probably built as a high status tower house by the de Hoptons in the late 13th or early 14th century near the confluence of two streams, one of which was diverted to fill the ditches that were dug around the site. The building was built more with an eye to convenience and comfort than to defence, with several fireplaces and garderobes, and its front door, in the north-facing wall, being designed to impress. (A 'porch' in front of this door was burnt during the Civil War.) There was also a secondary west-facing doorway. The surviving square 'keep' stands on a low motte, the ditch surrounding which has become somewhat eroded, perhaps due to flooding. The core of the building is of two storeys with a third floor in the south-western corner. It has been described as backwards-looking externally, considering its date of construction, but 'sophisticated and modern' internally. The doorway into the keep, which was probably served by a drawbridge across the ditch from the roughly rectangular inner bailey in which it stands, led into a small lobby which in turn led through an arched doorway, now lost, into a hall. Off this hall lay small rooms and recesses in the thick walls. The stairs were located in the north-western turret and led to a small lobby leading into a large room, with further rooms in the other corner turrets. The third, mezzanine, floor, contained a long narrow room, and there were probably further rooms in the top of each corner turret.

The inner bailey contains the sites of two rectangular (probably domestic) buildings, whilst scatters of stones suggest that the bailey was protected by a stone-built wall. The remains also suggest that a tower probably stood at the bailey's south-west corner. An L-shaped outer bailey lies to the west and south of the inner bailey, part of its protective ditch being widened to provide a fishpond.

The keep is built of thinly-coursed local rubble stone, with red ashlar sandstone dressings. Repairs undertaken by the Ministry of Works in 1960 stabilised the external elevations, but the rubble stone is highly friable (it was originally protected by a lime-based render) and subject to rapid deterioration. Two approximately triangular low platforms to the west of the castle may relate to Civil War activities or be ornamental features.

HOPTON CASTLE (cont.) A geophysical survey carried out in 2005 suggested that some structures in the baileys were used for industrial purposes, along with an area to the north of the keep. Excavations in 2009 found evidence of burnt structures, possibly resulting from the Civil War siege, a gold coin of the reign of James I, an iron cannon ball and evidence of stone robbing.

It is the Civil War which has given the name of Hopton Castle some notoriety. At this time it was owned by the Wallops, Parliamentary sympathisers. In early 1644 the Royalists decided to make a major assault on the one Parliamentarian stronghold in this area, Brampton Bryan Castle in northern Herefordshire, home of the Harley family. The Parliamentarians learnt of the Royalist plans, which involved as a prelude garrisoning Hopton Castle to limit ease of movement from Brampton Bryan, and decided to preempt them. In the event a small Royalist force got there first, but they meekly handed the castle to the Parliamentarians when they knocked at the door. Over the next couple of days 16 men under the command of Samuel More beat back a Royalist attempt to retake the castle, and were then reinforced by a further 14 men, taking the total garrison to 31. The Royalists made another assault and were beaten off, losing one or perhaps two officers, and sent for artillery. When these arrived, More was asked to surrender, his position being untenable, but he refused. A cannonade that lasted from 9am to 5pm on 11 March breached the castle's walls and another assault was made, but was beaten off with tens of casualties, perhaps even over 100; the Parliamentarians lost one man killed in the cannonade and three or four injured in the fighting. After further cannonades and with the outer walls badly breached, the defenders retired to the keep, losing some men to musket fire as they barricaded the main entrance. A short time later, hearing Royalists building a mine under the castle from which they could blow it up, More decided it was time to surrender 'to the mercy' of the Royalist commander, Sir Michael Woodhouse. More was kept a prisoner, but his garrison was disarmed and murdered, the excuse being that they had sought to defend an indefensible position given the weight and array of force opposing them. This form of 'mercy' became known as 'Hopton Quarter'.

Here you want to look ahead to the ridge that is on the far side of the River Clun. You will see three hilltops ahead of you along this ridge (see photograph below) and you now want to turn away from the wood to aim for the right-hand one of these. As you cross the field you will see a stile in the hedgerow below you; alter your course (if necessary!) accordingly. Across this stile, go down the steps onto the B4385.

🔴 **8** Cross the road and then go down the track on the far side. Don't go down the drive to the house, but head into the field to the left of the driveway, and follow the field boundary on your right. Just past the house you will find a stile in the boundary on your right, and you cross this, to then immediately turn left and follow the boundary down to reach a stile beyond various outbuildings and polytunnels. Cross this stile and the next one, just yards ahead, to enter a field.

Turn left in the field to follow its boundary along to the corner of the field and then right for some tens of yards till you reach some rails with a stile. Cross the stile, looking carefully at the yellow waymarking sign here to help guide your direction across the next field, in case the line of the footpath has not been reinstated by the farmer. On the far side of the field there is a hedgerow and you want to aim for its right-hand end. Once you have reached that point, the path continues across the field, roughly paralleling the field boundary (which also marks the line of the railway) on your right to a metal kissing gate into the next field. The path now heads across the corner of this field, aiming just to the left of a conifer plantation on the far side of the railway line where you will find a stile.

🔴 **9** Cross the stile and then carefully cross the railway line and then another stile to enter a small field. Here you want to head to the left of the conifer plantation to a gateway that will lead into the next field. Go through the gateway and then follow the field boundary on your left down to another gate. Go through this and keep ahead through the yard to a stile and gate which lead out onto a road.

Turn right on the road and this will lead you round to the Bird on the Rock tearooms, and you turn left to return to where you parked.

It is worth walking through the churchyard (and visiting the church if you wish), to leave it on its far left-hand corner and turn right on the track. You will soon reach the site of Clungunford motte which has a permissive path allowing you to visit it.

CLUNGUNFORD CHURCH AND CASTLE

The church dates from the 1300s (the roof timbers have been dated by dendrochronology to between 1329 and 1339) with a porch and tower dating from a Victorian restoration in 1895. There is a memorial window in the church which includes good representations of the local breed of Clun sheep.

The remains of the castle consist of a small originally circular motte, much mutilated by quarrying on its eastern and southern sides, yet with traces of the original ditch remaining on the eastern side. This would have connected with a stream on the south side of the motte which has probably been straightened in more recent times. Excavations have revealed layers of ash, some pottery of which pieces were identified as Norman, and fragments of stone mortar. The castle might have been built to protect a crossing of the River Clun.

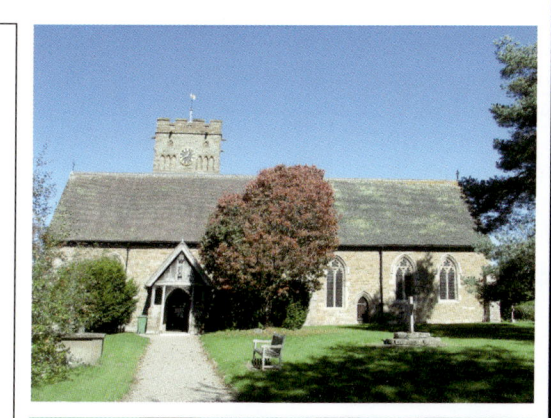

Walk 4
Offa's Dyke west of Clun

5.75 miles. Largely on tracks and lanes with some field paths, this walk follows one of the best preserved lengths of Offa's Dyke, with sweeping views in all directions. There are no stiles, unless you choose to walk along part of the dyke itself.

Head out of Clun on the A488 towards Knighton, and just past the church and up the hill, turn right on the minor road signposted Springhill and Anchor. You want to park near a crossroads reached in about a mile and a half.

❶ The walk starts by following the road signposted Springhill and Anchor, then immediately turning left onto a lane signposted to Burfield. Follow this lane all the way to Burfield farm, passing the house to its right and following the track out of the farmyard, through a gateway, and along into a field. Where the track forks, take the left-hand branch across a bridge over a stream and follow it up to the corner of a piece of woodland. Go through a field gate here and the track then follows a field boundary on your right. In due course it crosses the line of Offa's Dyke and continues on to meet a minor road.

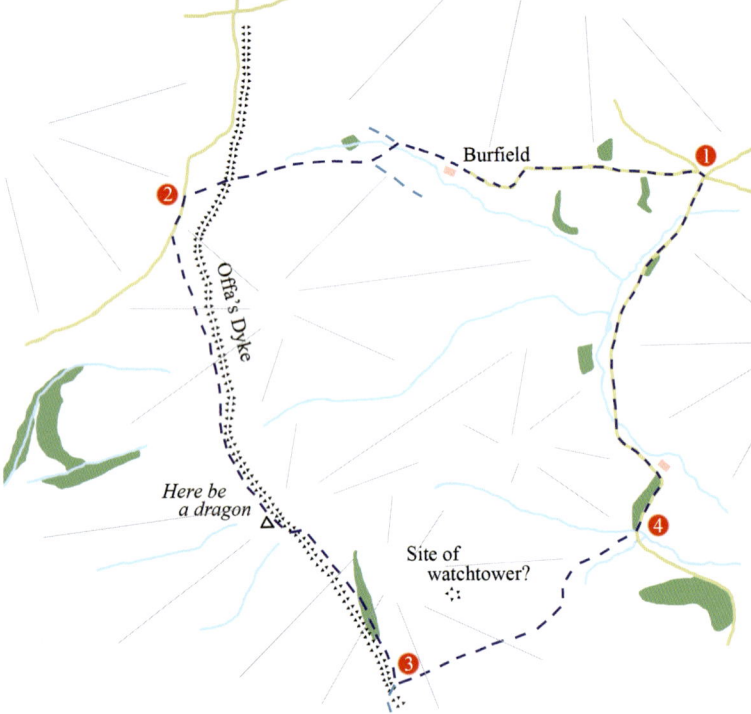

❷ Turn left on the road and follow it uphill, turning left onto a bridleway where the road bends to the right. Follow this grassy stretch along and it'll soon meet a stoned track on which you keep left. All this stretch gives you good views of Offa's Dyke to your left.

Keep on the track and it will gradually bring you ever closer to the line of the dyke, eventually crossing the

OFFA'S DYKE

'There was in Mercia in fairly recent times a certain vigorous king called Offa, who terrified all the neighbouring kings and provinces around him, and who had a great dyke built between Wales and Mercia from sea to sea.' So wrote Asser in his *Life of King Alfred* in 893, nearly a hundred years after the dyke's construction. The comment 'from sea to sea' has bedevilled the dyke ever since. Presuming the 'seas' to be the north Welsh coast and the Severn Estuary, antiquarians, historians and map makers have linked various dykes together and called the whole 'Offa's Dyke', but the dyke can only securely be said to run from near the north Welsh coast to near Kington, and possibly to the Wye to the north-west of Hereford. There is no evidence of any dyke that could form part of a 'sea to sea' structure over a 20-mile stretch in the vicinity of Hereford, and further south an assorted clutch of dykes have been suggested to form parts of Offa's structure.

Even the part which can safely be called Offa's Dyke because of a certain uniformity in its form and route across the landscape varies in its structure depending upon the type of soil, the lie of the land and, presumably, the numbers of workmen, their commitment and the skill of the foreman. Originally the V-shaped ditch on the west side was cut about 2 metres deep, and the bank raised to a height some 8 metres above the bottom of the ditch. Sometimes there is a small bank on the outer side of the ditch; this may simply have been created when clearing out debris from the ditch once the dyke had been constructed, although it does make the ditch deeper and even more of a barrier and so could have been part of the design. The ground was first stripped of its turves, which were placed in the bank as it was constructed to help hold the loose soil together. Turves were also taken from the area behind the dyke, sometimes creating the false impression that a ditch was also dug on the east of the dyke. No evidence for any palisade on the dyke has ever been found, but parts may have been faced in stone. Many of the current gaps in the dyke are modern creations, but in places the dyke has been angled to overlook where trackways (which have at times become minor roads) pass through the dyke, suggesting that these could have been controlled crossing places. Underneath the dyke have been found small marking out trenches and the occasional post hole, presumably where a stake was hammered into the ground to mark the line of the dyke.

What was the dyke's purpose? From its positioning, with areas of Saxon settlement already to its west in places when it was constructed, it might have been built as a 'backbone' to the Mercian border with Powys. Certainly its design, not least in the area of this walk, is such that it is very prominent when approaching from the west, so marking out an obvious line that needed to be crossed if travelling from the west and what that might mean in terms of a change of jurisdiction. It was never constructed to be a defendable line like Hadrian's Wall, but it could have been patrolled to keep an eye out for Welsh raiding parties, and its steep bank and ditch would have hindered rustlers marching away with oxen, cattle and sheep. Yet there is no strong evidence that the dyke was ever maintained; the ditch would have started to fill in from the day it was completed. Perhaps its real purpose lies in Offa's attempt to equate himself

OFFA'S DYKE (cont) with the greatest king of his age, Charlemagne. In or shortly before 789, Charlemagne suggested that one of Offa's daughters marry his eldest son, to which Offa responded that that would be acceptable if his own son, Ecgfrith, could marry one of Charlemagne's daughters. This so irked Charlemagne that he closed Frankish ports to English merchants. Could it be that Offa, in his own fit of pique and rage (his character suggests he was capable of both), decided on a project that would mark him out as an equal of Charlemagne, and that this project was the building of Britain's greatest dyke?

dyke just past a trig point on the right. Watch out for the dragon on the left at that point! You might at some point choose to walk along the dyke itself, but beware: badgers have created a lot of holes and unevenness in the dyke, not always easily spotted, and some of the stiles are not in the best state of repair. Also, walking on the dyke only helps to degrade it further. Keep on the track and follow it alongside some old coniferous woodland. As you start to descend, the stony track turns right through a gate and crosses the line of the dyke, but you keep ahead on a grassy track and so on through two fields, keeping the dyke to your right.

3 At the bottom of the second field, where the main track heads right to cross the dyke again, you want to turn left to follow the field boundary on your right and head at right angles away from the line of the dyke. When you pass through a gate into the next field, look up the hillside. On the skyline you'll see some bumps in the ground, marking the site of an old earthwork.

> ### EARTHWORK ON HILL
> Slightly on the south-eastern downhill side of the crest of the hill immediately 'behind' Offa's Dyke is a small, five-sided enclosure with rounded corners measuring some 50m across. The enclosing bank includes small stones and stands between 1.6 and 1.3m above the bottom of an outer ditch. The original entrance was on the eastern side. This could be the site of an Iron Age or Romano-British farmstead, but it is an unusual shape and size for such a feature, and it might instead be the site of a watchtower well positioned to send signals, perhaps using fire and smoke, to those behind the dyke, warning of an approaching raiding party.

Cross this next field and go through a gate just up from the field boundary on your right. In the next field, aim for a gate not quite halfway up the opposite field boundary and just above an area which hides a spring. Go through this gate and then follow the field boundary on your right to a gate and stile into the next field. Here the path follows the line of a ridge in the ground (as shown in the photograph above) that starts just in front of you and drops down to join a track. Turn left on the track and follow it round and then down the hillside, passing through gates, to meet a minor road. Facing you is the site of a small sandstone quarry which has been in existence since at least the late 1800s, from which time it has been marked on Ordnance Survey maps.

🔴 **4** Turn left on the road and follow it back to the crossroads near to which you parked.

Walk 5
Clun & Bury Ditches

7.75 miles in rolling countryside on a mixture of minor roads, tracks and paths, with none of the ascents being very arduous. Several of the paths in the first half of the walk cross fields and can be muddy in places, but most are in good condition and well used, and there is only the occasional stile. The hill-fort of Bury Ditches affords widespread views of the surrounding countryside, while Clun Castle features at the end of the walk.

❶ Park in Clun in the car park by the river. Walk back to the bridge and cross it, and walk up the road to the right to the point where it makes a sharp turn left. Here, turn right and walk past the Sun Inn.

> **SUN INN**
> This timber-framed inn, parts of which date back to before 1500, has previously been a house and a shop. In the ground-floor bar there is a panel between the timber framing that was painted in a floral pattern, probably during the 1700s.

Keep going until you reach Hospital Street on the left. (It doesn't have a street name plate, but the turning is just after the Methodist chapel.) Walk down Hospital Street and on the right you'll see Trinity Hospital (Clun's alms-houses), the garden and chapel of which are usually open for visitors.

TRINITY HOSPITAL ALMSHOUSES

These were founded in 1607 by Henry Howard, Earl of Northampton, who died in 1614 but left money in his will for their completion. They were built as a single storey block around a quadrangle, with a chapel added in the 19th century. Detailed statutes for the running of the almshouses stipulated that they were to house 12 poor men (nine from Clun and three from Bishop's Castle). They had to be at least 56 years old, be of good character, have lived in the prescribed area for at least five years and be able to recite the Ten Commandments, the Lord's Prayer and the Creed. There was also to be a warden, who was to be unmarried and aged at least 40. He had to collect the rents due to the almshouses, pay each resident 13s 4d a month, buy each resident a 'sad colour' gown of kersey to be worn each day, with a gown of blue broadcloth bought every fourth year for wearing on Sundays and festivals. He also had to equip the communal dining hall, keep the building topped up with firewood, repair walls, keep the accounts and much besides. It was from him that the residents had to obtain permission to go into Clun, which was only allowable at certain times of the day, and then they were not allowed to go to an alehouse. The residents had to go to the chapel twice a day, pray in their rooms three times a day and go to the parish church on Sunday. Despite these and other rules and restrictions, because residents were well catered for, living there was popular and bribery was sometimes involved in trying to obtain a place. On occasions the behaviour of the residents caused a local outcry, one drunken party when the warden was away lasting a week. With the funds endowed, the number of dwellings was increased over time to 16, and the building still functions as an almshouse.

Having visited Trinity Hospital, turn right to continue along Hospital Street, and at the top, turn right and follow the road round to the left, initially following signs to the Memorial Hall and the Youth Hostel, though fairly quickly you'll pass the former on your left and the latter on your right.

CLUN MILL/YHA

The youth hostel is in a former early 19th-century watermill, which was extended and re-equipped in 1850, ceasing working in 1926. The machinery from this date is still virtually complete inside the building, with an unusual Whitelaw turbine of c.1854 that drove three sets of stones which remain as features in the dormitories.

The road will then bend to the right, past a house on the right decorated with painted livestock profiles. A little further on, keep an eye out for a stile on the right.

❷ Cross this stile and bear left to cross a small corner of the field and reach another stile and bridge. Once over these, the path continues on the same line to another stile on the far side of the field. Cross this stile and turn right on the path you meet on the other side. This soon leads over a footbridge into a hollow-way which you follow uphill. At its end you enter a field in which you keep to the field boundary on your left. At the end of this field the path for a while regains an element of its hollow-way nature, and you keep following the field boundary on your left through another field to a corner of woodland which you enter.

❸ Just inside the wood the path divides and you take the left-hand option, dropping downhill to a gate into a field. Go through the gate, turn right and follow the edge of the wood to a gate into the next field. Through this gate, the path turns half left to drop down the hillside towards where the stream in the valley bottom 'elbows' into the field. Cross the stream by a footbridge to the left of a bridge used by farm vehicles. The path then heads uphill through the field on the far side, aiming for a gate on a track that runs along the bottom of a wood, the gate itself being just to the left of a large single oak that stands just inside the field boundary. Go through the gate and follow the track, it presently leading through Stepple farm.

❹ At the farm, pass to the right of the house and between ranges of barns. Continue on the track and it will lead briefly back to close to the edge of the woodland, before angling away once more and heading down the track towards a house in another small valley. (If the weather's been wet, keep to the upper part of the field, near the wood, to avoid the worst of the mud, and then walk downhill to rejoin the track.) Just before you reach the house, turn off the track to pass to the left of the house and cross the stream, then turn right and follow the course of the stream, now on your right. (If you have the OS map with you, it will show the path taking a course more in the middle of the field, but the route has been slightly diverted in recent years.) At the end of the field and immediately above the stream, go through the kissing gate into the next small field, and keep following the stream to another gate. Once you're through this gate and in the next field, the path slants up and across the hillside (passing to the left of a group of bushes) to a gate near the far top corner into a patch of scrubby ground beyond. Follow the path through this patch to a gate in the fence on your left that leads out onto the track that serves the buildings you've recently been passing to your left.

❺ Turn right on the track and follow it along to where it meets a minor road. Turn left on the road and follow this till you reach a parking and picnic area on the left. Turn left into this and then bear right on the wide path that slants up and across the hillside. This will lead you, via a gate near the top, into the ramparts of Bury Ditches. Not far into the hillfort you can take a path off to the right

BURY DITCHES

This is a roughly oval multivallate hillfort surrounded, from the south-eastern side round to the western, by two ramparts with a ditch in between, with three and sometimes four ramparts on the rest of the perimeter where the slope of the surrounding ground is less steep. A further low bank outside the fourth rampart is thought to be simply a boundary bank. There is an inturned entrance on the north-eastern side with a long passage, through which this walk enters the hillfort; this is best seen in the aerial photo below. Another entrance is on the south-western side (through which the walk leaves) where the additional ramparts running down from the north terminate outside the southern ramparts to form an entrance which is channelled between the ramparts. The ramparts would have been built in several phases and both entrances are probably late features that would probably have been protected by guardhouses. The good preservation of the banks, retaining steep sides, suggest that stone has been used in their construction, which is evidenced where the banks have been eroded. In the 20th century the hillfort was planted with conifers, many of which were blown down in early 1976, causing much damage to the ground surface, but scooped out hollows that back onto the inner rampart are likely to represent the locations of huts or other structures. Pillow mounds, representing the site of a rabbit warren, have also been identified, with a platform near the present toposcope possibly being that on which the warrener's house stood.

© CPAT 89-c-0224

which will lead you to a toposcope naming the various hills you can see around you. Return to the main path and turn right to walk through the hillfort to reach a gate on the far side.

❻ Go through the gate and follow the track to the right. Before long the track becomes wooded on both sides. About 20 yards after this, look for the small path off to the left that leads downhill (it's opposite an oak tree on the right of the track). Take this path and follow it downhill. It will cross an old track, after which it turns to the left and gently descends through the trees, making an

S-bend at one point. Further ahead the path divides and you keep to the main path, turning right and descending more sharply downhill to meet a stony track on which you turn right.

Keep following this track as it swings to the left, crossing the line of another path, and ignore other tracks to right and left. In due course your track will be joined by the Shropshire Way slanting in from your right, and it is the Shropshire Way you now follow back to Clun. Ignore another track off to the left and then, just before the stoned track bends to the right, the Shropshire Way slants off to the left. Follow this, and it will pass old quarry workings on your left, then cross other paths to become a track with woodland on your left and fields on your right. Later the track passes between fields on each side, bends to the left and then sharp right to join a tarmacked road near a house that serves teas at certain times of the year. Keep on the tarmac and it will lead you all the way back into Clun.

Once you're in the town, follow the lane all the way to where it comes to a T junction. Cross straight over to the track leading to the castle.

Having visited the castle, turn right onto the road and follow it along and round a corner into Clun's main street. Turn right and head back down to the river, cross the bridge and turn right to the car park.

CLUN CASTLE
The castle at Clun was commenced c.1090 by either Picot de Say, who fought with William the Conqueror in 1066, or his son, who held the Honour of Clun, a small Norman barony, at the time of the Domesday Survey. It was built in conjunction with the intended formation of a planned borough to its east. Initially it comprised the large motte (cut out of the hill on which the castle stands), a structure on the motte, probably of timber, and a curtain wall, perhaps also initially of timber. The castle passed to the Fitzalans by marriage c.1150.

CLUN CASTLE (cont) In 1195-96 the castle may have been attacked and burnt by Prince Rhys of Deheubarth in south-west Wales, though it is possible that the castle referred to in the records of the time is in fact Colwyn Castle in Radnorshire. In 1215 William Fitzalan was due to inherit the castle but was faced with payment of an enormous fee by King John for so doing. (One of the main clauses in the subsequent Magna Carta was to reduce such fees to previous levels.) William died and his brother took up arms in the general revolt against King John, taking Clun from royal control. In a surprise attack in 1216 John retook the castle. The castle was returned to the Fitzalans under Henry III, but their loyalty was found suspect in the wars against Llywelyn the Great in 1233 and the castle was once again garrisoned with royal troops, who saw off an attack by Llywelyn.

It was soon back in the hands of the Fitzalans, who built the mock keep sometime between the 1270s and 1290s, 'mock' as with its feet in the moat it would have been relatively easily undermined by a determined attacker and is thus not likely to have been built as a defensible structure, but more likely as a hunting lodge for guests, albeit in the style of a Norman keep. A description of the castle in 1272, before the keep was built, records that the roof of the existing tower wanted covering in lead, and the bridge between the inner and outer, southern, bailey needed repairing, and mentioned that a gate in the castle wall in the outer bailey was under construction. This suggests that the other walls and buildings probably underwent extensive remodelling at this time as well, after which the castle also included domestic buildings, stables, a bakehouse, a water garden and a fishpond. As well as serving as a hunting lodge, the castle would have also been the base for administering Fitzalan holdings in the Marches. In 1540 the castle was described by Leland as 'somewhat ruinous', and though it was abandoned by the time of the Civil War it was slighted by Parliament in 1646. It was nevertheless still mentioned as a residence in 1653, if for the last time.

In 1731 the court house, thought to have been built during the reign of Elizabeth I, stood on the site of the present bowling green and contained one court that dealt with the Lord of the Manor's cases and a second that handled borough cases. It was demolished in 1789 when the Town Hall was built. The Duke of Norfolk purchased the castle in the late 19th century and carried out some refurbishment work. The castle was used by Sir Walter Scott as the model for 'Guarde Douloureuse' in his novel *The Betrothed*, and was the third HQ of the Lone Piners in Malcolm Saville's stories.

The present remains include the keep, which is four storeys high (the lower floor being used as storerooms and the upper three as domestic quarters for the family), a pair of 13th-century wall towers and a fragment of the curtain wall. One small bailey stood to the east of the castle and now holds an unusually-shaped bowling green, whilst a larger bailey lies to the south of the castle. To the west of the castle, on the far side of the River Clun, are the slight earthwork remains of a water garden that included a square moated area in which would have stood pavilions around a central formal garden. There are also remains of fishponds.

In 1991 English Heritage took the castle into guardianship and began to plan a programme of repair.

Walk 6
Bishop's Castle

6.25 miles on paths and minor roads in the main, with largely good conditions underfoot, though this can depend upon whether any field has been recently ploughed or where cattle are stationed. After leading you through Bishop's Castle the walk takes you out to the Bishop's Moat, the site of an early Norman castle, and back again, with wide views of the surrounding countryside from the vicinity of this castle. The countryside is gently rolling and the ascents and descents are pretty kind on the body. There are a few stiles.

Park somewhere in the main street; it's often easiest down at the bottom, near the church.

🔴 Walk up the main street, taking the alleyway to the left of the recently modernised Town Hall and past the House on Crutches. Turn right on the road at the top of the alley, then left at the junction quickly reached and then on up the hill along Bull Street, with the large stone-carved Clive coat of arms in its little square to your right.

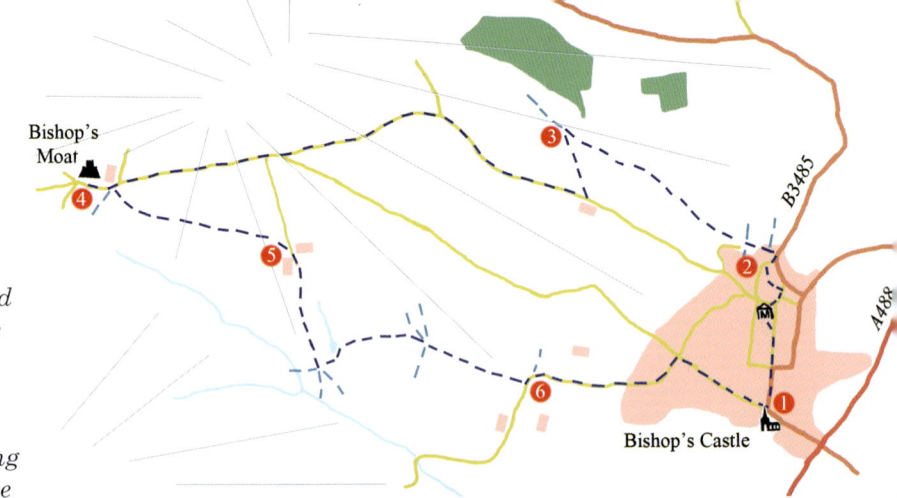

BISHOP'S CASTLE

Around the end of the 8th century the bishop of Hereford was given the Lydbury North estate, which included some 18,000 acres of land. By c.1080 a castle had been built on a site to the west of the town to provide some form of protection or warning system for those living in the area, a site reached on this walk. In c.1127, the bishop built a castle within the town whilst laying out burgess plots down the slope to its south towards but not as far as the church at the foot of the hill, which had probably been founded earlier as a chapelry of Lydbury North.

By the mid 1150s the town was thriving, with some 46 burgesses, and in 1167 the Lydbury North estate was providing about a third of the income of Hereford diocese. It was around 1167 that the timber castle was replaced in stone, but the town only received a market charter in 1248. In 1263 the castle and town were seized by John Fitzalan during the period of upheaval when Simon de Montfort amongst others was trying to find a way of controlling the king's excesses and developing Parliament in so doing. The castle was damaged in the process but was restored by Bishop Cantilupe, and when, in 1356, Bishop Trilleck, following the advent of the Black Death, sought to reduce the number of manors that the diocese maintained to six, Bishop's Castle was one of those retained. In 1539 Leland noted that the castle was still well maintained, if not 'very high'.

In 1559 Elizabeth I acquired the town as a result of a forced exchange of properties with Bishop Scory, the castle then being described as comprising 13 rooms roofed with lead, a tower on the east with stables, two rooms roofed in tile and two further rooms in a new building located between the gate and the prison tower, along with a dovecote.

In 1573 a new charter was granted to the town which made it self-governing with a chief bailiff and chief burgesses. The charter also granted the town the right to elect two MPs. At the time of the 1584 election there was an eligible electorate of just 40, and soon elections became notorious for the quantity of bribery, treating and threats issued by the candidates, especially as contests moved from being between Independents to being between Tories and Whigs. In 1701, 81 votes were cast, one burgess saying he was to receive £5 whichever way he voted. In a by-election of 1753, electors were treated to 1,781 gallons of ale and 'other liquors'. In 1763 Clive of India took up residence in the vicinity and, with the riches available to him, Bishop's Castle soon became his 'pocket' and rotten borough. By 1802 the electorate had expanded to c.170 who each expected some 20-25 guineas in order to vote the 'right' way. The rotten borough was abolished with the passing of the third Reform Act in 1832.

The story of the Bishop's Castle railway is one of stop-start for most of its life due to continual financial difficulty. Conceived in 1859, its route was surveyed in 1860, and it was opened (as far as it ever reached) in 1866. It struggled through to 1935 before finally closing. Its story is told as part of the display in the House on Crutches Museum. This tends to be open in the afternoons on spring and summer weekends; check on hocmuseum.org.uk.

BUILDINGS

As you ascend the street the houses are initially a mixture of cottages, typical urban dwellings and handsome town houses. As the steepness of ascent increases, these are replaced by more commercial and public buildings, and then comes Porch House on the left. The building dates to the 1560s and the first-floor lozenge work is almost entirely original, but the ground floor studding is largely a replacement of c.1990. The porch was added in the early 1600s.

The Town Hall faces down the street. Built c.1765, the building initially contained the town lock-up in the basement, an open arcaded market space at ground level and a council chamber above. It has recently been restored, retaining a space for local markets, along with a visitor information service (except on Sundays) and meeting rooms.

To the left of the Town Hall is the House on Crutches, spanning a cobbled lane.

The carved stone displaying the heraldic crest of Clive of India – note the Indian elephant – is all that remains of what became known as the old market hall and subsequent Powis Institute. This building, constructed in 1781, was the gift of the Clive/Powis family, the 'institute' essentially being a reading room over the market hall. It fell into disrepair and was pulled down in 1951.

The Castle Hotel dates to 1719. The Three Tuns Brewery, which began life in 1642 and now occupies a building constructed in 1888, was, by 1970, just one of four pubs in Britain that still brewed beer before CAMRA helped inspire a renaissance of local brewing.

All that is left of the castle is the shape of the bailey, a circular bowling green on the site of the motte and some reconstructed walling in Castle Street.

Just past London House/5 Bull Street on the left, turn left on a footpath which is waymarked for the Shropshire Way. The Shropshire Way is what you follow for the next few hundred yards, the footpath soon becoming a track past the bowling green on the left (there are information boards about it on the wall), which is on the site of the castle motte, and then back as a narrow footpath between the walls of two houses.

🔴 **2** When you reach a road at the end of the path, turn right and keep ahead at the crossroads quickly reached. Just 20 yards beyond the crossroads, follow the Shropshire Way off to the left down a track and then through a gate onto a path. Shortly after this gate the path divides and this is where you leave the Shropshire Way, taking the left-hand path, following it round to the right as it approaches a road to follow the edge of a group of garden plots or allotments to your right and then enters some woodland.

The path shadows the road on your left for a while but when this bends to the left the path keeps ahead across a grassy patch to cross a track and then head between two hedges to a gate out onto another track. Cross this track too onto a track on the far side and follow this up to a gate and stile. On the other side of these, the path continues ahead and uphill, under an arch of vegetation formed by the hedges on each side. At the end of this path cross the stile, and then follow the field boundary round on your left till you reach another stile immediately past a pair of field gates. Cross this stile and then turn right up the hedgerow and follow it to the top of the field where you'll find another stile. Cross this and turn slightly left to cross the next field, aiming for a point just to the right of all the free standing trees in the field. Here you will find another stile (close to a telegraph pole on the far side of the field boundary) which you cross. The path crosses this next field aiming just to the right of a low dark barn on the rising ground ahead.

As you cross the field you'll see a field gate in its far hedgerow which is your target. Once through this gate you are going to take an interesting route through the field so as to stay on public paths! Initially your target is the right-hand end of the hedgerow you can see on the far side of the field above you (and to the left of a solitary oak tree in the field).

❸ Once here, you turn sharp left in front of the hedge and shadow it across the field, in due course heading for the left-hand gate of two gates at the end of the field. Through this you'll find yourself on an old track with overgrown hedgerows to each side. Follow this along to a gate into the next field and then down to a road.

Turn right on the road (which is part of the Kerry Ridgeway) and walk along it till you reach the Bishop's Moat on the right-hand side: this is near the crest of the ridge, just past a house on the right and shortly before you reach a road leading off to the right.

❹ Having seen the moat, turn back along the road and opposite the house now on the left take the stile alongside a farm gate into a field. Two paths cross the field from this point and you want that to the left, which crosses a corner of the field aiming for a kissing-gate on your immediate horizon that leads into the next field. Once through this gate, you cross the next field, aiming for a point just to the left of Titterstone Clee, the hill which is hopefully visible on the far horizon. As you cross the field you will see a large group of farm buildings down the slope and your specific target becomes a kissing-gate alongside a field gate in the hedgerow on the far side of the field at a point to the left of this group of buildings. Once through the kissing-gate head across the next field, still aiming just to the left of the group of farm buildings. As you near the hedgerow at the bottom of this field you will see it has

BISHOP'S MOAT
A castle was developed here *c.*1080 by the bishop of Hereford on the route of the Kerry Ridgeway and gave wide views across the Camlad valley. The motte stands some 9m high above the ditch with a diameter at the top of *c.*12m. The surrounding ditch is best preserved to its south-west and north-east. The castle could well have been designed to serve essentially as a watch tower, though its 90 x 60m bailey to the east would suggest a more permanent occupation. The bank that surrounds the bailey has an entrance on the eastern (English!) side. The castle may have been captured by Llywelyn ab Iorwerth in 1233.

a slight kink, and immediately beyond the kink a footpath gate leads into the corner of a field on the far side of the hedge. Go through this gate and then diagonally cross the field to its far corner, where you will join a lane that serves the farm.

⑤ Turn right on the lane and go past the house and a barn into the farmyard, to then take the second of the two field gates on your left. Through this gate, the footpath follows the line of the farmyard on your right to a kissing-gate. Through this, keep following first the farmyard and then the fence on your right, heading gently down the curve of the hill. At the end of the field you come to a stile, in front of which you turn left and follow the field boundaries on your right, passing first below a dammed pool and then above it and round to the left. At a right-angled corner you reach in the fence by some hawthorn trees, turn right to keep following the fence, soon passing through a small gate into the next field. From here, keep following the field boundaries on your right, ignoring signs for paths to left and right, and passing through two more fields. Near the end of the second of these you join a track which you follow to a gate out onto a road.

⑥ Turn left on this and follow it along into the outer edges of Bishop's Castle, turning right when you reach a crossroads. Follow this road back to the church and the bottom of the town's main street.

CARRIAGE WORKS

On the left just before you reach the Six Bells is a carriage works of the early 1900s. A workshop in which the upholstery was made, together with other items for furnishing the carriages, was supported on cast-iron pillars, the carriages being assembled on the ground floor underneath. The site also included a forge.

CHURCH OF ST JOHN THE BAPTIST

A church probably existed here from the early days of Christianity in the Marches, to then be rebuilt by the Normans. This church was partially burnt during the Civil War by the Royalists in 1645 following a skirmish with Parliamentarian forces, the Royalist commander justifying the act by saying that the church had been used 'for the preaching of sedition'. It was heavily restored and much altered in 1860, and even the tower is now of doubtful Norman heritage. The Norman tub font survives, however, as does the top half of a figure of an Elizabethan priest carrying a Bible. There is an interesting range of Victorian stained glass.

Walk 7
Mitchell's Fold, Ladywell & Grit Mines

5 miles along two hillsides on either side of a valley, one side served by wide tracks, one by a section of minor road and field paths, and all tending to be in good condition. There are several stiles in the latter part of the walk. There are good views to be had, especially from Stapeley Hill, the ridge on which sits Mitchell's Fold stone circle, whilst on the other side of the valley there are some impressive and varied remains of lead mining to be seen. If you wish to see the Hoarstones, a second stone circle, with any clarity, you will need to bring binoculars.

Turn west off the A488 between Lydham and Hope, on a road signposted to White Grit, Priest Weston and Chirbury and with a brown sign indicating 'stone circle', and near the remains of a mine building. Where the road bends to the left to cross the Welsh border, as indicated by a sign marking the start of the county of Powys, you want to park on the gravelled area on the right near the start of a track.

❶ The walk starts by heading down this track, crossing a cattle grid. Keep left at all the main junctions you come to (ignoring those that simply serve houses, of course!) At one point you'll pass a sign to Laburnum Cottage off to the right.

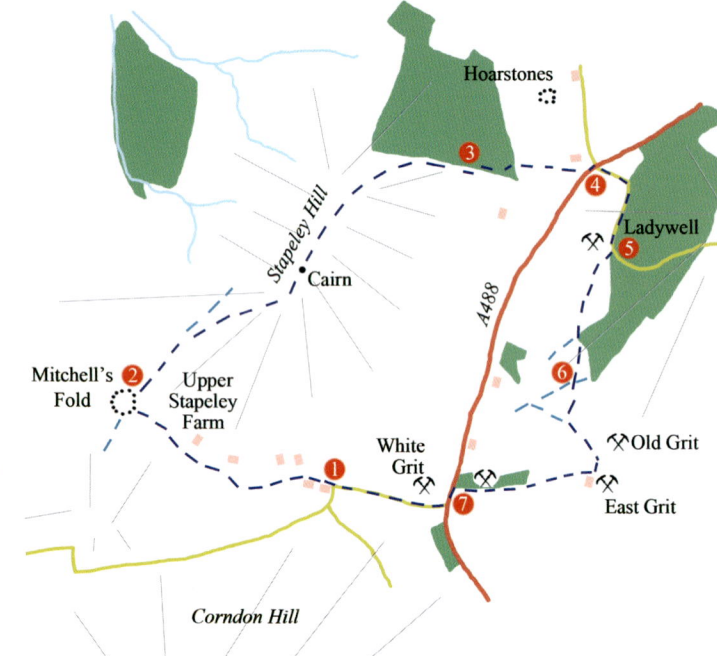

This is now a red brick bungalow, but it started life as a squatter's cottage in the late 18th or early 19th century, as no doubt did some of the other houses in the area. Past Laburnum Cottage the track will lead you gently uphill to the entrance to Upper Stapeley Farm. Keep to the left of this, following the now slighter track first briefly downhill and then uphill. As you approach the crest of the ridge you'll start to spot some of the stones of Mitchell's Fold stone circle against the skyline.

62

MITCHELL'S FOLD STONE CIRCLE

The name Mitchell is believed to derive from the Old English *micel*, meaning large. Although most of the stones rise only a little above ground level, this stone circle is one of the 30 largest regular stone circles in England, and a monument believed to date to the Late Neolithic or Bronze Age. It is believed that there were originally 30 or so stones, of which 15 still survive, the circle suffering from damage as recently as 1994 and again in 1997. Its function is believed to have been of a ritual or social nature, perhaps a gathering point for festivities or rites of passage. There were once more elements to the Neolithic/Bronze Age landscape in the vicinity: documentary evidence survives for three possible standing stones near Mitchell's Fold, two of which survived into the 19th century but all of which have now disappeared. The mutilated remains of a Bronze Age burial cairn still lie 90m south-east of the circle (on the rise in the ground in the direction of Corndon Hill), whilst an information board to the south of the circle details some of the lost monuments.

Of later date than the circle and standing stones, banks and ridges in the nearby landscape indicate an abandoned field system of uncertain date. They include a linear bank close to the west of the circle and another running north-south, the line of which you cross shortly after continuing the walk. The remains of ridge and furrow (from years of ploughing a single furrow with oxen) with an average width between ridges of 3m can be seen to the immediate north-east of the circle.

There are legends that tell of a giant using the circle as a milking parlour for his cows. Another story has it that a bountiful cow used to appear each night and could be milked by the local population on the one condition that she was never milked dry, which wouldn't happen if everyone only took a pailful. But if she was milked dry she would disappear. A malevolent 'witch' who lived not far away heard the story and was aggrieved at how well her neighbours were flourishing as a result of all the milk, and so went with others one night, but took a pail with a sieve for its bottom. Of course when it was her turn, the pail could never be filled, and the cow ran dry and vanished. The 'witch' was called Mitchel (spelled with one 'l' in the original tale) and divine vengeance turned her into one of the stones – hence the name of the circle, of course!

Some 300 yards from Mitchell's Fold once stood another stone circle, Mitchell's Fold Tenement, but this had been destroyed by the end of the 1800s.

❷ The walk continues by turning right (from the direction from which you approached the stone circle) and going gently uphill. Follow the main track for a way, then bear right along a smaller path and head for the summit cairn on the ridge. From here walk along the ridge to the next summit cairn, looking out for the remains of a prehistoric burial cairn that lies in the saddle between them. This is marked by a low mound of turf and stones surrounded by a shallow ditch and low outer bank; the path goes straight across it (see photograph on page *viii*).

Keep following the track along and then downhill towards a wood. At the bottom of the hill the track you're on turns right, but you want to bear left to join the track that follows the fence that marks the wood's edge. Follow this track until you reach a stile in the fence on your left.

❸ Cross this stile and turn right to follow the fence-line for about 25 yards, then pick up a path that wends its way between the conifers on your left and the fence on your right. Keep following the path, which starts to swing gently to the left and will lead you to a kissing gate into a field. Here, if you have brought binoculars, you might want to use them to search for the Hoarstones in the fields to your left; unfortunately no public path passes near the stones. (Look across the fields in a line slightly to the right of the wooded knoll on the skyline. The low standing stones are on the far side of the fields in an area of rough grass, just to the right of a cottage that lies in the trees behind the stones.) The path follows the fence on your left to the next corner of the field, where you pass out by a gate onto a track. Keep ahead on this, passing over a stile and through a gateway to reach the A488.

4 Turn left on the road, and then immediately right on a minor road. This will soon bend to the right in front of a wood. Continue walking along the road till you reach an old building belonging to Ladywell mine.

HOARSTONES
Hoarstone means boundary stone and the circle stands near the junction of three parishes, though it is also known as the Marsh Pool or Blackmarsh Circle. It is made up of 37 stones standing up to 3 feet high, with a single stone at the centre. Lines drawn from this to three gaps in the circle extend to three prominent hilltops, suggesting that it was aligned on these. Two Bronze Age barrows lie to the north of the circle. None of these three sites has been excavated.

There was a local belief as late as the 1880s that the stones were a fairies' ring where they danced on moonlit nights. Two of the stones have small holes and miners would fill these with a powder which they would set on fire when celebrating a wedding. An earlier story has it that Catholics, when needing to clandestinely celebrate mass, would give the sacrament from these holes, but that seems somewhat unlikely.

LADYWELL MINE
Lead-bearing ores were discovered here in the late 1700s during work to create Wood Level (see next page) which was serving mines to the north. It was usually worked as part of Grit mine, for which you'll see workings later in the walk, but in 1867 a company was formed to mine it as a separate entity. By 1872 a new company was formed to take the mine forward, but this folded in 1884 in a flurry of accusations: one of the principal promoters of the new company was thought to have given insufficient detail to the potential backers and lawsuits might have followed. The mine seems to have been in production, if only intermittently, between 1862 and the early 1880s. Some lead was produced and a little zinc, with a workforce that peaked at 43 in number, dwindling to just 8 by 1881. The surviving building is the engine house (the engine running pumps to keep the shafts and tunnels clear of water) – see the top photograph on page 66 – and this testifies that little expense was spared in equipping the mine, which was worked from a series of shafts, the mining tunnels often only just missing those from Grit to the south and Roman Gravels to the north.

SHROPSHIRE'S LEAD AND BARYTES MINING HISTORY

The history of many of the lead mines in west Shropshire is similar. A handful were certainly mined by the Romans as three lead pigs inscribed with Roman text have been found at mining sites in the area. The Romans were probably searching for silver, which often comes from lead ores, but the percentage of silver in the local ore is below commercial viability. Nevertheless, lead was mined by civilian enterprises and continued to be mined in small quantities throughout the medieval period, often to be used for water pipes and cisterns and also for roofing material. With the expansion of commercial enterprise following the Civil War, the restoration of the monarchy and the start of an overseas empire, the pace quickened. Subsequent years saw an increasing use of steam power to drive mining machinery and run pumps to keep the mines clear of water, the latter working in combination with levels – large underground drains that took water out from the mines and were built to service several mines. These were sometimes made large enough to carry small boats which could ferry ore out of the mines. The appropriately named Boat Level (at just over 2 miles long) was one such, Wood and Leigh Levels two others, though not designed for use by boats. By 1883 Shropshire was producing 12% of the country's lead. Sometimes zinc and silver were also produced; very occasionally, and given the right geology, copper too. But the price of lead fluctuated widely, mining was not easy, the veins of ore were unpredictable, and companies were constantly going bust or being taken over by others. With veins crisscrossing each other, some ground was worked at two different levels from different shafts or even different mines. Towards the end of the 1800s, as the quantity of lead mined diminished, some mines adapted to the mining of barytes, also known as spar – the source of barium compounds used in a variety of products – an industry that lasted widely into the 1920s and at some mines a little longer.

GRIT MINE

This was the name given to a group of mines, sometimes individually known by names such as Old Grit, (see the bottom photograph opposite), East Grit and White Grit. Ladywell, (see the top photograph opposite), as mentioned earlier, was also often part of this group, as was Roman Gravels to the north. The veins may indeed have been worked by the Romans, and again during the 12th and 13th centuries, though it is not certain which veins may have been worked at these dates. Again, the mines may have been worked in the 1600s, but during the 1760s a company was formed with the specific intention of mining this area. Some 17 named lead-ore bearing veins cross the land on which the mines stand, most running east-west but two running north-south, and by 1780 White Grit (for photographs see pages 68 and 69) was being developed, its engine house built at the junction of Squilver and Rider veins. By 1783 the shaft was ten yards long and a pumping engine was acquired to help sink the shaft to a depth of 60 yards, but this proved unsuccessful. There was a short boom in the early 1820s, but the future depended in part on constructing Leigh Level to help drain the mines, with mining intended across the area and over to Stapeley Hill (on which sits Mitchell's Fold stone circle), but law suits over the construction of a level and associated leases for mines only drained resources rather than water. Nevertheless, over time, across the area of the Grit mines a total of 25 shafts were sunk, several 120 yards deep, some 200, not all worked at the same time. The principal shaft remained at White Grit, where the buildings included an office, smithy and carpenter's shop, which are now the private dwellings alongside the A488 near the engine house. In between times, some of these buildings comprised the More Arms public house for about 70 years.

In 1827 the group of mines employed 160 men, some of whom worked in 32 'bargain' companies. These were headed by a miner who struck a bargain with a mine owner or agent to dig ore from a part of the mine for a set price per ton. Usually such companies comprised up to five men, but sometimes as many as 19. As for production of ore, some records suggest that the Grit mines together with those known as Gravels produced between 300 and 700 tons of ore a year between 1835 and 1845, whilst official figures for these same mines show a total of c.2,500 tons mined between 1846 and 1858. Certainly White Grit's engine house was extended and heightened c.1840 to house a new engine.

By 1882, however, much of the mining simply involved a couple of men working over the old tips, and in the 1920s the tips were again worked over, this time for barytes. A handful of men were employed in some years thereafter, with a new shaft sunk and the tips continually being worked over.

As for Stapeley Hill, which this walk went along earlier, veins of ore were wrongly assumed to extend westwards to the hill from Grit. Some trials were dug in the 1820s and for a while in the 1860s a mine called Stapeley formed part of the Grit family. Grit was put up for sale in 1865 and by 1866 Stapeley mine ceased to exist on the ground, if it ever had existed.

⑤ Carry on along the road for a few yards past the mine building and a very small copse, then cross the stile on your right into a field. From the stile the path heads down the field to join a track that runs alongside the fence below, on which you turn left and follow it along and gently up the hillside. At this point you are roughly following the course of Wood Level below you, built to follow New Briton vein and provide drainage. This part of the level, which has its outlet considerably further north at Hope, was constructed *c.* 1844-48. At the far end of the field you come to a clutch of gates and you go through the left-hand one or over the adjacent stile into the next field. There are two paths here and you want the left-hand one which heads a little to the right of the line of trees that jut out from the wood on your left. As you cross the field you'll see two stiles in the opposite fence, and it is the left-hand of these you want.

⑥ Once over the stile, there are again two paths and you want the left-hand one that heads to the far left-hand corner of the field. There are good views of the Stiperstones to your left. At the corner of the field, cross the stile on the left and follow the fenceline down the hill. Go through the gateway at the bottom into the field that contains the ruins of Old Grit mine, where Foxhole, Eider and New Briton veins meet.

Keep following the line of the hedge on your right towards a cluster of farm buildings that contain more old mine workings, these of East Grit, and so to a stile. Cross this and keep following the hedge on your right. At the end of the field pass out on the track on the far side, on which you turn right. Walk up the track past a house on your left to enter the next field. Once in this field, aim for the left-hand end of the wood at the top of the slope. There are disused mine shafts and old spoil heaps on the right.

Cross the stile at the top and then follow the left-hand edge of the wood: you are following the course of Rider Vein, pockmarked with mine workings on the surface. Cross the stile at the bottom of the field and walk straight ahead, passing the ruins of a powder house under swathes of ivy (top photograph opposite). This consists of two circular walls, one inside the other, which would have supported a lightweight roof, so that if the powder should ignite and explode, the walls would thrust the force of the explosion upwards, taking the roof with it. Remains of old shafts lie further to the right. Walk down to a stile which will lead you onto the A488.

7 Turn left on the A488 and immediately right to return to where you parked, passing round the remains of the engine house of White Grit mine (pictured above and left) as you do so.

Walk 8
Stiperstones, Tankerville & Bog Mines

5.25 miles largely on wide tracks with some minor roads and sections of connecting footpaths. It is a steep climb in places to the Stiperstones ridge, from which wide views are obtained, and please note that the path along the summit of the Stiperstones is very rocky in places and good ankle-supporting footwear is particularly advisable for this walk. Gates have recently largely replaced stiles on this walk. As well as part of the Stiperstones ridge with its various features, the walk includes the remains of Tankerville and Bog mines.

Park at the car park near the Bog Visitor Centre. (The car park is a short way along the road for Bridges.) We suggest heading for the visitor centre at the end of your walk, when you might also value some refreshment which can be acquired here.

❶ From the entrance to the car park, turn right on the road and walk uphill. Where the road bends sharply to the right, turn left down the gravelled track, almost immediately passing Hill Cottage to your right. When the track splits just beyond the cottage, keep left. You later pass on your right a single-storey building clad in timber together with some stables, beyond which you ignore the track to the left and keep straight

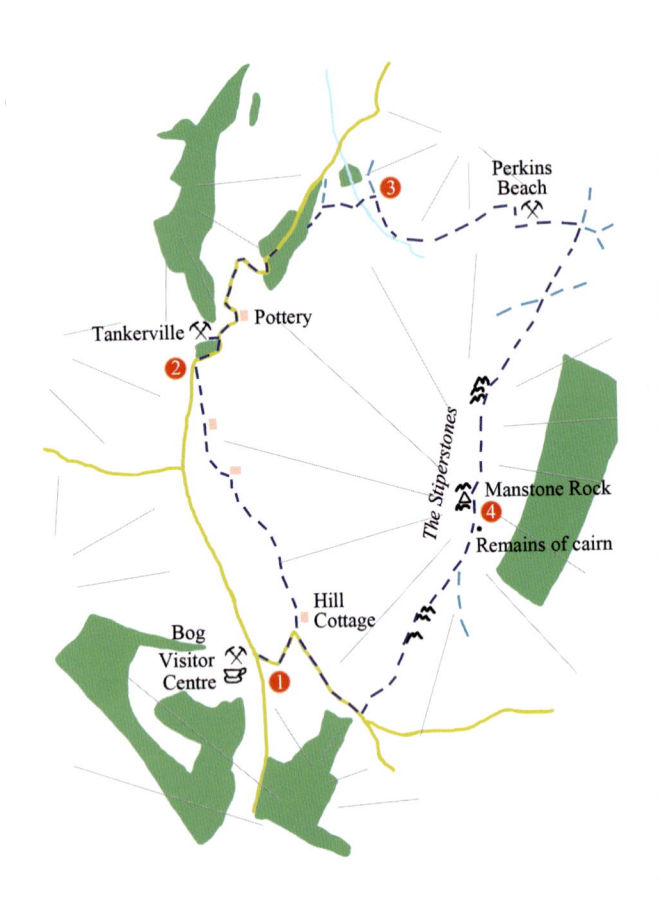

70

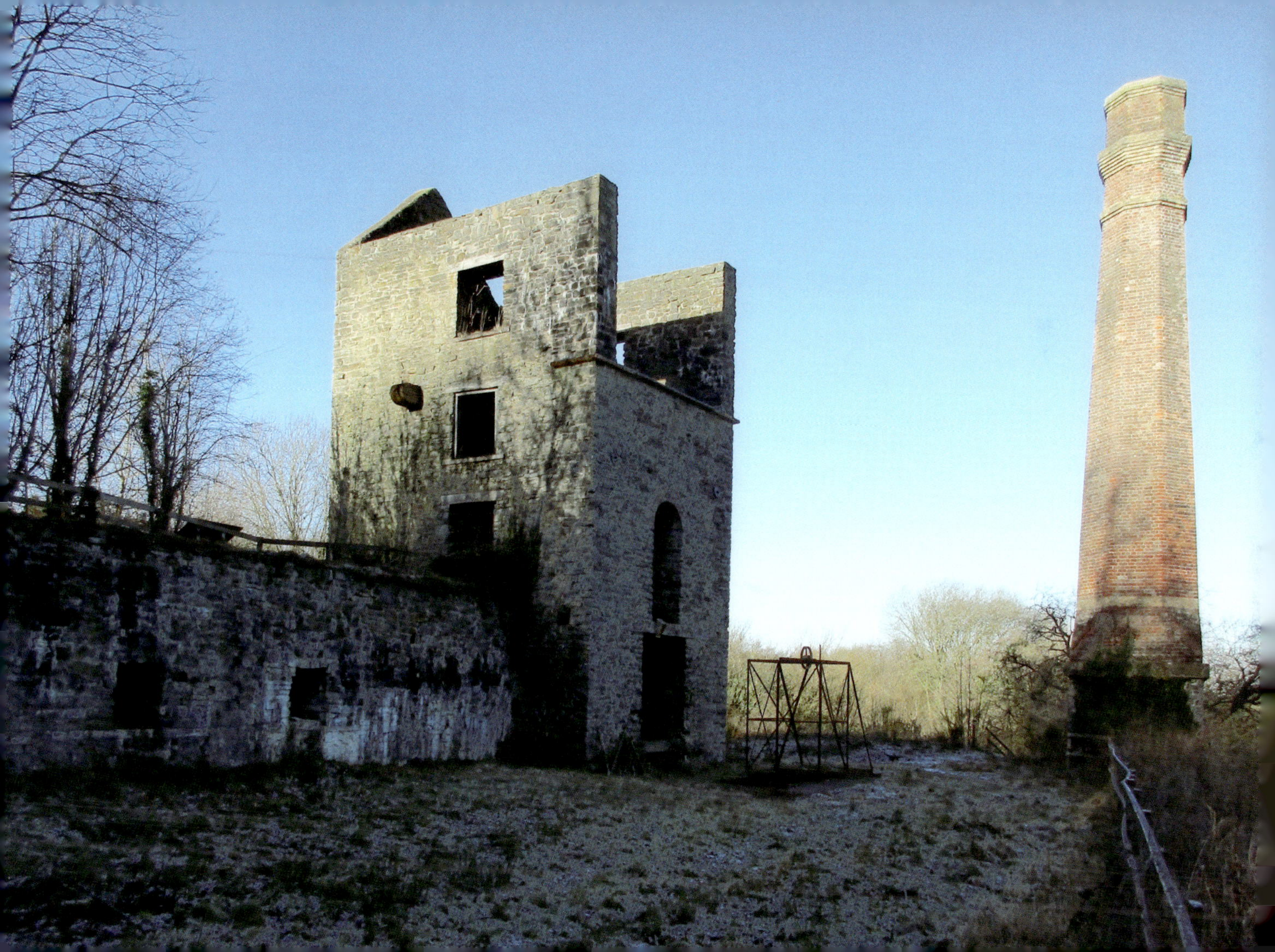

TANKERVILLE MINE

For a brief overview of mining in this area see page 66. This mine was first mentioned in 1830 when it was known as Ovenpipe mine and formed part of the Bog mining enterprise. This enterprise ran into financial difficulty and was sold c.1844 but it was not until the mid 1850s that the mine was really developed. During the 1860s it was run in conjunction with Bog, Perkins Beach and Pennerley mines, but came into separate ownership in 1869, when it was known as Tankerville mine. Further investment was raised and in 1871 Watson's Shaft was sunk, passing through almost pure galena, possibly the richest vein of lead ore then known in the world. For a brief few years the mine was hugely successful. In 1871 and 1872 it produced nearly 2,000 tons of lead ore each year (many mines then producing less than 100 tons a year), 1872's production representing over a quarter of Shropshire's total and 2.6% of national production. The years 1872 to 1883 also saw 23,000 ounces of silver produced, with a peak workforce in 1875 numbering 171. But the company running the mine over-expanded, digging new shafts and spending money trying to drain Pennerley mine, which they also owned but where they found no further ore. The price of lead fell and in May 1884 the company went into liquidation. Further licences were granted by the landowner to search for ore, but without success and in 1902 the mine equipment was sold by auction. Some barytes was mined between 1910 and 1923, and calcite from the tips during the inter-war period. During the Second World War stone from the tips was used to build runways at RAF airfields.

The mine tunnels were reached by ladders and 'kibble-riding', this despite Watson's Shaft being the deepest single shaft in the minefield at over 1,600 feet, nearly 600 of them below sea level. However, the veins have been described as being like fingers and did not spread far horizontally. The ore was sent to smelters at Pontesbury and later to Pontesford, and then, as the railway network expanded, further afield. The mine site was donated to the Shropshire Mines Trust in 1996. With the aid of grants, the Trust stabilised and repaired the remaining buildings. Around the dressing floor, the remains include metal headgear at the top of Watson's Shaft (now flooded for most of its depth and in any event blocked a short way down), the engine house, which ran a pump, an octagonal chimney that served the boiler house and a set of ore bins next to the engine house. (See photograph on previous page.)

ahead. Keep ahead at the next junction of tracks and the track will take you in a gentle arc past Brook House on your right and some sheds to your left. The track then reaches a 5-way junction of tracks. Keep straight ahead here, leaving two tracks to your right, and follow the track down to where it meets a road, ignoring yet another track off to the right.

❷ Turn right on the road and just before a sign for Tankerville Lodge near a small metal gate on the left, you'll see a footpath sign and a footpath that leads down to a stile. Take this footpath, but turn right immediately in front of the stile, then left down a set of steps and this will lead you to the remains of Tankerville mine and a board picturing the mine as it once was.

Return to the road and turn left, soon passing the Tankerville Pottery and Gallery on the right. Keep on the road past a wide kerbed lay-by on the right and just after the road bends to the left beyond this, take the footpath up the bank on the right into an area of recently cleared woodland. This is Bergam Wood, a sign telling you a little about the wood and the mine that once operated here. Follow the track through the wood, keeping to the right when the track forks, the track later becoming a path and leading up to the edge of the wood, where you go through a gate and turn left. The path now curves around the hillside following the fenceline on your left (ignore all paths to the right) and then drops downhill to pass close by some barns on the left, crosses a stile and rises up some steps to meet a track.

❸ Turn right on this track and follow it past some houses to a gate onto the open hillside. Go through the gate and follow the track up the hill. To your right is the site of another mine, Perkins Beach.

PERKINS BEACH

At times known as New Venture or simply Venture, and even as Top Ventnor, this mine was worked with another mine (itself usually known as New Venture) further up the valley, and sometimes on its own under its own company. The mine was first worked c.1842 and has a history of being worked for a few years before the company then owning the lease was sold, often to clear debts or as a result of going into liquidation. Lead mining in the valley came to an end in the 1890s, but barytes were mined haphazardly from the mid 1880s until 1925, after which activity seems to have been restricted to groups of men working often new mines for small amounts of barytes. Veins were often worked from adits in the steep-sided valley. Production was always small: in only two years from 1870 was more than 100 tons of lead ore mined, and usually it was under 50. Barytes production usually exceeded 100 tons a year, rising to just over 1,000 tons in 1911 and continuing a bit below this level during the First World War and even rising by 1921. For most of its life the mine was worked by fewer than ten men.

Keep on the track uphill and above a wide grassy area, and just in front of the moss-covered ruins of a building it will meet another track. Turn right on this and it will soon swing left and head more directly uphill, soon leading you onto the summit ridge of the Stiperstones, a ridge of quartzite shattered into a variety of shapes during the last ice age. At the recently-formed cairn on the crest, turn right on the track that roughly follows the ridge summit. The first major rock outcrop you reach is called the Devil's Chair; further on, the one with the trig point perched on top is Manstone Rock.

THE DEVIL'S CHAIR

The name derives from the belief that the devil sat down here to take a rest when carrying stones in his apron with some evil intent in mind. When he stood up, his apron strings broke and scattered the stones hereabouts instead.

In December 1938 a geologist by the name of George Vardy, who was studying the rocks, ran out of daylight and began to descend the hill. As he did so he felt the air become unnaturally cold, then he saw several shadowy figures not far off. Mist was rising and the figures seemed to be swaying in the air, and he felt that there were others he could not see, but they all seemed oblivious to him. Then a light seemed to illuminate the hilltop, enabling him to see that the figures, of both sexes, were completely naked and seemed to be performing a ritual dance. He was unaware how long he stayed there, but was literally frozen to the spot till the ritual came to an end and the figures disappeared. Making subsequent enquiries, he discovered that others had had similar experiences, locals telling him that on the longest night of the year the ghosts of witches and warlocks assembled by the Chair to perform rituals.

Alongside the path are the remains of several prehistoric burial mounds probably dating to the Bronze Age, but these, often disturbed over subsequent centuries, are difficult to pick out from natural rock formations. However, just past Manstone Rock is one that is fairly easy to spot.

④ From Manstone Rock carry on along the path towards the next rock outcrop, but as you approach this, walk a few yards into the heather on the left of the path. Here you will find the remains of a small round cairn. It is a partially turf-clad, stony mound some 5m in diameter and 0.4m high. A surrounding ditch, no longer visible as a surface feature, would once have surrounded the cairn and have provided much of the material from which to build it.

Return to the main track and continue to follow it along towards Cranberry Rock, the last major tor on this stretch of hill. As you approach this, the main path will swing left, gain a more grassy surface and start to descend towards a car park on the eastern side of the hill. You don't want this path: instead, take one of the more minor paths that keeps you to the right of Cranberry Rock and other smaller tors. A narrow path can be found here which weaves its way through the rock and heather, gradually taking on a larger form and near the final tor swinging gently to the right and leading you downhill in the direction of the Bog. This path will lead you out onto a road on which you turn right to return to your car and the Bog Visitor Centre.

BOG MINE

Lead ore once outcropped at this mine, making it a good candidate for early mining, possibly in Roman times. It was almost certainly commercially mined from 1684 and was worked during the 1700s, but always suffered from flooding. As a result Boat Level, though above many of the workings, was extended to the mine in the early 1800s, as is known from a record of the death by drowning of two men in 1812 when water from some of the old pits at the mine burst into the level. Deaths had not been uncommon in earlier years, with some men being killed when working the winding gear (due to equipment such as the capstan breaking loose, or ropes becoming detached, so that men who were using them to come out of the mine fell back into it), from rock falls during blasting, from falling out of kibbles, and from 'suffocation by damp'.

Law suits concerning the Leigh Level and renewal of leases left the owners bankrupt in 1830, when the lease of the mine was put up for sale. This was for 3,000 acres of land and mentioned a navigable level for boats that also served as a drain (the Boat Level) extending 115 yards, with 2,400 tons of lead ore calculated to remain. There was also much equipment. All was acquired for £20,000, but water remained a problem and even though new engines were installed, mining ceased in 1845 and the company running the mine lost £78,000. Leases were taken out in subsequent years, often only for a year or two, with little mining taking place. In 1864 the lease was acquired by the Stiperstones Mining Company which already ran several other mines in west Shropshire, and though this company and its successor first restructured and then went into liquidation, and subsequently changed hands on more than one occasion, mining managed to carry on at a low but regular level till the mid 1880s, and haphazardly thereafter. Barytes were subsequently mined, notably during and after the First World War, the mine closing in 1925, with a couple of half-hearted attempts to recommence mining in subsequent years.

As the lease for 3,000 acres would suggest, the mine and its shafts spread over the best part of a mile, with a principal centre near where the Bog Visitor Centre now is. The quantities of ore produced were never great, and fluctuated wildly. Some zinc ore was mined from 1871, and some silver produced, notably 1,400 ounces in 1882/3. At its height in a boom in the 1880s, it employed around 120 men. At its close in 1925 just 18 were employed. Many of the tips were used for roadstone in the 1960s and buildings were cleared in the 1970s.

BOG VISITOR CENTRE

In a gas-lit former school the Centre has information boards about the Bog Mine and local history, as well as serving tea and home-baked cakes. The Centre opens from 10am to 5pm seven days a week (except Mondays, when they open at 12 noon) between the end of March and beginning of November each year. To check opening times and see what events may be on, go to www.bogcentre.co.uk.

Walk 9
Bridges & Ratlinghope

5.25 miles. This walk starts with a length of minor road on which cars can travel fairly fast, so you need to take care, but in our view the rest of the walk more than compensates for its inclusion. There is a very satisfying return walk following the Darnford Brook, and a great pub as the walk's base! It is probably the walk in the book where the history is least discernible – the earthworks on the hill can only be made out against the skyline, all evidence of the priory at Ratlinghope has vanished and more recent mine workings are difficult to descry – but it has the feel of an ancient landscape. There is one steepish ascent, but few stiles.

Park in the car park of the Bridges Inn, Ratlinghope.

❶ Turn left out of the car park, left again at the road junction immediately reached, and then right at the T-junction encountered soon after. You now walk along this road for a bit over a mile, passing Hillside Farm on the left, then a turning for Near Gatten also to the left. Keep on the 'main' road until you approach another farm, this time on the right (Upper Stitt Farm), just before which there is a turning to the right signposted to Picklescott and Thresholds.

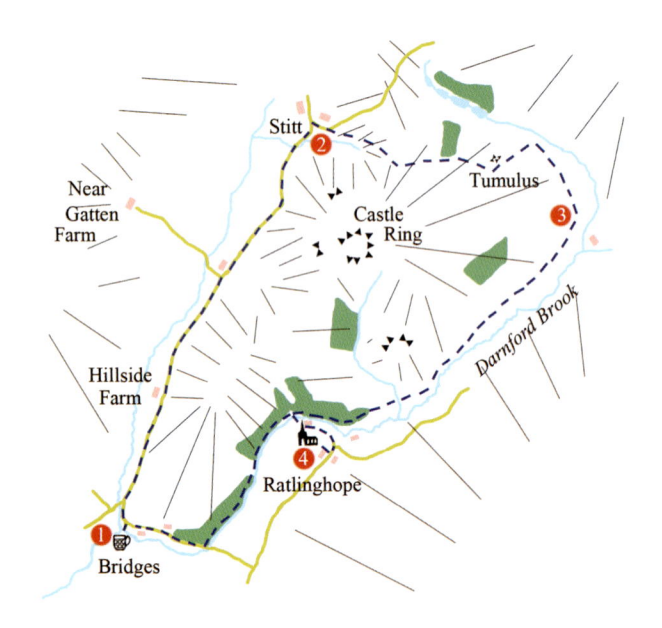

STITT
The township of Stitt or Stutte was granted by Henry II to Haughmond Abbey and a church was built c.1180 by agreement with the bishop of Hereford in whose diocese it lay. At the Dissolution the church passed to the Crown. By 1840 all trace of the church and most of the surrounding houses had gone, with the exception of Upper and Lower Stitt farms.

➋ Take this turning. The road soon bends to the left, but here you want to walk up the bank on the right to a gate and stile. Once in the field, look out for a lone tree on the skyline to the right, just to the right of which you'll make out a slight bank. This is a cross dyke.

The path continues on the track directly up the hill. As you climb, if you turn round and look behind you, you'll see the Stiperstones on the horizon (see photograph above). Also keep an eye on the summit of the ridge to your right, for you should be able to make out the earthwork bank delineating the settlement known as Castle Ring (see the horizon of the photograph below). As the course of

CASTLE RING AND CROSS DYKES

The main earthwork is roughly triangular-shaped and encloses c.1ha. The largest section of rampart is on the north, facing the higher ground and may originally have been a cross dyke to which ramparts on the other sides were later added. Its entrance lay on a spur on its south-western side, in front of which three small banks cross the spur linking to steeply-sloping ground on either side of the spur, presumably to provide some sense of 'presence' when approaching the hillfort. Other cross dykes have been formed on spurs of the hill, such as the one seen as one ascends the hill. No evidence for habitation has been found, and such hillforts are believed to have served as stock enclosures or places for ritual or ceremonial gatherings towards the end of the Bronze Age or in the early Iron Age.

On the southern slopes of Ratlinghope Hill a similar shape and size of hillfort has also been built, again its northern bank being the largest in scale facing, as it does, the higher ground to the north. This hillfort is difficult to see from the path that the walk follows in the valley to its east and south.

the track peters out, shadow the lip of the appropriately named The Dingle to your right to reach a gate (alongside a pair of rather overgrown stiles) into the next field.

Once through the gate and in the field above The Dingle, the path roughly follows the contour of the hillside. Cross the field, aiming for a field gate just to the right of a small wood near the valley bottom to your half left. Go through this gate, then head for the two tall beech trees that stand on the far side of this next field. Here you will reach a fence. Turn left and follow the fence along, almost immediately reaching a tumulus just inside the field boundary. Ahead of you on the next ridge, at right angles to your direction, a line of trees marks the course of an ancient track known as the Portway, as seen in the photo above with the tumulus in the foreground. (This is a long-established trackway which crosses the Long Mynd from north to south; worked Stone Age flints have been found near it.)

Towards the end of the field, the fenceline turns right and you drop down to join a track on which you leave the field through a gate. Keep on the track and this will lead

> **TUMULUS**
> A Bronze Age round barrow with a surviving diameter of 21m and a height of 1.5m, the barrow has been damaged and reduced in size over the years by ploughing. It would originally have been surrounded by a ditch, the material from which would have formed the mound.

you, as you turn to the right, through a kissing gate into the valley of the Darnford Brook. Once through another field gate, a little further down the track turn right and go through a kissing gate onto the appositely named Darnford Walk.

🟠 **3** This path leads you parallel to the Darnford Brook on your left, passing through some gates and stiles to the village of Ratlinghope. En route, keep a lookout for a rocky outcrop on the ridge to your right, just past a piece of woodland. If you then look further along the ridge you might be able to make out the bank surrounding another ancient settlement site, but this one is much harder to spot as the main bank runs over the crest of the hill and the banks are anyway shrouded in bracken.

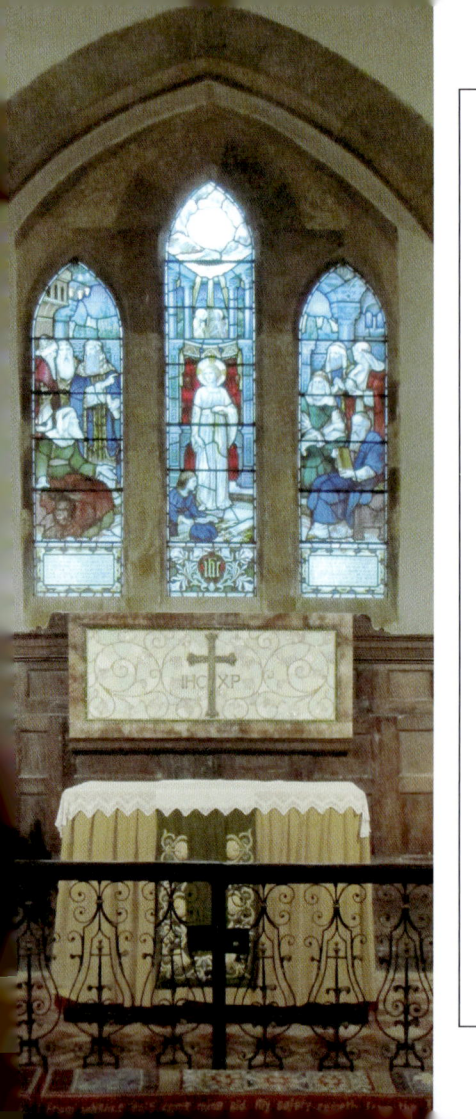

RATLINGHOPE CHURCH AND PRIORY

Sometime between 1199 and 1209 the manor of Ratlinghope was acquired by Walter Corbet, a descendant of the tenant at the time of Domesday. Walter was a canon of the Augustinian Wigmore Abbey in north Herefordshire, to which he subsequently transferred about 60 acres of land. By 1209 Wigmore Abbey had founded a small cell at Ratlinghope for a prior and seven brethren. Walter was a relation of Llywelyn, Prince of Gwynedd, and this connection afforded some protection from Welsh raids. Over the following decades the monks gradually extended the cultivation of the valley, even on the lower slopes of the Long Mynd. By 1291 there is a reference to a corn mill and by 1301 Ratlinghope had been released from the forest law that controlled the Long Forest which encompassed the Long Mynd.

At the time of the Dissolution it was a very small establishment and there are now no remains of any conventual buildings. Tradition holds that some remains of these were still visible in the early 1800s north of the church and in 1992 excavations carried out in this area duly found remains that probably relate to the priory buildings.

It is unknown whether the present church of nave and chancel owes anything to the original priory buildings, but it would appear that none of the architectural detail is medieval. The inscription above the door shows that it was made and given by the then churchwardens in 1625, and it is probable that the rest of the church dates from this time.

The tall monument to the left of the path that approaches the church is a memorial to the Munslow family. Richard Munslow, who died in 1906, is thought to have been the region's last sin-eater. A sin-eater was usually a poor person who would essentially pawn their soul to take on the sins of the deceased in return for some food and financial recompense from the family. There would be a small ceremony conducted around the deceased's body during which the sin-eater would recite some words taking the sins upon himself (it was usually a he). Richard Munslow was unusual as a sin-eater, not only in that he was comparatively wealthy, but also because he was doing it at a time when the tradition had largely died out. It's possible that it was the deaths of three of his children at a young age within a week of each other from scarlet fever that set him on this course.

4 The walk itself continues by crossing this gravelled track and going through the small gate on the far side and following the embanked path just above the brook. (A campsite operates in the field on the far side in summer months, hence the bridge across the brook soon reached and the gate on its far side into a field.) Keep on this path close to the brook – more kissing gates will need negotiating – and the path will lead you through woodland to a road.

Turn right on this and keep an eye out to your right: at the edge of the woodland and possibly also buried in the patch of scrub further along the road there are the remains of 19th- and 20th-century test pits and spoil heaps from when the area was investigated for ores containing copper. The results, however, were poor and no actual mining took place. The road will then lead you past Ratlinghope Youth Hostel back to the Bridges Inn.

As you approach Ratlinghope, ignore the concrete footbridge that crosses the Darnford Brook by a large red-brick barn, keeping on the Shropshire Way with the brook still to your left. If you want to visit Ratlinghope Church, once you have passed the rendered and off-white painted Yew Tree Cottage to your left, turn left on the gravelled track you meet on the far side of a field gate across your path. This will lead over a narrow V-shaped bridge to a track that leads up to a minor road on which you turn right and then right again through the churchyard gate. (To then continue the walk return the same way and recross the V-shaped bridge.)

THE BRIDGES INN
This was probably built in the late 18th century as a house and was extended in the mid 19th century, roughcast now hiding some of the original timberwork and its brick infill. The building became the Horse Shoe Inn and more recently the Bridges. The nearby youth hostel was built in 1868-69 as the parsonage.

Walk 10
Church Pulverbatch

3.5 miles. The shortest and one of the flatter walks in this book, many of the paths cross fields and so conditions are a little dependent upon what the farmer(s) may have recently done in the fields, or what stock has churned up wetter patches of ground. Lengths of the walk are also on minor roads and well-kept tracks. It includes one church and two castle sites, one of which is easy to explore. There are good views to be had, and you can seek refreshment at the White Horse Inn near the end of your walk if you time it well.

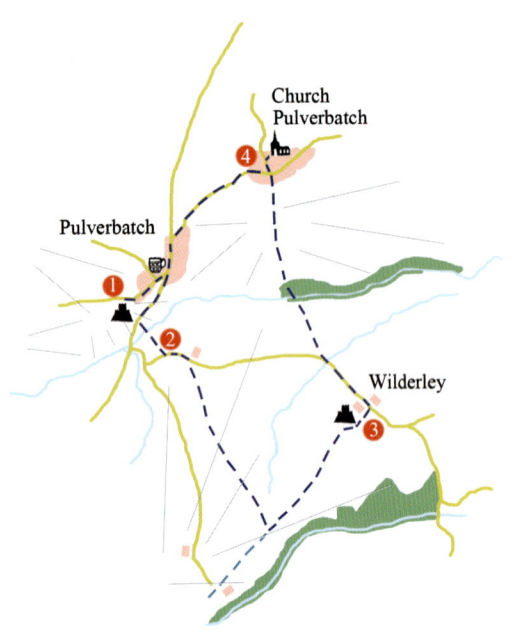

Park at the little car park near the castle site in Church Pulverbatch. To reach this, take the road in front of the White Horse Inn that is signposted to Habberley, Minsterley and Pontesbury and then take the next left quickly reached (in effect continuing straight ahead) and continue uphill to the castle site on the left with its car park.

❶ Having had a look around the castle site, head to the road and turn right, following it down to the road junction at the White Horse Inn. Here, turn right and walk along the road till you reach a point where a footpath crosses the road (and before you reach the road junction in the valley bottom). Cross the stile on the left into the field and walk ahead to a footbridge across a stream, over which you cross another stile then head up a bank to enter a field. Once in the field look across it towards a new barn beyond its far side. To the right of the barn you'll see a set of steps and a small gate in the hedge on the far side of the field, and these you want to head to, passing to the left of a telegraph pole as you do so. Leave the field by the steps and the gate to reach a road.

PULVERBATCH CASTLE

The remains include a castle motte still standing some 8m high, though dug into on its south side, defended by a ditch to the north-east and west. The absence of a ditch on the other sides suggest that the builders felt the natural slope was a sufficient additional defence. A rectangular inner bailey lies to the north-east, partially destroyed by quarrying on its eastern side, and a larger roughly triangular outer bailey to the north-west. No evidence for stonework has been found on the motte, which presumably therefore supported a simple wooden tower, but the outline of two rectangular buildings in the northern part of the inner bailey can be seen as cropmarks in dry weather.

An old route between Shrewsbury and Bishop's Castle once ran through the valley and the castle may have been built here as a result. The manor was held by a Roger Venator in 1086, but a castle is first mentioned in 1153 when it was held by the appropriately named Herbert de Castello. It was still in existence in 1202 and is mentioned again in 1291 on the death of its then owner, Philip Marmion. It seems to have remained in use well into the 14th century, and the castle chapel is mentioned in 1427.

② Turn left on the road and follow it up to the crest of the hill. Here, go through the second of two adjacent gateways on the right into a large field (if you turn round and look back as you start to walk through the field, you should get a good view of Pulverbatch Castle, as in the above photograph). Hopefully the footpath sign will still be standing to help guide you across the field, but in any event look across the field to the high ground on its far side. To the left of this are two large trees standing in a nearer hedgerow, and to the left of them a forked tree (also hopefully still standing). Just to the left of this tree are a gate and a stile which are your targets, to be reached by walking across the field in a straight line. Once over the stile the path turns slightly left to cross the next field, aiming for a field gateway in the hedge on the far side which you will only see part way across the field. Go through this gateway, and then turn slightly right to cross the next field, aiming for a stile in the hedge on the far side that will become visible as you cross the field.

Having crossed what turns out to be a pair of stiles with a bridge in between, you cross the next field to the far hedgerow, on a line slightly to the right of straight across; as you approach this hedgerow you will hopefully see a footpath fingerpost pointing at you: this is your target. Once you reach this, you turn left to follow the hedgerow, now walking on the Shropshire Way. The path will lead you down the field edge (ignore a waymarked bridleway off to the right) and funnel you down to a gate in the bottom angle of the field. Go through this gate onto a path which soon becomes a track. As you pass a small block of woodland on the left you may be able to make out the motte and surrounding ditch of Wilderley Castle, earthworks relating to its bailey surviving in the field between this wood and the farm buildings you soon reach. The track will lead you to a road that passes through the farm.

❸ Turn left on the road (and so leave the Shropshire Way) and carry on along the road till it bends to the left, where you take the track that bears off to the right. Follow this between fields and then through a wood where it crosses a stream and on into the village of Church Pulverbatch. Cross the road you meet to take the road that approaches the church, soon taking a path off to the right to reach the church itself.

WILDERLEY MOTTE AND BAILEY

Towards the eastern end of a shallow spur a motte still stands some 5m high above its surrounding ditch. To its north-east is a bailey measuring some 110m by 80m that would have contained the castle's domestic buildings. This is divided into a higher and lower bailey by a bank cut across the slope.

Wilderley Hall Farm is the sole survivor of the former hamlet of Wilderley, first recorded in 1066. It appears to have shrunk to its present size during the 18th century.

CHURCH PULVERBATCH CHURCH

The church was apparently destroyed by the Welsh sometime before 1414, presumably when the border area was much troubled during the times of Owain Glyndwr, and the building that followed it was remodelled in 1773. The Georgian style tower of this rebuild survives, but the existing nave, north aisle and chancel were built in 1854 in the Decorated style of the early 1300s.

If you head to the northern side of the churchyard and look beyond the wall you can see the remains of an arc-shaped bank and silted-up ditch running around the churchyard. It is not known when this was constructed: it may be the remnants of a prehistoric enclosure, perhaps surrounding a settlement, an earlier churchyard boundary, or even a rather large field boundary.

❹ Having visited the church, return to the road and turn left and return to the road junction. Turn right and follow the road into Pulverbatch, turning left at the road junction on the edge of the village. This will return you to the White Horse Inn and thence to where you parked.

Walk 11
Picklescott, Woolstaston & Smethcott

4 miles on a mixture of minor roads, tracks and paths, some of which can be muddy in places in winter to the extent that Wellingtons could be advisable in wet conditions. It is a walk of much historical variety – churches, castle sites, deserted medieval villages, tales of ancient manors – over a short distance, with some half dozen stiles, and a good pub.

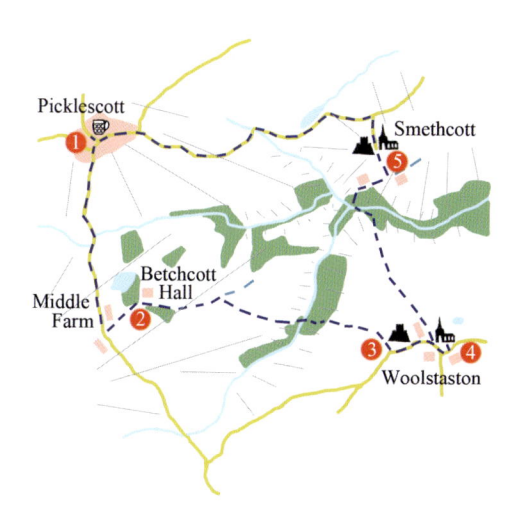

THE BOTTLE AND GLASS PUB, PICKLESCOTT
This timber-framed building dates to the mid to late 17th century and was originally a farmhouse. Its first licence was granted in 1837 and it continued as a pub until 2011, when it was in a dire state of disrepair. It was left empty for a while and then restored, and it's now open again – every day except Monday.

1 Park near the Bottle and Glass pub in Picklescott. To start the walk, turn left out of the pub car park, then cross the road at the junction ahead to take the road signed to Betchcott. Follow this road past the entrance to Betchcott Hall Farm, and then past Middle Farm (with accommodation and farm shop) on the left to reach the entrance to a bridleway off to the left. Turn down this (it can be thick with vegetation and muddy at times) and it will lead you to the drive that leads to Betchcott Hall. Turn right on this to reach the hall.

BETCHCOTT VILLAGE, MIDDLE FARM & BETCHCOTT HALL

Betchcott is mentioned as a township in 1253, and there appear to have been three principal farms together with several smaller holdings, along with fields worked in common. Middle Farm (alongside the road from Picklescott) is thought to occupy the site of the medieval manor house. The current Middle Farm and Betchcott Hall (formerly Lower Betchcott Farm) both date to the 17th century. Middle Farm has an interlaced scrolled design painted in black on one windbrace that probably dates to between 1550 and 1575, but the timber appears to have been reused (the painting was once part of a larger scheme) so the painting's provenance is unknown and it may have adorned the earlier manor house. Probate inventories between 1557 and 1637 suggest that the house was then occupied by the Wilding family, Matthew Wilding in 1627 describing himself as a yeoman. To the west of Middle Farm there was a chapel that was a dependency of Haughmond Abbey from 1183, which may have begun life as the oratory of a hermit by the name of Bletherus (though he is also reputed to have lived at Leebotwood). The chapel was still in use in 1545, and still standing in 1614.

❷ The bridleway swings to the right at the entrance to the hall, and you follow this downhill, the track presently having fields to both sides. Shortly after the track bends slightly to the left look out for a yellow footpath sign on the right. (The sign is on the left gatepost of a field gate, the gate also having yellow tape wrapped round a short section of one of its bars). Go through the gate and follow the field boundary on your immediate right. At the far end of this field you will reach a stile which will lead you into the next field. The path now descends almost straight downhill, aiming for a stile to the immediate left of a group of trees protruding into the field. Cross the stile, descend to a bridge which you cross, and then ascend the hillside through the woodland on the far side. This path, which swings to the left halfway up the hill, will lead you to a pair of stiles that you cross into the next field. Head up the slope in front of you and then roughly diagonally across the field to its far left-hand corner near a small barn. Go through the gate you'll find here and then through another gate into a small stableyard. Follow the lane that serves this to a road. As you walk along the lane and then the road, you are passing round the well-hidden motte that was once the core of Woolstaston Castle.

> **WOOLSTASTON CASTLE**
>
> The castle remains comprise a low motte built in the western side of a triangular-shaped bailey. This bailey runs along the top of a hill, the slope of which was cut away to form a steep ditch, most notable now where the road to its south which you walk along forms a hollow-way along what was probably the ditch bottom. Excavations in 1965 revealed that the motte had been surrounded by a ditch, the material from which had probably been used to form the motte. Pottery from the 12th and 13th centuries was also found, suggesting that that was when the castle was occupied. A house built in the early 1980s has cut into the motte, its garden encroaching further onto the motte and also into the bailey.

❸ Turn left on the road to reach the village of Woolstaston. Walk into the centre of the village to see its houses and church (the latter reached along a footpath that starts up the drive to the Rectory).

WOOLSTASTON HALL

On the west side of the village green (known as The Square), the present building is the south wing of what was once an H-shaped house comprising 37 rooms built or enlarged by Roger Pope c.1671. It ceased to be the residence of the lord of the manor on the death of Catherine Pope in 1754 and was partially demolished c.1784. The house would originally have been entered on its eastern side, meaning the existing doorway has probably been brought from another part of the house when the rest was demolished. Much of the panelling was removed and dispersed amongst other houses, but the 17th- and 18th-century fittings in the old south wing largely survive *in situ*.

BOWDLERS HOUSE

Also located on the village green, Bowdlers House (so named after the family that once occupied it) was built as a two-bay cruck hall with a contemporary box-framed solar crosswing in which timbers have been ascribed a felling date of 1398-1400. In the mid to late 16th century alterations were carried out followed by some remodelling c.1878 when the local vicar, Revd E.D. Carr, refurbished it for his coachman. At some stage part of the hall was used as a smithy. There is also a late 20th-century addition. Part of the building has been rebuilt in red brick painted to imitate timber framing. It was Revd Carr who also laid out the village green and planted it with trees.

WOOLSTASTON CHURCH

The church is of the late 1100s and early 1200s, so spanning the transition from Norman to Early English architecture, hence the mixture of round-headed and pointed arches. The font is unusual, with one bowl set inside another, the inner one Norman, the outer thought possibly to be the re-cut base of a Roman column. The church was restored in 1864-66 when the small south transept was added as were the north vestry and the bell-tower, whilst the chancel roof was rebuilt in the hammerbeam style by William Hill, a local man. The pulpit, lectern and reading desk are all his work too. Revd E.D. Carr paid for most of the new fittings out of the proceeds of a pamphlet he wrote describing his experiences on the night of 29 January 1865, when he was lost in a snowstorm on the Long Mynd when returning from holding a church service at Ratlinghope. Such snow had not been seen for a good fifty years. The storm blew him over several times and he not only lost his way but also his hat, boots and gloves. After a night and day of struggling in snowdrifts he was eventually found by children playing in the Carding Mill Valley near Church Stretton. He was fortunate, for several people lost their life that night due to the conditions.

Walk along beside the black and white house to your left to reach another stile which you cross; then, at the top of the field, cross another stile. Keep straight on, keeping to the right of the fenceline. At the end of the field, once through a gate bear slightly right across the next field to a stile next to a field gate. Through the gate cross a small grassy area and take the path down through the woodland. The path is well waymarked. Cross a stream by a footbridge, then go up the path on the other side to a stile, which you cross. Turn sharp right on a path which can at times be very muddy. In due course, go through a gate and then turn right onto a lane. After 50 yards or so, turn left on a path between two hedges (it's just before a red-brick building that bears the nameplate 'Spring Coppice'). Follow the path along till you meet a road. Smethcott Church is on the right at this point.

④ Start to walk back out of the village up the road by which you entered it. Within a few yards you'll come to a footpath sign off to the right. Ignore this one, but in about 20 yards you'll come to another footpath sign to the right; this is the one you want to take. Climb the bank and go over the stile.

SMETHCOTT CHURCH

Comprising a nave, chancel, south porch and western bell-turret, this originally Norman church was substantially rebuilt in 1850. Of the Norman structure a blocked doorway survives on the north side and a priest's door in the chancel's south wall, on either side of which are two sections of Norman nail-head ornament. The tub-like font must be Norman at the latest.

SMETHCOTT MOTTE

The surviving earthworks include a low motte with an oval bailey marked by banks to its south, which have both suffered from ploughing in the 20th century, though the top of the motte had already been removed and used as road building material in the mid 1700s. Excavations in 1956-58 revealed a ditch around the motte as well as around the outside of the bailey. Evidence for a timber structure on the motte was also found, together with stone foundations for a building outside the motte ditch to the east, which might have been a barbican tower. Finds, including some entire cooking pots, indicated that the castle was in use in the 12th and 13th centuries. It was probably abandoned in the 1270s when the manor passed to the Burnells of Acton Burnell. The photograph above is taken from the footpath that crosses the field from near the church. (You may want to go down the path a little way for a closer look.)

 The medieval village lay around the church, its centre of gravity shifting over time, probably beginning in the 13th century, and then shrinking in size.

THE GATEHOUSE, PICKLESCOTT

This cottage in the centre of the village was once an inn, almost certainly that known as The Gate Hangs Well (hence its current name), and possibly even the site of the first inn recorded in the village in 1616. Whatever its earlier history, by the late 19th century it had become a wheelwright's shop. It has a pair of conically-roofed bread ovens projecting from one of its gable end walls.

❺ Leaving the church, turn right on the road, and cross the stile quickly reached for a look at the castle site, before returning to the road. (Though the footpath continues across the fields and cuts off a corner of road walking, one stile is in a poor state and another is apt to be wildly overgrown.) Keep on down the road, turning left when you reach a T-junction, and walk to Picklescott, turning left at the junction at the edge of the village. To return to the pub, turn right in the middle of the village, noticing the gatehouse on your right just before the turn.

Walk 12
Church Stretton & Caer Caradoc

7 or 7.5 miles, depending upon which route you choose near the end of the walk. The paths are all in good condition with few stiles, and there is some road walking in the town itself. The summit of Caer Caradoc with its rock outcrops, hillfort banks, cave and wide views is a wonderful spot to spend time in good weather. The once landscaped Rectory Wood and an adjacent sculpture trail offer a choice of routes with which to end the walk, and there is refreshment en route to be had in a pub or at the National Trust tea rooms in the Carding Mill Valley.

❶ With your back to the entrance to Rectory Wood and the church on your right, walk down Churchway to the Square. Turn left along the High Street, then right down Sandford Avenue. The Victorian building on the far side of the junction was once a hotel, being built on the site of a former late 17th-century coaching inn. Walk down the avenue until you reach the A49.

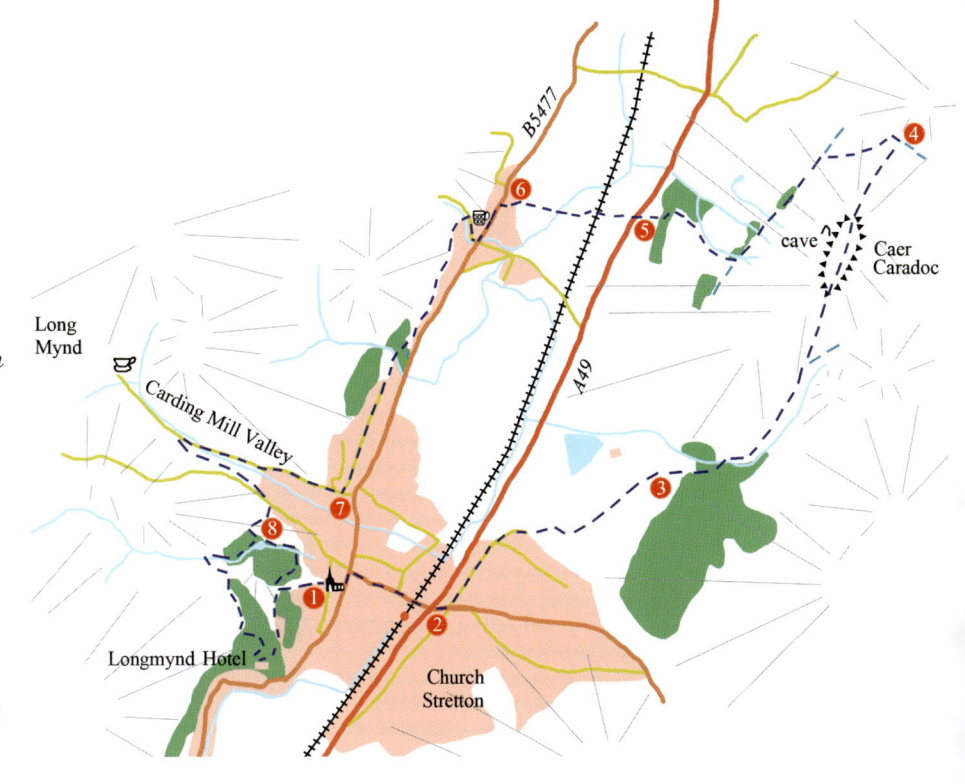

❷ Cross the A49 by the traffic lights and continue along Sandford Avenue, turning left down Watling Street North, the first left turn just past the Catholic Church. On a bend in the road you will come to a little nature reserve managed by Church Stretton Town Council on the left. The walk continues past this, and past the entrance to Leasowes Close, also on the left, to take the tarmacked

97

CHURCH STRETTON

Despite being on the old Roman road that ran south from Wroxeter through the Stretton Gap (between the Long Mynd and Caer Caradoc) the town probably began as a Saxon settlement, but it was only in 1214 that King John granted a weekly market to be held at the royal manor of Stretton-en-le-dale and an annual fair. Whilst further market grants and charters followed, a fire in 1593 set the town back when much of the central area was burned down. The church survived, its graveyard acting as a firebreak, along with the Buck's Head Inn, which was built mainly of stone. Most of the other buildings in the central part of the town post-date this event, but it was not until the arrival of the railway in 1852 that the town really began to thrive. A local syndicate bought 300 acres to develop and laid out roads along the slopes on both sides of the valley, setting a value that a house had to reach for each plot. Several plots went unsold, so in 1908 those involved tried to encourage the town to become a spa destination, buying and extending the Longmynd Hotel, which had been built a few years previously as a hydropathic hotel, planning to pipe water from a saline spring near Wentnor, but these plans came to nothing.

To the north of the church is the Square, the original market place near the church. This was once home to a timber-framed market hall built in 1617, which was replaced by a red-brick hall with ashlar quoins and detailing in 1839. This was in turn demolished in 1963, being deemed unsafe, and the space was left open to the weather for stall holders. At no.19 on the High Street side of the Square the frontage of 1901 hides the fact that over time the site has been a wheelwright's, a blacksmith's, a stonemason's and latterly a shop. Further south along the High Street (and so not on the route of the walk) the Buck's Head Inn has been built in phases, some timbers in the roof of part of the building having felling dates between 1287 and 1321, other parts of the building dating to the 1600s. It was substantially refurbished in 2008. The Silvester Horne Institute at no.60 was built in 1915-16 as a religious, social and educational centre, Silvester Horne being a Congregational Church minister and one-time Liberal MP for Ipswich who is buried in Church Stretton. Further along the street, on the east side, is Tudor Cottage, deemed by Pevsner to have 'the best exposed half-timbering in the town'. It has a rare hewn jetty, as opposed to one created by joining timbers at right angles.

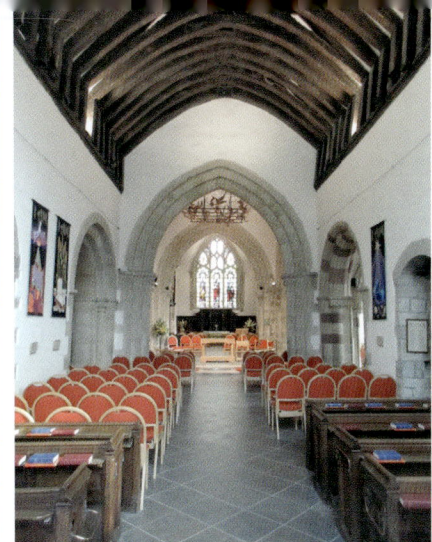

ST MILBURGA'S ROMAN CATHOLIC CHURCH
(see photograph on opposite page) This is the first Roman Catholic church in the town since the Reformation. It was built in 1929, funded by a local benefactress. St Milburga was an early prioress at Much Wenlock (see page 128) and the church contains a wall hanging commemorating one oft-told story of her life: she is shown surrounded by birds that she is said to have prevented from eating the crops that had been planted to feed the monks and nuns at Much Wenlock.

CHURCH STRETTON CHURCH
The church is large, consisting of a nave, a chancel, a crossing with central tower, east and west transepts each with a westward extension, as well as an organ chamber projecting from the chancel. The core of the nave is Norman; above the north doorway is a re-set sheila-na-gig. The central tower was added late in the 1100s (except for the top storey which was added later in the Perpendicular style) followed by the transepts and the rebuilding of the chancel. The extensions to the transepts were added in 1866-68. That there was formerly a rood screen that held an altar is evidenced by the piscina on the sill of a square window in the south wall of the chancel some 11 feet above floor level. The reredos behind the altar is composed of pieces of Jacobean panelling. Some of the stained glass is composed of Flemish roundels of *c.*1600.

> ### BATTLEFIELDS
> The area around the start of Cwms Lane, but now covered by housing, has long been known as Battlefields. Said locally to be the site of a skirmish between the English and the Welsh in the 1200s, fragments of broken swords that have been unearthed suggest a probable Roman date, c.51AD. As Tacitus refers to a hillfort playing a key part in the battle between the Romans and Caratacus, and as the site is in the vicinity of Caer Caradoc, Caradoc being the old British name for Caratacus (though there are several hillforts so-named), this might suggest that the defining battle in the Roman conquest of Britain, when the Celtic leader Caratacus was defeated, took place here.

> ### HOLLOW-WAY, CWMS LANE
> The continuation of this hollow-way can be traced to Cardington and indeed such a road is shown on Ordnance Survey drawings of 1817. It was abandoned as such during the late 1800s, and a footpath established instead on its lip.

lane immediately reached on the left (a footpath post stands just inside the lane entrance) known as Cwms Lane.

Walk down the lane and just before you would cross a cattle grid, cross over the stile on your right to then follow the field boundary on your right (below which is a hollow-way which is deeply sunken for much of its route).

❸ Before you reach the end of the field your route and that of the hollow-way join and you follow the track out of the corner of the field into some woodland. Keep on the track and it will take you through a short stretch of woodland. At this point, take a path off to the left and cross the stream by a small footbridge. Follow this path along the hillside and in due course rejoin the main track on which you turn left. You will see ahead of you the sharp outline of Caer Caradoc and the small path you will be taking to reach its summit. Keep on the track, and just after it starts to bend to the right, go through the small gate on the left and follow the path up to the summit. As you pass the first rocky tor near the top, notice the three ramparts to your left.

Continue straight on, following the line of the ridge, dropping down through the ramparts on the northern end of the hilltop and then heading steeply downhill. Where the slope starts to become gentler you start to shadow a fence line on your right.

CAER CARADOC HILLFORT AND CAVE

Named after the British leader of the Silures who led defiance of the Roman invasion that began in 43AD, Caer Caradoc is a multivallate hillfort protected by between one and three banks at different points on its circumference that often incorporate natural rock outcrops; the hill itself is of volcanic origin. The ramparts enclose c. three hectares. and can be appreciated from the aerial photo. It is thought that the inner bank was created first and it remains well defined along its north-eastern, northern and western sides. It was formed by cutting into the hillside, so creating a steep and high outer face and a lower inner face. A series of hollows inside the rampart suggest that the ground here was dug and the rock and soil thrown down to help face the outside of the rampart, each hollow perhaps reflecting the work of a different gang of labourers. At its south-western end the rampart turns east and crosses the neck of the hill to meet a large basalt tor. Just north of this tor, the bank curves to form a simple inturned entrance, an oval platform set in the bank on its south side possibly being the site for a guard chamber; a 300m long and 4m wide causeway was created as the approach to this entrance (it heads roughly north-east down the slope from the entrance). The outer rampart runs roughly parallel to the inner rampart apart from on the east and south-east where the natural hillslope is already steep. It appears to have been made in the same manner as the inner rampart. The part of the circumference least well protected by the natural slope is its southern end, and here there is a third, outer rampart.

There are a number of levelled platforms in the south-east part of the hillfort that may represent the sites of buildings, a small spring-fed pond within the area enclosed providing a water supply. In the north-western section of the hillfort and close to the outer rampart is Caratacus' Cave, its hewn roof indicating that it has been man-made at some time in the past.

© CPAT 84-c-0488

④ When you are adjacent to the first farm gate in this fence (before the bottom of the dip in the line of the ridge), turn left on the recently laid stone track which leads from this gate. After a few yards you'll see a much fainter track bearing right and soon heading downhill. Take this over the crest of the ridgeline, where it gains a more prominent form, and slants left and downhill across the hillside. Follow it down to where it meets another path just inside the boundary of the open hillside with the fields below, and turn left.

After a while, and having crossed a couple of streams, the path forks and you want to bear right to drop downhill a little more steeply to enter a dell. There are two small streams on the far side of the dell, and having crossed both of them, you'll see a stile in the fence now immediately to your right. Cross this, and once in the field, follow the field boundary on your right to the far-right-hand corner where you will find a metal kissing gate into the woodland beyond. Go through this gate and then down some steps to join a track. Turn left on the track and when it enters the field beyond the wood, turn half right to cross the field down to a stile in the hedge alongside the A49.

⑤ Cross the A49 with care, then a stile on the far side of the road, then another field to a stile just to the right of a house that stands on the far side of the railway line. Cross the stile and then the railway line, again with care, followed by another stile. Then follow the fence on your left to a stile in the hedge ahead which you cross and drop down onto the track that serves the house on your left. Turn right on the track and this will lead you to a footbridge which you take to cross a stream. Go over a stile, then follow the field boundary on your right to another stile which you cross to join another track. Turn left on this and follow this down to the road.

6 Turn left on the road and follow it past Stretton Hall nursing home, after which you turn right on the road signposted to the Village Hall. Just before a no through road sign and a bench on the left, take the footpath off to the left that heads over a stile next to a field gate. Over the stile, take the path that initially follows the walls at the back of houses on the left, then heads through what resembles parkland at the foot of a rise in the ground to your right and which shadows the rear boundaries of properties to your left, and then shadows a track on your left. At the far end of this 'parkland' go through a gate, cross a lane and take the narrow footpath that continues to pass behind a number of properties. This will lead you into some woodland where the path divides, and you want to take the right-hand fork, which leads you slightly uphill and then down and through a gate to meet another lane. Turn right on this and then immediately left to go through a kissing gate onto a path that leads along the bottom of some woodland. This will lead you out onto a road that serves as access to a number of houses including some very individually designed properties.

7 At the end of this road, turn right and take the lower of the two roads into the Carding Mill Valley. You will soon enter onto land in the care of the National Trust, the road crossing the stream that flows through the valley. After crossing the stream, the walk continues by making a hairpin turn left up a track reached in a further 200 yards or so (opposite a bungalow on the right), but you might first want to head on to the National Trust Chalet Tearooms reached by walking another ten minutes or so up the valley and open between 10am and 4pm throughout the year.

Follow the track uphill until it meets a road. Cross the road and take the stony path on the far side. Follow this along the boundary of the common land till you reach a wooden footpath gate on your left, just before where the track starts to head downhill. Go through the gate and follow it down to a pond. You are now in Rectory Wood.

🔴 From here there are two options, one to the left, which is a shorter way back to the church and so into town and which follows a stream for part of the way, and one to the right which also starts by following a stream, but involves walking steeply up a small hillside on the edge of some

RECTORY WOOD

In 1749 Professor John Mainwaring of Cambridge became rector of Church Stretton. The living was in the gift of the Crown and was one of the most valuable in Shropshire, able to retain its tithes and having a quantity of glebe land. Later to become Handel's first biographer, Mainwaring's Society friends, including Lancelot 'Capability' Brown, were soon visiting the Old Rectory. About 1767 Mainwaring began to improve the landscape of Rectory Wood, no doubt incorporating some of Brown's suggestions. It was probably Mainwaring who modified the brook flowing along the northern boundary of the wood to form a pool and who laid out the formal walks. T.B. Coleman, rector between 1807 and 1818, remodelled the Rectory to improve its views, but it was his successor R.N. Pemberton, rector until 1848, who was credited with further enhancement of the park and the erection of various buildings and features, many of which have since been lost. There are still some ruins of the folly or hermitage which was later used as a pumping house, and the site of an ice house, but only the platform survives where a summerhouse once stood. What does remain is a new approach to the Rectory from a lodge on the southern edge of the property and created by Revd Coleman, even if the lodge itself was heavily modernised in 1994. The wood, covering 20 hectares, is now owned and managed by Church Stretton Town Council, who have recently taken over responsibility for it from Shropshire County Council.

mature woodland and further on following a sculpture trail.

The shorter version is described first:

Cross the bridge to the left of the pond and head down the path which follows the stream for a while, then runs past garden walls on the left. Keep going; the path rises gently, and at the point where there's a bench on the right, turn left through a kissing gate, walk down the steps and follow the path across parkland to a gate. Go through this and then the park gates and you'll find yourself back at the church.

For the longer version, you might want first to head round the left of the pond to an information board to read about the area. Having done so, turn right and follow the path round the pond, keeping the pond to your left and so passing the ruined 'gothic' building which was once a pump house providing Church Stretton with water from the reservoir higher up. Beyond the pond keep the stream to your left, ignoring the two bridges across it, and follow the path till it reaches a kissing gate back out onto the common land. Keep on the path ahead to walk alongside an artificial cascade, and then turn left to cross the cascade by the bridge at its top. Now follow the well waymarked path (at times you might also spot signs to the Hundred Steps) which soon curves to the right and heads steeply uphill, before bending to the left and making a more gradual descent. In due course you'll reach a small wooden gate positioned at the corner of some fencing. The path goes through this gate to immediately descend the Hundred Steps (actually more like 125) to emerge onto a tarmacked lane.

Turn right on the lane and after about 20 yards you reach a gate on the left onto the Allen Coppice Trail. Go through the gate and keep on the path ahead and uphill which is waymarked with a green Allen Coppice Trail waymarker. When you meet another path, bear right and downhill, soon coming to a crossroads of paths. Here turn left, to immediately pass a bench with acorn carved ends and a carved toadstool just beyond. At the next junction, make a hairpin turn left and slant uphill.

At the next junction turn right and head into the glade with a circle of carved standing bears. Go through the middle of the bears, keeping an eye out for the stag off to the left just beyond the bears, and then turn left on the tarmacked lane in front of the Longmynd Hotel. Follow the lane down to the hotel's entrance gateway and cross the road beyond into a small car park. Walk through this to a gate into the grassy valley beyond, and head down this back towards Church Stretton. This will lead you to a stony path which will take you back to the church.

Walk 13
Acton Burnell & Langley Chapel

6.25 miles. Much of this walk is on minor roads and good quality tracks, with shorter sections of footpaths in fields. The walk is fairly flat and has few stiles. In Acton Burnell there is the castle and church to see, whilst Langley chapel is a building of quite individual character. In between lies Acton Burnell Park, which you circle round.

Park near the castle in Acton Burnell. To reach this, at the crossroads in Acton Burnell take the lane that serves Concord College. Immediately before its white gates, take the lane to the right (through gates that a sign says might

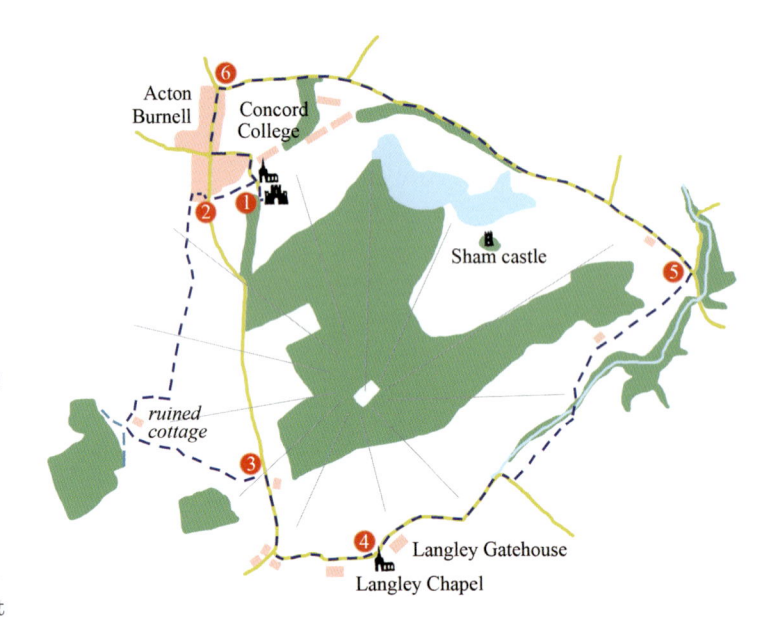

> **ACTON BURNELL SETTLEMENT**
> Acton usually infers a 'settlement by oaks' and Shropshire has five 'Acton' settlements, four of which are defined by the name of the key family involved in the local manor's early history – in this case that of Burnell. At the time of Domesday the manor was actually held by Robert son of Corbet, but by the late 1100s it was held by the Burnells, with whom it remained till 1316. Their most famous scion was Robert Burnell, who became chaplain and secretary to Edward I when he was Prince of Wales. In 1269-70, in the closing years of the reign of Henry III, Robert was granted a weekly market and two annual fairs and set about founding a borough. In 1283, following his second campaign in Wales, Edward I summoned a parliament at Shrewsbury, adjourning it to Acton Burnell, the Lords sitting in the castle's hall, and the Commons, tradition supposes, in the nearby tithe barn. By 1301 there were 47 burgages in the borough, but this had reduced to 36 by 1315 and the borough was never very successful. By 1379 it appears to have had a similar proportion of tradesmen to most surrounding villages and had lost any pretence of becoming a town.

be closed at dusk) and follow it past the church on the left to a parking area about 100 yards further on.

🟠 You can use the path from near this parking area to visit the castle either at the start or end of your walk.

ST MARY'S CHURCH, ACTON BURNELL
The church is unusual in having been all but built c.1275-80 in one style, that of Early English, at the time when Robert Burnell was trying to create a town, and he used superior craftsmen compared to those used in most local church construction. The chancel and small tower were added to the original building in 1887-89. In the outside wall of the north transept is the remains of an 'anchorhold', part of the cell of an anchorite recorded at Acton Burnell in 1280. Anchorites might be male or female, and were ritually walled up so as to lead a contemplative life free from temptations of sin and become closer to God. Usually there would be a window into the church so that they could witness Mass at the high altar, and through which they could be passed food, and they also needed a patron who would provide them with that food.

    The church contains many elaborate memorials: a tomb chest and memorial brass to Sir Nicholas Burnell (d.1382); an Elizabethan monument with alabaster figures of Sir Richard Lee (d.1591) and his wife; a Jacobean wall-mounted monument to Sir Humphrey Lee (d.1632) and his wife (both pairs of Lees were ancestors of the American Confederate general, Robert E. Lee); a wall tablet to Lady Mary Smythe (d.1764) and a tablet to William Smythe (d.1794).

ACTON BURNELL CASTLE

Robert Burnell became bishop of Bath and Wells as well as chancellor to Edward I and, beginning in 1283, remodelled the estate having already created a deer park. In 1284 he was granted a licence by Edward to crenellate and fortify his property, and work commenced on the castle building, the remains of which are those seen today. The castle, built in red sandstone, was designed as the main dwelling for Robert Burnell and his household, including manorial staff and guests. Other buildings such as stables, barns and a brewhouse probably occupied the space between the castle and the remains of the tithe barn, one gable wall of which can be seen standing in the grounds of Concord College. Archaeological work has also discovered evidence of a short-lived timber building to the north of the castle that probably formed part of the complex, together with evidence of smelting. The castle itself was probably still incomplete when Robert died in 1292. The property stayed in the family into the mid 1400s, but had probably ceased being used as a residence by 1420. It passed by marriage to the Lovells, who were supporters of Edward IV and then Richard III, but was taken into royal hands by Henry VII after the Battle of Bosworth. Henry VIII gave it to the Earl of Surrey after his victory over the Scots at Flodden in 1513. In the 1600s it passed into the hands of the Smythe family, who may have restored the castle sufficiently to live in, though if so they had abandoned it by 1672. The building passed into the care of the Department of Works in 1934 and then into the hands of English Heritage. The larger tower, on the north-east of the rectangular building, contained the chapel and was partially demolished in the 1700s 'to give the ruins a more symmetrical appearance'. The north-west tower collapsed in 1914. In the mid 18th century Acton Burnell Hall was built to the north of the castle (see page 116).

> **TITHE BARN**
> The remains consist of two gable ends 13 metres wide and 152 metres apart. It is traditionally the building in which the Statute of Acton Burnell was passed during the parliament of 1283 and although usually spoken of as a tithe barn, it may have been a domestic building, possibly the manor house superseded by the castle, although the surviving stonework appears to date from the time of Robert Burnell.

The walk itself starts by returning down the lane to the church. Having visited the church, head for the layby on the far side of the lane from the church. Here, with your back to the church, look to the left, where you will see a tree around which are four posts linked by a chain. On one post you will see a footpath waymarking sign indicating the direction to take (slightly to the left) across this grassy and treed patch to a stile. Cross this and take the right-hand of the two waymarked paths, to initially follow a wall on your right to another stile. Cross this, and then turn half left to cross a small field to gate and stile on its far side. Leave the field and walk down the tarmacked lane ahead of you to reach a road.

❷ Turn right on the road and immediately left to enter the farmyard of Home Farm. The waymarked path turns right and left round a barn, at the end of which it turns left and right to leave the farmyard and meet a wide track. Turn left on this and follow it past the red-brick farm buildings on your left, looking back to see the magnificent dovecote entry at the end of the range. Follow the track as it undulates up and downhill, always keeping field boundaries to your immediate left. In due

> **DOVECOTE**
> The right to build a dovecote was tightly controlled until 1619, restricted to manorial lords and the clergy. The purpose was to provide a home that would attract and retain pigeons, the squabs they produced in the spring providing a supply of fresh tender meat, often partaken of at Easter, and by-products including dung for fertilising the land and feathers for bedding. The ending of the common law manorial prerogative in 1619 led to an upsurge in the building of pigeon houses. The fashion for dovecotes waned from the 1750s onwards. They were usually built within the range of farm buildings to make it easier to deter thieves and predators, and took some looking after: the pigeons would need feeding – a pair of pigeons eat about 4 bushels (some 240lbs or 110kg) of grain a year (we haven't been able to find out how many nesting boxes this dovecote contains) – and cleaning out.

course the track turns right and then left, still following field boundaries on your left, and goes through a gate near a ruined cottage. Here the track again bends right and left to emerge at the high point of a wide grassy patch of ground. From the corner of the ruined cottage, head downhill to the first field gate on your left. Go through this gate and walk across the field. The farmer tends to reinstate the path well, its line following the dip in the field, keeping it to your left. Go through the gate at the far end of the field, and turn left to follow the field boundary on your left to a gate at the far end of this field.

Once through this gate, the line of the path is less clear. Look along the field boundary to your right, and then follow the boundary on the far side of the field till you identify the first large tree (an ash) in that hedgerow. Your path heads across a corner of this field to a gateway just to the right of this tree, and then carries on in much the same direction diagonally across the next field aiming for its far 'corner', though the hedgerow to the left of this corner has no practical use in forming a field boundary any more! Once at this corner, the path passes through this 'hedge' and then follows once again the rather 'ex' field boundary on your right up to one gate followed by another through which you pass to meet a minor road.

❸ Turn right on the road, and then left at the next junction, following the brown sign to Langley Chapel.

LANGLEY CHAPEL

The parish of Ruckley and Langley apparently had two chapels for many years, but from Elizabethan times only Langley is heard of. Langley was a manorial chapel, for which a licence had been obtained by 1313. The present structure was built c.1564 (though may retain the three-light east window from the earlier chapel) and re-roofed in 1601. Walking into the interior is like stepping back into an age of which we hear much but experience little these days, Puritan England, for as the settlement around Langley Hall shrank and the congregation withered, so the chapel remained fossilised in time. The squire's pew, box pews, rough benches, musicians' pew at the west end, reader's desk and movable pulpit are all original, but the communion table had to be replaced after the original was stolen. A plaster frieze of roses and fleur-de-lys adorns part of the south nave, and small coarse carvings decorate the bottoms of some of the roof trusses. The chancel is decorated with some relaid medieval floor tiles laid haphazardly. The chapel came into the care of the then Ministry of Works in 1915 and is now cared for by English Heritage.

LANGLEY GATEHOUSE

The L-shaped Langley Hall which stood to the north-east of the present gatehouse had 16 hearths at a time when most houses had one, yet had declined to the status of a farmhouse by 1717. It was still standing in 1846, but was demolished later that century. It had stood on a roughly square moated island. Part of the moat was formed by two substantial ponds on the north-east, with more ponds outside the moat on the south-east, some of these almost certainly serving as fishponds. The water supplying moat and ponds was also used to power mills, the sites of which are now marked by low earthen banks. The presence of fishponds and mills would have aided the economic well-being of the medieval community, and there is evidence of ridge and furrow ploughing in the surrounding landscape.

Excavations in the 1990s revealed the foundations of a curtain wall along the northern limit of the medieval courtyard and it is thought that this was built in the late 13th or early 14th century. A gatehouse was added to this wall in the mid to late 15th century, centred on an existing archway, enlarged in the 16th century and remodelled in 1620 when a timber-framed upper storey and rear elevation replaced parts or was added to the existing building. The gatehouse was lived in during the 18th century and survived the demolition of the hall in the 19th century to become a grain store and barn in the 20th. A southern extension of the gatehouse was demolished in 1961. In the late 1980s and early '90s the gatehouse was restored to provide accommodation managed by the Landmark Trust.

LANGLEY PARK

Langley Park is said to have existed in 1249 but it is not recorded in surveys of the later 1200s and may have been created afresh after 1319. It is shown on maps of 1577 by Saxton and of 1610 by Speed, was still stocked with deer in 1688, and is shown on the map of 1751 by Bowen, but by the later 1700s appears to have been restricted to the area east of the road from Langley to Kenley, having earlier included an area to the south of Langley Hall. It was disparked sometime between 1785 and 1805.

❹ Having visited the chapel, turn right on the road and pass Langley Hall gatehouse to your right. Near a bungalow the road will make a right-angled turn to the right, and 20 yards or so past this turn, take a bridleway off to the left, which may not be waymarked. It starts through a field gateway then follows a boundary on your left. Just before it reaches the far end of this large field, the bridleway turns left and heads down to a new bridge. Cross this, then follow a faint track to the bottom of a bank in the field, then follow this (on your left) past a marker post. The path then heads to the right of a stone barn on the far side of the field, its course picked out by marker posts, first down the field and then across it. On the far side it joins a track on which you turn right and follow it along the hedgerow on your left to meet a road.

❺ Turn left on the road, which runs along the boundary of Acton Burnell Park, and once you have passed Evenwood, look out for the sham castle on your left. Keep

SHAM CASTLE
This building was erected by Sir Edward Smythe in 1779-80 to the design of Samuel Scoltock of Shrewsbury, who was a bricklayer by trade, in part as a prospect tower and in part to contain a large room in which his family could listen to musical concerts. The building is triangular in plan with circular corner towers and is appropriately built of brick, although that has been rendered. It became known as the Keeper's Tower when the keeper of the estate lived here and has relatively recently been restored for residential use.

ACTON BURNELL PARK
The park was first enclosed by Robert Burnell (for whom see under Acton Burnell Castle on page 110), c.1270 and extended in 1759 and 1814. It has a circuit of nearly four miles, fences and stone walls enclosing some 300 acres; walls delineated the south side of the park as early as 1379. Fishponds, probably the later Shadwell Lake and Black Dick's Lake, were mentioned in 1292. By 1752 the park was largely wooded (as a medieval deer park it would have needed a mix of woodland and open glades). In about 1779, near the crest of the hill to the south of the castle, a grotto was built of squared sandstone blocks with a corbelled roof of flatter stones. Its ceiling is covered with shell designs and the walls have remains of Chinese-type glazed picture tiles. At about the same time what became the gate lodge to Acton Burnell Hall (now Concord College) and the sham castle were also built. By 1808 the park had been reduced in size by about half but still had 180 fallow deer in the late 19th century.

ACTON BURNELL HALL / CONCORD COLLEGE

A small house that existed in 1731 was enlarged in 1753-58 by William Baker for Sir Edward Smythe, a member of a leading Catholic family. Refugee monks from Douai were given space in the house between 1795 and 1814, the Smythes building the west wing for them, the monks subsequently settling at Downside in Somerset. In 1814 Sir Joseph Edward Smythe commissioned John Tasker to give the house new façades in the Neo-Classical style. It was Tasker who added the portico seen from the road as you pass round the building to its north; this would have been at the centre of the façade until the building was extended since it has become Concord College. A fire caused extensive damage in April 1914 after which the house was rebuilt by F.W. Foster, the exterior being stucco painted to resemble ashlar masonry. The interior design dates almost exclusively to the 1915 rebuild, though the west wing and the chapel survived the fire, the latter retaining many of its fittings dating to 1846 when it was enlarged and is now the College's library. The College describes itself as 'a highly academic independent international school for day and boarding students' that welcomes girls and boys between the ages of 13 and 19 from the local area and all over the world.

on the road all the way back to Acton Burnell, passing the buildings of Concord College en route.

6 Turn left at the T-junction on the edge of the village and walk up to the crossroads, where you turn left and retrace the route you drove along to return to your vehicle parked near the castle.

Walk 14
Holdgate, Shipton & Wilderhope Manor

7.25 miles on minor roads, tracks and footpaths in good order. The countryside is rolling with no steep ascents or descents and there are few stiles. With churches, manors and deserted medieval village sites, it is a walk with many interesting features. Refreshments can be had at Holdgate Church on a self-service arrangement.

Park near the church in Holdgate.

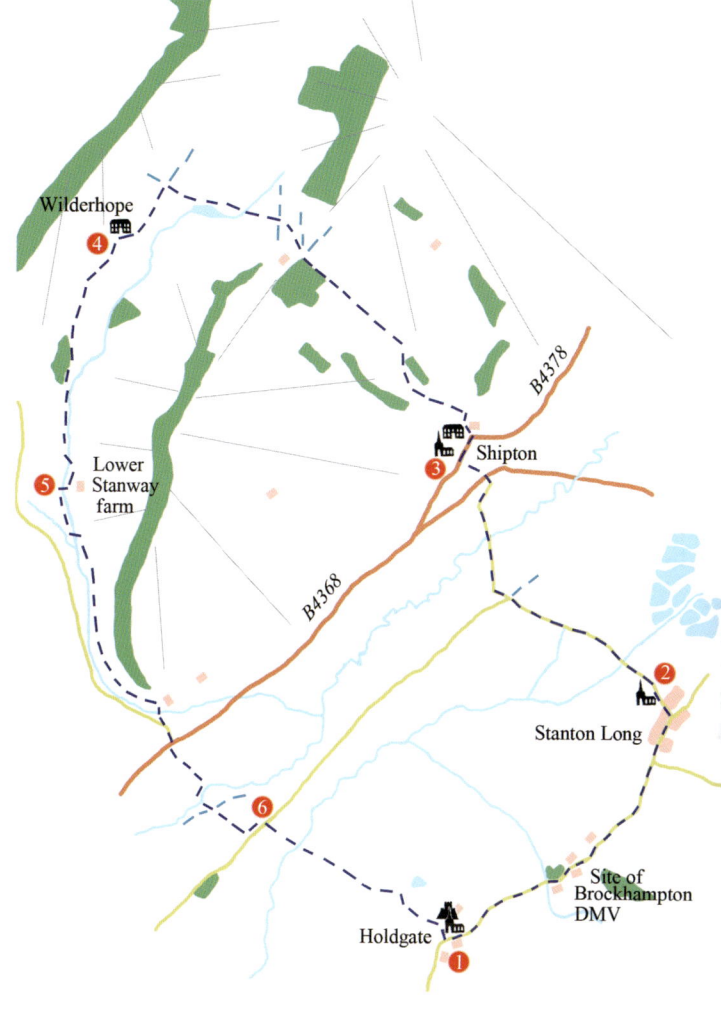

117

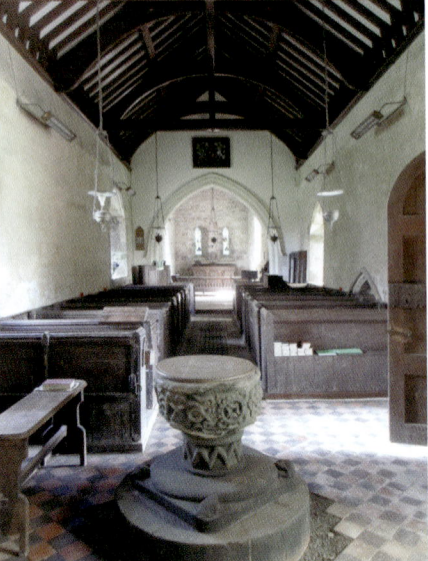

HOLY TRINITY CHURCH, HOLDGATE

Holdgate is one of the few manors in Shropshire mentioned in the Domesday book as having a church and a priest, indicating that a Saxon church once stood here. The nave of the present church is Norman and has a south doorway carved with a mixture of geometrical designs, foliage and other ornamentation. The Norman font is crowned with cable moulding below which are carved serpents and patterns of interlace, and below them some foliage. At the base are four curious heads. In the nave are some medieval benches and a Jacobean carved family pew. The base of the tower dates to the 1200s, but the upper part is Perpendicular and has some weathered gargoyles. The west end of the nave was partitioned off in 1793 for use as a schoolroom, the partition removed when the church was restored in 1894-95. During this restoration the roof was renewed and new windows were installed in the Decorated style.

❶ With the church on your left, walk along the road. Having crossed a stream and risen up the far side, keep an eye out for a stile on the right just past a house (Kingscroft) and its

HOLDGATE CASTLE AND DESERTED MEDIEVAL VILLAGE

The current remains are of a motte, some 20 feet high, standing towards the western end of what was probably a circular bailey. (If you go round the back of the church you might be able to get a view of the motte, best seen in winter when leaves are not a visual obstruction.) There are traces of a rectangular building, presumably a tower, having once stood on the motte. When a new barn was erected in the area of the bailey, stone rubble was found which suggested that the bailey might once have been surrounded by at least a defensive bank and possibly a curtain wall, but nothing datable was unearthed.

The initial castle had been built by the time of the Domesday Survey by Helgot (from whom Holdgate takes its name) and was in the hands of Herbert fitz Helgot in 1109 when Henry I visited. It had passed to the Maduits in the early 1200s from whom it was taken by King John in 1216, though it was restored to them the following year. It was briefly in the hands of the Knights Templar before being sold to Bishop Burnell (for whom see page 110), who it is believed built the tower *c.*1290 that now comprises part of the farmhouse on the far side of the motte from the church. It continued to pass through a variety of hands. At least some of it must have survived until the time of the Civil War for in 1644 it was fortified for Parliament and besieged by the Royalists, resulting in considerable damage. It was after this that the remains were probably used to build the farmhouse. In the 18th century an icehouse was built into the eastern side of the motte. The icehouse is now blocked off, but the vaulted steps leading to it remain.

Earthworks that can be seen in the field on the other side of the road from the church and castle site relate to the deserted medieval village and include seven possible building platforms, a number of hollow-ways and the remnants of old field boundaries and ridge and furrow ploughing. Domesday records a minimum of 11 households here and in 1222 a licence was granted for a weekly market and an annual fair. The settlement then continued at much the same level – 12 tenants were assessed for tax in 1333 and in 1672 there were 18 houses recorded – until the 1700s. By 1793 there were only eight dispersed farms and a scattering of cottages in the parish.

garden. Go over this to the next stile to see the range of earthworks that are what remain of Brockhampton medieval village in the field ahead.

> ### BROCKHAMPTON DESERTED MEDIEVAL VILLAGE
> The field contains six possible building platforms linked by hollow-ways and a possible fishpond, together with ridge and furrow. Depressions in meadows on the other side of the lane may relate to brick-making activity.

Return to the road, turn right and carry on, ignoring a road off to the right. When faced with a no through road a little further ahead, follow the 'main' road round to the left and you'll soon reach the church in the village of Stanton Long.

> ### STANTON LONG CHURCH
> Consisting of just a nave and chancel with a western belfry, its south door is dated to *c.*1200 set in a late Norman doorway. In the south wall of the chancel is a Decorated tomb recess. There are two piscinae, one in the chancel and one in the east end of the south wall of the nave, indicating that the church once had two altars. The building underwent a major restoration in 1869-71 which included a new chancel arch and east window. The stone reredos dates to **1888** and is to a design by F.R. Kempson.

❷ After visiting the church, return to the road and turn left, following it over a crossroads with a road off to the left and a track to the right, and on up to a junction with the B4368. Cross this, heading slightly to your left, to take a wooded path which soon becomes a track; this is not designated a public path but avoids walking on some short sections of B roads, so is much more pleasant and also safer. When you meet the B4378, cross it and go up the path to visit Shipton Church.

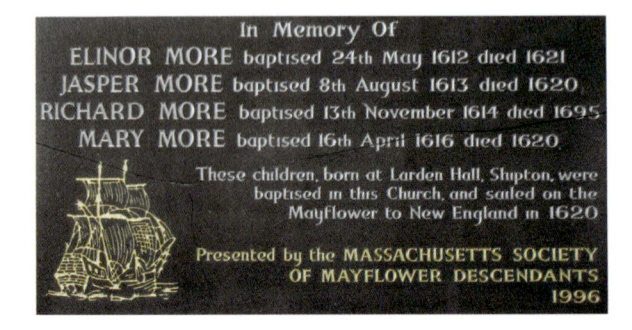

SHIPTON CHURCH

The nave (with windows of later date inserted) and lower part of the tower date to the late 1100s, but the chancel is of rare Elizabethan build, albeit with Decorated windows of pure 1300s style. The eastern window still contains some Elizabethan glass in its lower part. A curate's house once stood in the churchyard, but it was a poorly paid job; in 1879 the parish was reputed to have the smallest stipend in England.

   A modern tablet tells of the departure from Shipton for the New World of four children of Samuel More on board the *Mayflower* in 1620. The story is a sad one. Through an arranged marriage, Samuel More had married his cousin Katherine, over seven years his elder, so that two branches of the family could consolidate their landholdings. By the time of the birth of his fourth child, Samuel believed he was not the father of any of them and accused his wife of having an affair with a Jacob Blakeway. It is possible that Samuel spent much of his time in London as secretary to Lord Edward Zouche, in which case the coast might have been clear in Corvedale for such a romance. In 1616 Samuel began steps to separate from his wife. On 8 July 1620, after an appeal by Katherine which failed, Samuel was granted a judicial separation, which gave him control of the children. Edward Zouche was an ally in the next move, having cast aside his own wife and with 'little sympathy for errant women'. A member of the Virginia Company which was looking for people to help build the colony on the eastern coast of North America, he helped arrange guardians for the children with whom they were quickly packed off on the *Mayflower*, due to sail that August from London (it left Plymouth for the New World on 6 September). Two of the children, Jasper and Mary, may well have died during the crossing, the ship being blown far north and then anchoring at Cape Cod, the 'pilgrims' eventually settling at what was to become New Plymouth. Over half the ship's complement died over what was a miserable winter, including another child, Elinor. The other child, Richard, survived and became a sailor, but never sought to make subsequent contact with the Mores of Shipton.

SHIPTON HALL

Shipton was for many years in the hands of Wenlock Priory, but after the Dissolution the hall was built in yellow limestone by Richard Lutwyche. The over-arching symmetrical plan is broken by the positioning of the front porch together with its four-storey tower. This was initially partially balanced by a two-storey window bay on the left of the building, but this was removed c.1762 when the house was remodelled by Thomas Farnolls Pritchard for Thomas Mytton. A terraced garden was laid out in front and a bowling green to the rear. A library and dining room was added in the early 18th century. Inside are ornate plaster ceilings, oak panelling and a massive staircase.

The stable block to the front of the house was built in 1756-57, also of local stone. A circular dovecote with walls four feet thick that stands to the rear of the house is believed to have been built in the 1590s; it was definitely re-roofed in 1962.

The village was largely cleared during the later 1700s so as to improve the view from the hall, something achieved by not renewing leases when they fell vacant. It was during this period that a Picturesque park with firs and rhododendrons was laid out to the rear of the house. When a pool to the east of the hall was drained in 1978 the entrance to a tunnel was exposed. The tunnel was explored for 55 yards till it was found to be blocked by a roof fall. It is believed that the tunnel formed part of a mining venture led by William Reynolds, a partner in an ironworks in Coalbrookdale, who reported he had found lead at Shipton in the first years of the 19th century.

❸ Having visited the church, return to the B road and turn left, walking in front of Shipton Hall (you can get a good view of the dovecote to the right of and behind the hall from here), and then take a footpath off to the left where the B road swings to the right. This path (it is also signed for the youth hostel on a plaque on the wall of a barn) follows a track through the farm buildings and out by a field gate. Beyond this, follow the track, which has a tarmac surface for a while, in a gentle arc; the dovecote of Shipton Hall will again be visible on your left at this point.

Entering the next field, keep on the line of the track to the corner of a strip of woodland on your right, and follow the edge of the woodland uphill to reach the top right-hand corner of this field. Here a sign on a stile to the left of the gateway suggests you cross this to stay on the left-hand side of the field boundaries ahead, (and indeed the OS maps suggest that this is where you should walk), but we would suggest going through the field gate and joining the track with the field boundary to your left, for further on the route of the path as shown on the OS map has become overgrown through a stretch of woodland, and at that point you will need to be on the right-hand side of the boundary. Follow the track and keep the field boundaries on your left, eventually reaching the crest of Wenlock Edge. Keep going alongside the wood on your left. Go through the kissing gate at the bottom corner of the wood and then drop down the hillside keeping to the right of an old hedgeline now marked by large individual trees. Keep to the right of a spring and its outflow at the bottom of this field and cross a stile into the next field.

WILDERHOPE MANOR

The manor, built largely of Aymestrey and Wenlock limestone for Francis and Ellen Smalman, was commenced some time between 1584 and 1591 and completed by 1593, the year that Ellen died. Built to the usual H-plan of the time, a central hall is flanked by a parlour wing for the family and a service wing. It remained with the Smalmans until sold to the Lutwyches of nearby Lutwyche Hall in 1734. In 1785 the estate was broken up and by the mid 1800s the manor had declined to the status of a farmhouse and in the early 1900s was heading towards semi-dereliction. But in 1936 it was bought by the William A. Cadbury Charitable Trust, was carefully restored and in 1937 was passed into the care of the National Trust on the condition that it was used as a youth hostel in perpetuity. Some 16th-century fireplaces remain, as do several lightly ornamented plastered ceilings. The brick stable block was built *c*.1700.

Follow the field boundary on your left down to the corner of the field and cross a stile and footbridge into the next field. Again follow the field boundary on your left, behind which lies a small lake, and keep following it as it bears right and heads uphill. In the top corner of the field, cross a stile and turn left on a wide track, to follow this to just before Wilderhope Manor, where the path reaches a crossroads of tracks. Go straight across and through a field gate that leads onto a track below Wilderhope Manor, another gate leading out below a retaining wall into a field. Here, good views are to be had of the house. The path then turns uphill to a fingerpost indicating an assortment of paths.

❹ Turn left along the Shropshire Way, passing just to the left of a small range of barns. The path then heads down a narrowing strip of field. Cross a stile to enter the next, much larger, field (shown in the photograph above). The path now heads towards the far right-hand corner of this long field, passing to the left of an area of scrubby woodland, then keeping on down the field, past a field gate on the right and past another patch of woodland.

When you reach the far corner, go across the bridge into the next field and follow the field boundary along on your left. Towards the end of the field, keep an eye out for a stile on the left. Take this and cross a bridge and another stile into the field on the far side of the stream. Keep following the stream on your right and in due course you will meet the track that services Lower Stanway farm (right-hand photograph on page 124).
.

5 Turn right on the track to re-cross the stream, and then left over a stile into a field. Once more follow the stream, now to your left. Some way into this field, you again cross a stile on your left, then a bridge, and go over another stile, to then turn right and once more follow the stream which is back on your right. Soon you'll cross out of this field over a stile to walk straight along a long meadow, keeping the stream on your right and crossing another stile in due course. At the end of the meadow you'll join a track that services a house. Turn right on the track to cross the stream (for the last time!), and then turn half left to walk up the slope to a stile in the hedge ahead of you.

Over the stile turn left on the lane and walk up to the B4368, on which you turn right and almost immediately cross to go over a stile into a field on the far side of the road. The path now follows the field boundary on your left, first down the slope, then to the right and above the River Corve to a farm bridge. Cross this bridge, then follow the field boundary on your right away from the river, ignoring a stile in that boundary as you go. Cross into the next field and keep following the field boundary on your right, turning left at the far end to walk along till you come to a gate in about 100 yards, through which you leave the field to meet a minor road.

6 Cross the road and go over a stile into another field, following the field boundary on your left. At the end of the field you cross two footbridges in quick succession and then follow field boundaries on your right uphill, the Holdgate church tower in due course being a landmark ahead of you. Go across the stile at the top of this field and walk up this next field to leave it by a gate to the right of the church. On this stretch of the walk you might be able to make out the large motte of Holdgate Castle between the church and the farmhouse.

Walk 15
Much Wenlock

6.25 miles on a mixture of very quiet minor roads, tracks and paths, most of them in good order. The walk heads out into the rolling countryside near Much Wenlock to see the remains of a deserted medieval village and the lynchets left by medieval ploughing, before returning to explore some of the town. Wenlock Priory, in the care of English Heritage, can be visited en route. There are no steep ascents or descents but in wet weather some parts can become pretty soggy and in these conditions Wellingtons might be advisable.

❶ The walk starts from the car park owned by English Heritage near the entrance to Wenlock Priory, which you may wish to visit at the start or end of your walk. Walk on down the lane with the priory to your right. This will take you along the edge of some woodland on your left, towards the end of which you should be able to make out that there was once a quarry here. This was dug for limestone, some of which was burned in a kiln on site for agricultural use, and some taken by a short railway line to the Much Wenlock and Severn Junction Railway built between 1860 and 1862.

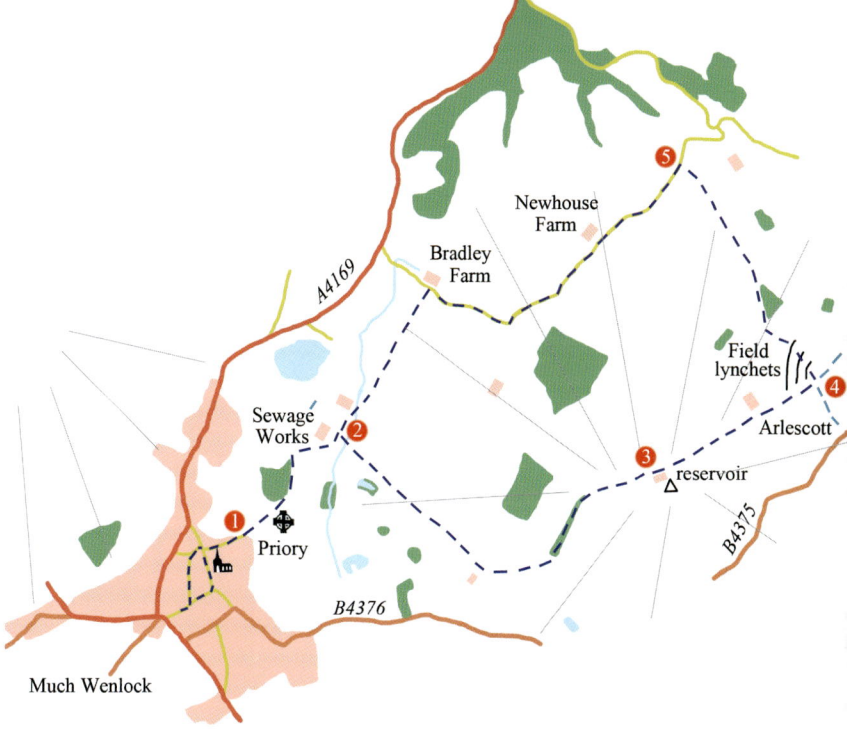

Just past the quarry, the lane turns right to pass a sewage works, also on your left. The lane then bends to the left to reach a gateway to a couple of houses. However, you want to turn right just before you reach this gateway on a footpath accessed through a metal kissing-gate.

127

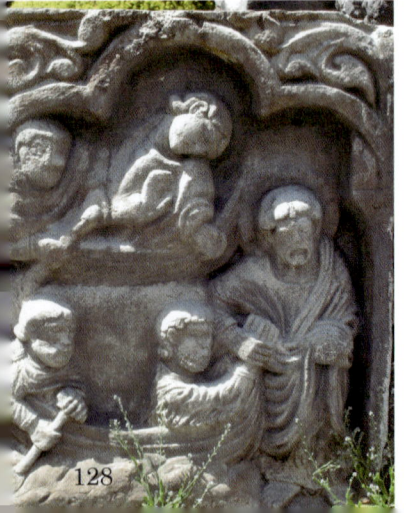

WENLOCK PRIORY

The original foundation was of a nunnery c.680 by Merewalh, king of the Anglo-Saxon sub-kingdom of the Magonsaete, part of early Mercia. His daughter, St Milburga, was abbess (though it is possible that it was founded some 20 years earlier still, with Milburga its second abbess). She died c.722 but the nunnery continued for over another 150 years until it was destroyed by the Danes c.874. It seems to have then become a monastery for monks or perhaps a house for canons until it was refounded by Leofric of Mercia in c.1050 as a minster church, and finally was established as a Benedictine/Cluniac priory under the Normans c.1080 as a daughter-house of the priory at La Charité-sur-Loire, itself a principal daughter-house of the abbey of Cluny. St Milburga's body is supposed to have been found in Holy Trinity Church in the town c.1101 and was moved to a shrine in the priory, which encouraged pilgrimages to the site and an associated flow of revenue. (The footings of the north porch to the nave suggest a large area perhaps built for the use of pilgrims, who would have been kept separate from the monks, with the shrine to the saint perhaps in the north transept.) By the late 1200s the priory had 40 monks. Because of its connections with La Charité, Wenlock was classified as an alien priory during the Hundred Years War and its estates were confiscated. It managed to buy these back and severed its links with La Charité in 1494, only to be dissolved in 1540.

The existing remains include a lavatorium (washing place) with copies of fine relief figure carving (the originals are in storage) and a chapter house with decorative arcading, remains both dating to c.1150-90; parts of the main church dating to the 1200s (the roof is recorded as being constructed in 1232); a lady chapel added in the 1300s; and a sacristy or library which, because the rebuilding of the south transept in the 1200s left no room between it and the Chapter House, occupies a unique position parallel to the cloister walk. Another unusual feature is the upper room over the western three bays of the south aisle alongside the nave, which might have been a chapel to St Michael, perhaps for the use of the prior as it had no access from within the church. Alongside the site, but not open to the public, is an infirmary, dormitory range and the 15th-century prior's house, acquired by the Lawly family at the Dissolution.

In 1901 an apsidal structure was identified by excavation to the east of the existing crossing: this is probably part of a building that dates to Earl Leofric's refoundation.

129

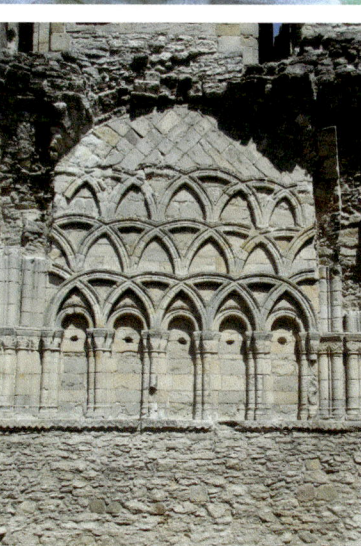

❷ The path heads away from the lane to cross a small bridge over a stream, after which the path follows the field boundary on your left. When this makes a slight turn to the left, the line of the footpath continues ahead, aiming for the far right-hand corner of the field. Here you will find a kissing gate into the next field. The path now follows the field boundary on your right, eventually reaching the far right-hand corner of the field. Here you go through a kissing gate and take a path which passes between two fields to enter another field.

Here the path turns left and crosses the corner of the field to reach a line of trees that marks an old field boundary. Turn right in front of this old boundary, and follow it as it rises uphill and bends round to the left. In the far left-hand corner of this field cross the stile and follow the field boundary on your left to walk up through the woodland (see photograph on opposite page) past a couple of redundant stiles, then emerge into the next field. Once again follow the field boundary on your left and this will lead you to another stile at the end of the field. Cross the stile and walk down a path between a hedge on your left and the banks that cover a reservoir on your right.

❸ Past the reservoir you will emerge to find the end of a hedge facing you, with a track to its left. Walk down the track with this hedge on your right, but when the track bends to the right, the footpath continues across the field, aiming to the right of the white-painted Arlescott Farm on its far side (see photograph above). Here you cross the track that leads to the farm and go through a metal kissing-gate. The path then heads just to the right of the cottage you can see on the far side of the field, leaving it by a gate. As you cross this field you'll see the uneven ground that represents the remains of the medieval village of Arlescott (see overleaf).

Through the gate, walk ahead up a path to meet the track that serves the cottage. Follow this track up to the corner of the field. Here the track you are on turns right, but you turn left and go through the gate into the field on your left.

ARLESCOTT DESERTED MEDIEVAL VILLAGE

Earthwork remains of the deserted settlement are crossed to the south-east of Arlescott Farm, which itself dates from the 17th century. The remains focus on a hollow-way that runs from the north-east to the south-west (i.e. that roughly parallels the line of the footpath to its right for about 150m), but platforms which might identify the locations of houses within the settlement are not easily distinguished.

④ Follow the track in the field, keeping the hedgerow on your right, and notice the old cultivation terraces as you start to cross the field; these have been formed from ploughing in medieval days so as to form level 'lynchets'. As you approach the wood at the far end of the field, the track slants down the hillside and passes through a gap in the old hedgerow where there is a marker post in the bottom of the little valley. Turn right to follow this old hedgerow to a gate into the next field. Through this gate, once again follow the field boundary on your right to reach a gate into the next field. Through this, you again keep following the field boundary to your right. Near the far side of this long field, the path enters a small patch of woodland through which it passes to cross a stile out onto a minor road.

⑤ Turn left on the road and follow it past Newhouse Farm. Keep going until you pass a new barn on your right and then reach the red brick buildings of Bradley Farm. Here you take the bridleway off to the left, which starts as a wide track. This ends at a gateway through which you pass and then follow the field boundary on your right. At the end of this field you go through a kissing gate and enter another field. The path goes straight ahead, crossing a corner of the field to then follow the field boundary on your right down to a bridge and thence onto a path past two houses. Leave the gravelled parking area that serves the houses by the driveway, and this will return you to the lane near the sewage works. Retrace your steps into Much Wenlock; depending upon the season, you might be able to catch some glimpses of the priory to your left as you approach it.

Continue past the priory car park and at the top of the Bull Ring turn right and then immediately left up Queen Street, and left again at the fork quickly reached to walk up Back Lane. At the T-junction with the High Street turn right to see Ashfield House. (For information on Ashfield House and other buildings see overleaf.) Then about face and head down the High Street to the Square, an area largely rebuilt in the 1980s, with Barrow Street off to the right. However, turn left to see the timber-framed Guildhall and also Holy Trinity Church, turning right in the Bull Ring to return to the car park near the priory entrance.

HOLY TRINITY CHURCH

This may have begun life as the nuns' church and part of the priory, the church on the current site of the priory originally being a priests' church. The nave and western part of the chancel with its wide arch are Norman, the western tower dates to the late 1100s (with battlements added in the Perpendicular period together with a since demolished spire) and obscures an impressive Norman west face to the nave that includes three tiers of blind arcades. In the early 1200s a south aisle was added, with an eastern Lady Chapel. The porch was probably added in the 1300s, towards the end of which the chancel was extended in the Perpendicular style. A Victorian restoration replaced windows, for instance in the aisle. The pulpit is Jacobean, the original Norman font is in the Lady Chapel (the other is Victorian), there are memorial brasses in the chancel and in the nave a memorial to Dr William Penney Brookes, for whom see overleaf.

MUCH WENLOCK

Excavations at the rear of no.5 High Street showed foundations of a wall that predate the laying out of the medieval town and may be of Saxon date. Other evidence for a Saxon town comes from excavations at 23 Barrow Street (see overleaf). The settlement entered a period of prosperity when the priory was granted an annual three-day fair in 1138 and a weekly market in 1227. These would have been held outside the gates to the priory precinct, the space near the surviving three-storey stone tower of the priory gatehouse becoming the site of the subsequent cattle market. By 1247 the town was referred to as a borough and in 1468 the borough took over the priory's market rights. The town flourished in the 1400s and 1500s producing and dealing in woollen cloth and having a thriving tanning and leather industry as well as two papermills outside the town in the mid 1600s. It stagnated somewhat from the late 1600s, but in the 1800s the quarrying and haulage of limestone for use in lime kilns for agriculture and in the iron industry and latterly for road building led to economic revival. The older buildings are a mixture of timber-framed structures and those constructed using the local limestone.

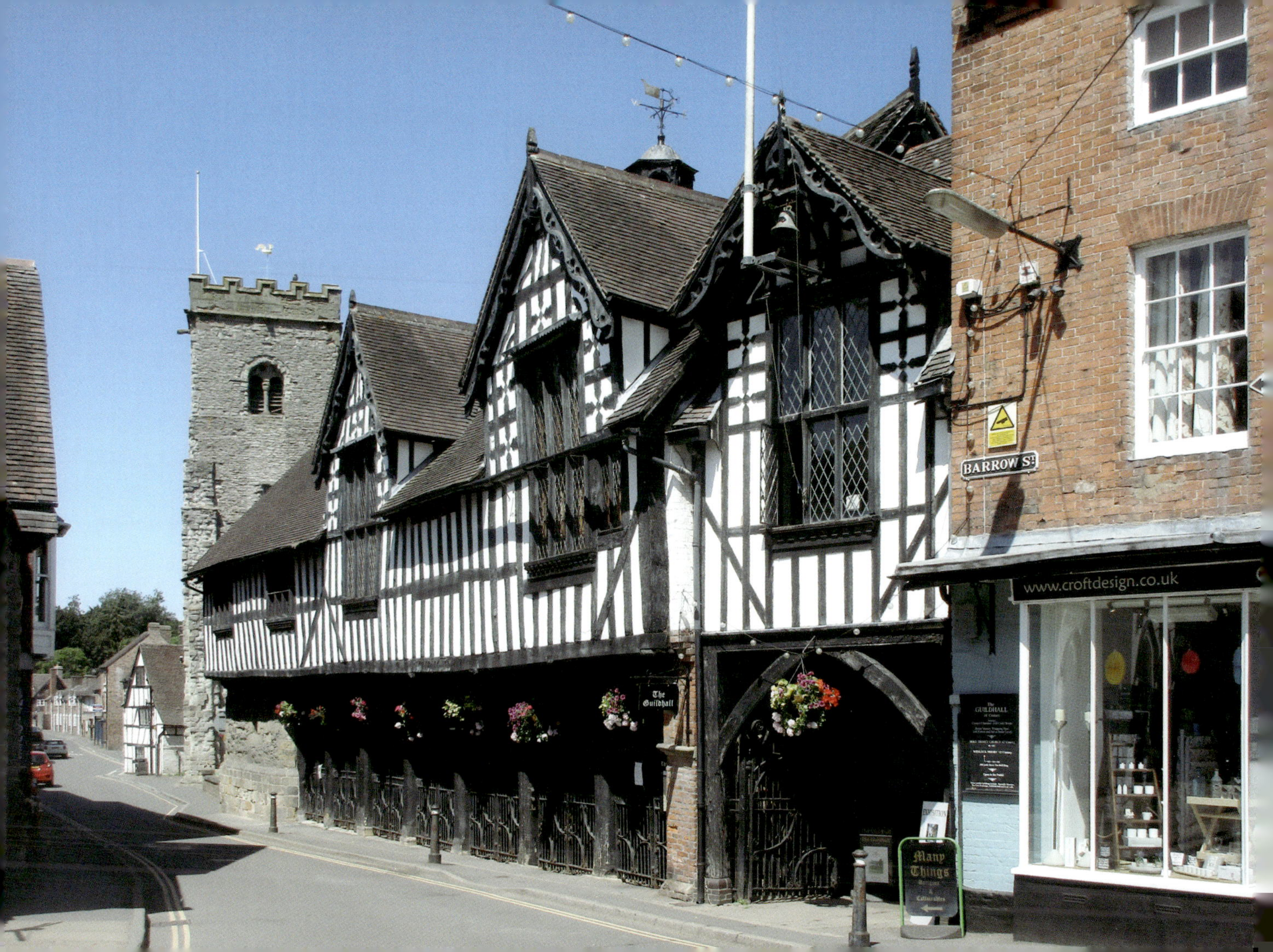
BARROW St
www.croftdesign.co.uk
The Guildhall
Many Things

ASHFIELD HOUSE

This is thought to incorporate the medieval St John's Hospital which provided for 'lost and naked beggars'. The house was bought c.1853 by Dr William Penny Brookes, a surgeon. He founded the Olympian Games in Much Wenlock, following many of the traditions of the Greek Olympic Games, with winners being presented with laurel crowns, and odes being composed in their honour. These served to inspire the revival of the Olympic Games we know today.

HIGH STREET

The timber-framed Raynald's Mansion contains timbers which were felled between 1425 and 1450, though the street frontage dates from the 1600s, with balconies possibly dating from the 1800s. Other houses of similar date are masked by later frontages. Further along, the public library building on the left started its life as the Corn Market and Agricultural Library, built on the initiative of Dr Brookes.

BARROW STREET

Some of the houses here are not what they first appear. No.23 on the right hides a two-bay cruck-framed hall of the early 1300s with a box-framed cross-wing on the street end. Excavations in 1983 showed that this was constructed on top of a cemetery that had existed sometime between the 2nd and 6th centuries AD. Next to No.23, the row of cottages numbered 25-28 hide a five-bay cruck hall for which the timbers were felled in 1435. It was probably originally built either as a row of shops or as almshouses.

GUILDHALL

This was erected c.1540 and some 35 years later extended over the prison that lay to its north. Restoration and additions over subsequent years (such as the gable over the passage to the churchyard that was added in 1868 and the Victorian bargeboards) have produced the building now seen. Upstairs is a courtroom used for the assizes and a council chamber, the latter having 'a riot of Jacobean woodwork' acquired in the mid 1800s by Dr Brookes.

Walk 16
Morville, Upton Cressett & Aston Eyre

5.5 miles. This walk takes in three villages or settlements with distinctive and substantial historic features, including churches and mansions. There is a short section of B road to navigate, but most of the walk is on quiet minor roads or footpaths through fields. But please note: some paths across fields in the latter part of the walk have not been reinstated by the farmer(s) concerned after agricultural operations, and some gates and stiles are not in the best of repair. We have written to Shropshire County Council (as the highway authority and so with responsibility for maintaining paths) to point out these problems so they may have been resolved by the time you come to do the walk.

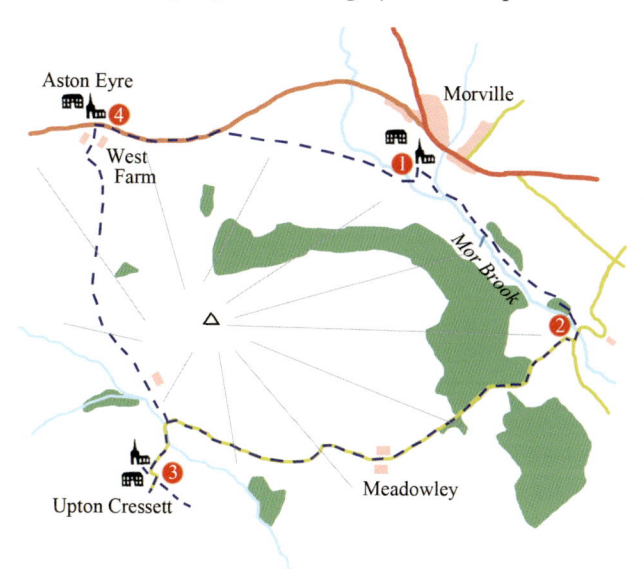

At the junction with the B4368 and A458, turn down the driveway set between pillars that leads through 'parkland' to a car park at Morville Church.

137

ST GREGORY'S CHURCH, MORVILLE

Morville was the centre of a large Saxon parish that included Bridgnorth, but its Saxon church is no more. After the Norman Conquest, Earl Roger of Shrewsbury made it a dependant of Shrewsbury Abbey and in 1138 the Abbey established a Benedictine priory here. This was done away with in 1540 at the Dissolution and some consider that Morville Hall was built on its site, others that the foundations of the priory buildings await discovery in the environs of the current church. A stub of robbed walling has been found extending into the graveyard from beneath the north aisle, which may be part of the cloisters one would expect to find in this position in a priory, and into which the blocked north doorway in the church would have led. Yet others consider that the priory may have functioned largely as a grange, farming the local land, and that it was simply grange buildings that stood where Morville Hall now stands. Indeed, the monks may never have numbered more than two or three, with the grange providing accommodation for the bishop of Hereford on his travels around the diocese. Some certainty arises in 1372 when the prior appears to have been living on his own, as the abbot's representative, collecting tithes and other dues. But then at the Dissolution four fishponds were valued, which suggests a largish establishment at least at one time in its existence. (The fishponds subsequently became part of the landscaping around Morville Hall when they were merged as a 'canal' feature, then became a coarse fishing lake in the mid 1900s.) The original site of the village may have been between the church and the river, perhaps cleansed when Morville Hall was built so as to 'improve' the view from the mansion.

Returning to certainties, the present church of St Gregory's was consecrated in 1118 (20 years before the priory was established) by the bishop of Hereford, an event that saw two women and five horses killed by lightning on their journey home. The tower was built, or at least raised in height, later (as can be seen by the Norman window that looks out from the west wall of the nave into the tower), followed by the aisle in the late 1100s. The font is Norman and includes carvings of human faces. In the north chancel window is some medieval stained glass depicting the Crucifixion. In the nave hang four wooden carvings of uncertain date depicting the four Evangelists and their associated symbols. These were probably once ornamental brackets supporting the roof, placed here when the roof was renewed in the 19th century. They still retain some of their original red and blue paint.

1 With your back to the church door, look half right to see a small gate in the churchyard boundary between a hedge to its left and fencing to its right. This is the gate by which you need to leave the churchyard. Through the gate, turn left and follow the boundary of the churchyard to its corner, then head towards the far right-hand corner of the field where you will find a bridge across the stream on your left. Cross the bridge and then go through two gates either side of a track.

The path now follows the banks of the Mor Brook on your right, passing through a number of small fields and ignoring a footbridge across the river before rising up a bank at the end of one field to leave it by a gate into the next field. Here the path crosses the field to the right of two oak trees standing inside the field to leave it by a wooden field gate and enter a small piece of woodland.

UPTON CRESSETT HALL

Upton Cressett was known as Ultone in the Domesday Book, a name derived from the Anglo-Saxon word 'Upton' meaning 'higher settlement'. It was for many years held by the de Uptons who, in the 13th century, were verderers of the Royal Forest of Morfe. The Cressetts succeeded to Upton through marriage in the 14th century.

Whilst there may have been an even earlier house on the site, the earliest surviving part of Upton Cressett Hall has been dated to 1431 by dendrochronology. It then comprised a timber-framed open hall with a solar wing to its north-west and presumably at least a service wing and was built for Hugh Cressett. He and his son, Robert, were successively Members of Parliament and Sheriffs of Shropshire. In 1580 the house was substantially remodelled by Richard Cressett; it was encased in brick, large brick chimneystacks were added and the hall was ceiled over to create first-floor rooms. The separate gatehouse with octagonal towers (that interestingly face the house rather than having any outward-looking defensive purpose) was built in diapered brickwork c.1580-1600. Richard was succeeded in 1601 by Edward Cressett, a prominent Royalist who was killed at the Battle of Bridgnorth in 1646. Upton Cressett Hall was itself used as a Royalist base.

The Cressetts built Cound Hall near Shrewsbury in 1703-04 and this became their principal seat from 1792. It was at about this time that some parts of Upton Cressett Hall were demolished and the building became a farmhouse, albeit a rather magnificent one. In 1937 it was bought by Sir Herbert Smith, a carpet manufacturer and owner of Witley Court in Worcestershire, to use as a shooting lodge. After his death in 1943, the house was left unoccupied and gradually deteriorated, and valuable panelling and chimney pieces were stolen, with others left damaged by vandals. The ground floor of the gatehouse meanwhile was for many years used for agricultural purposes and this building also fell into a state of some disrepair. Both buildings were bought by the parents of the current owner in 1969, since when much repair work has been carried out, including to the plasterwork ceilings in the gatehouse, assisted by funding from many sources. It was discovered during these repairs that the Elizabethan mortar in the brickwork needed little attention.

Once again follow the Mor Brook, passing through another gate in the woodland. As you emerge from the woodland you will see a redbrick cottage ahead and slightly to the right, and before you're tempted to go through the gate into the field above this cottage, you in fact need to turn right and drop down the bank to a small gate out onto a road.

❷ Turn right on the road and follow it along, passing through Meadowley, and following it round to the left where a brown sign points to an historic church and mansion. The road then drops downhill to cross a small stream and then uphill to reach Upton Cressett Hall, with the church to the right. If you continue along the road to the next corner, a metal kissing gate leads onto a path which takes you into the site of the deserted medieval village, and if you continue round the corner on the road you can gain a good view of the entrance gateway building (see photograph alongside).

UPTON CRESSETT CHURCH

The church comprises a nave, chancel, south chapel and belfry with a short spire. The church dates from the latter 1100s, the chancel arch being built with three orders of zigzag and other mouldings. The nave south doorway is also richly ornamented, ornamentation rather hidden by the porch. The font is also Norman and is carved with cable moulding and rounded arches. In the early 1200s a north aisle was built, since demolished (its junction with the main building can be clearly seen by the blocked archways in the outside of the north wall), the south chapel also being built then or a little later. The chapel's west wall features a painting (rediscovered in 1968) depicting an angel and an enthroned king as well as less clear features. This was probably carried out soon after the chapel was erected. Restoration was carried out in 1858 which included alterations to some of the windows, notably those in the chapel. The church was closed for worship in 1959 due to its being in a dangerous condition and is now in the care of the Churches Conservation Trust under whose auspices (as the earlier Redundant Churches Fund) extensive repair work was carried out.

❸ Having seen what you want to see of the church and the deserted medieval village site, return to the brown sign on the bend in the road, and take the footpath off to the left which follows the track through the farm buildings, leaving the farmyard with a Dutch style cattle barn on your left and a concrete and metal 'store' on your right. This will lead you out through a gate into a field where you then keep ahead, following the hedgerow on your right to the corner of the field.

Go through the kissing gate here and again follow the hedgerow on your right. Where this makes a 90 degree turn to the right, the footpath aims for the telegraph pole in the middle of the field and thence keeps straight on to the field's far side – the path may not have been reinstated by the farmer (see the warning at the start of the walk), so you may need to use whatever tramlines help you. Once across the field, you should find yourself near a dog-leg in the fence where there's a stile into the next field. Once in the field, turn right and go through a gateway you immediately come to on your right. Follow the fence on your left downhill till you reach a gateway which you go through. Cross the corner of this field to a gateway into the field below. The path then cuts across a corner of this field to a gateway in the opposite hedgerow. Through this, follow the line made by two large trees in the next field to a broken footpath gate on the far side, possibly again needing to follow tramlines through the field.

UPTON CRESSETT DESERTED MEDIEVAL VILLAGE

The site of the deserted medieval village to the east of the hall is bisected by a broad hollow-way up to 3m deep, just to the right of the photograph above, which represents the course of the main street through the village. The greatest concentration of earthworks lies in the field crossed by the footpath and includes a series of building platforms of various sizes, as well as banks and other linear features possibly defining small paddocks or enclosures. On the other side of the hollow-way are further building platforms and a series of linear earthworks, including a long curving bank, possibly the remains of a trackway, which, although less well defined, represent further features associated with the settlement. A small excavation unearthed several pottery sherds of 12th- and 13th-century date. The village was probably abandoned before 1517, either due to the intention to create a deer park of Thomas Cressett, who that year was alleged to have imparked 40 acres of arable land, to 'improve the view'. Other earthworks that might represent another part of the settlement lie to the north of the hall and church.

ASTON EYRE CHURCH

The church consists of a nave, chancel and bell-cote. Probably built *c.*1138 and in the years shortly following, it soon became a chapelry to the church at Morville, where all burials are carried out (hence there are no gravestones around the church here). The triple east window is a Victorian replacement. The particular joy of the church is the tympanum above the south doorway which depicts Christ's entry into Jerusalem and is a work of the Herefordshire School of Romanesque Sculpture.

Through this gate the path turns left on the track, then almost immediately right through a kissing gate and down a track to another kissing gate through which you turn right and follow the farm lane past the white-painted West Farm and so down to the B4368. Head across this to Aston Eyre Church.

④ Having visited the church and perhaps peered over the wall behind the church to see Aston Eyre Hall Farm, turn left out of the churchyard to follow the B4368. You need to follow this for almost half a mile; at first you can walk on a wide grass verge on the far side of the road from the church, and most of the rest of the way is at least within a 30 mile speed limit, but take care. Beyond the 30 mph speed limit, the road bends to the left and not

ASTON EYRE HALL

Looking over the wall behind the church you can see the buildings that comprised Aston Eyre Hall. The hall itself (which is the large stone building – undergoing repairs in 2018 – on the left of the group of buildings), the gatehouse (which now has a timber-framed rear added to it and is on the right of the group), and probably other buildings all stood within what may have been a moated site measuring some 100m by 75m. The southern boundary of this lies adjacent to the churchyard and is marked by a scarp some 1.5m high, while the eastern arm has been filled in to provide for a drive and garden. It is unclear whether any wall or other defensible structure was built above the moat.

At the time of the Domesday Survey the manor was owned by the Ayer family (hence part of the name of the modern village), who retained it until 1314 when it passed to the Charltons through marriage. It was probably they who built the first stone hall, no doubt replacing an earlier house on the already existing moated site, and also the gatehouse (for which a felling date of 1341-52 for some of the timbers in the oldest part has been ascertained), work on these structures appearing to finish with the advent of the Black Death in 1349. Work recommenced in the mid 1400s on more or less the same design when the manor was acquired by the Cressetts; a felling date of between 1469 and 1471 has been found for the timbers used to complete the hall. In the early 1600s the hall was relegated to agricultural use associated with the keeping of stock and the gatehouse was converted into the main dwelling, felling dates of between 1596 and 1616 being obtained for timbers in the timber-framed extension. This now forms Hall Farm. Some repairs and modifications were carried out to the hall in the 1700s (which included replacing the roof which may well have collapsed) and 1800s, before a milking parlour was installed in the mid 1900s. Early in this century plans were drawn up to return the hall to residential use.

MORVILLE HALL

This building started life as an Elizabethan house built by the Smyth family. It was then 'classicised' c.1748-49 for Arthur Weaver after he had been elected MP for Bridgnorth; at that time the building was also extended by walls linking to service buildings. Later in the 1700s a third storey was added, which makes the building appear more sombre, heightening the effect of the grey stone of which it is built. The polygonal Elizabethan stair turrets that once rose above the two-storey building can still be seen on the eastern elevation. The left-hand service building as you look at the front of the house used to be the stables. In 1965 Morville was given to the National Trust, who rent it out.

As well as rebuilding the house, Weaver also made changes to the grounds described in a letter dated July 1760 from Thomas Percy to William Shenstone, a poet and early practitioner of landscape gardening:

'Last year died a Mr Weaver who had a Seat near Bridgnorth and who was possessed by the very demon of Caprice: He came into possession of an Old Mansion that commanded a fine view down a most pleasing Vale, he contrived to intercept it by two straight rows of Elms that ran in an oblique direction across it, and which led the Eye to a pyramidal Obelisk composed of one single board set up endways and painted by the Joiner of the Village: this obelisk however was soon removed by the first puff of wind. In view of one of his windows grew a noble large, Spreading Ash, which tho' the spontaneous gift of Nature, was really a fine object: and by its stately figure and chearful Verdure afforded a most pleasing relief to the Eye; you will stare when I tell you that Mr W had this Tree painted white, leaves and all: it is true the leaves soon fell off, and the tree died, but the Skeleton still remains, as a monument of its owner's Wisdom and Ingenuity.'

far along here you reach an opening in the hedgerow and a track into a field. Go into the field here and then turn half left to follow the line of the path (again you may need to follow tramlines) which initially heads across the top of the 'pimple' in the ground immediately ahead of you and then roughly parallels the field boundary on your right. You cross the long length of this field to meet the banks of the Mor Brook on your left and then follow the river along, with views of Morville Hall on its far side, till you come to a stile which you cross. Shortly afterwards you'll come to an old bridge across the Mor Brook which you take to then join a footpath which will take you back to the gate into the churchyard by which you initially left it.

Walk 17
Bridgnorth and south

9 miles. This walk is quite long, though relatively flat, with lots to see and visit. Out of Bridgnorth, much of it is on well-maintained tracks and paths, but some of the woodland paths can be arduous due to trunks of fallen trees and boggy patches of ground. In addition, the walk passes under the Severn Valley railway line through a culvert. This can be dry (as the photograph taken in November and included on page 155 shows), but it can flow with water. In April we managed relatively comfortably in hiking boots, but after recent heavy rain, perhaps Wellingtons would be better. But it is a wonderful and intriguing walk, with lots of kissing gates rather than stiles, and especially memorable if you happen to coincide with the passing of a Severn Valley steam train!

① The walk starts from the North Gate at the northern (unsurprisingly) end of the High Street. This is a recent building of 1910, the previous gate having been built in brick in 1740. It adjoins nos.3-4 High Street once a single timber-framed house dating from around the time of the Civil War.

Walk down the High Street and through or past the Town Hall. This is an easily identifiable building as

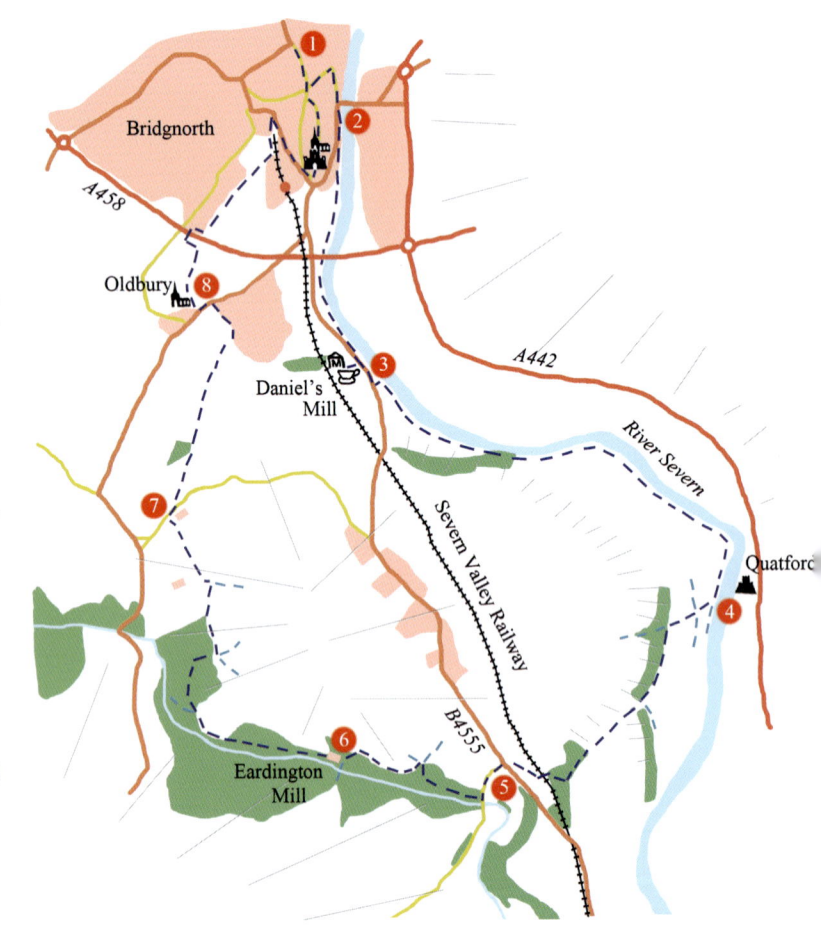

THE TOWN

The origins of Bridgnorth are obscure. The town is not mentioned in the Domesday Survey and it would seem a settlement only began to develop when Robert de Bellême, the third Earl of Shrewsbury, began to build a castle in 1101 to replace his earlier one at Quatford. Bellême rebelled and the castle was taken by Henry I in 1102. Over the next few years the town grew in stature: although a bridge had crossed the Severn here as early as AD896, the Norman crossing was at Quatford but when a new bridge was built at Bridgnorth, borough status soon followed. For several centuries the bridge at Bridgnorth was one of just two crossing points on the river between Shrewsbury and Worcester, encouraging the development of the town as a centre of trade and commerce. Trade along the Severn also boosted the town's fortunes, with 75 vessels regularly using the wharves in 1756, though the focus of trade and its speed of passage changed with the coming of the railway in the 1860s.

it stands in the middle of the road. It was rebuilt at the end of the Civil War, its stone arcades since encased in brick. It was restored in 1887. Continue down the High Street, turning left near the Victorian market hall down Waterloo Terrace. The market hall was built in 1855-86 in a Victorian Italian style in yellow, blue and red brick but never served its purpose well, with traders refusing to move in when it opened. Until recently it has been the town museum but in spring 2019 the building was undergoing renovation.

As for the houses that make up Waterloo Terrace itself, the façade disguises a late medieval timber-framed group of buildings. Continue down Waterloo Terrace, noticing, on the left, the bricked-up mouths of several caves that were inhabited until 1856, and the turning on the left, Friar's Street, which commemorates the location of a Franciscan friary. Your route continues to the right down Cartway, near the bottom of which is Bishop Percy's House, the most richly decorated timber-framed building remaining in Bridgnorth (see photograph alongside). It was actually built by Richard Forrester, a bargemaster, in 1580. As you reach the road junction ahead you'll come to the lower entrance for the Castle Hill Railway on your right. (The photograph on the left shows the upper entrance of the railway, which you can see on your return.)

CASTLE HILL RAILWAY

This is Britain's only working inland cliff railway and was built in 1891-92, partly as a tourist attraction (50,000 people used it in its first three months of operation), to link the High and Low towns, and is a sophisticated version of the inclined planes that had been built around the county to serve coal mines and quarries. It initially used water (stored in a reservoir at the top station) to balance the weights of the upbound and down-bound cars but was converted to an electric system in 1944. The Upper Station is built in a mock Jacobean style, whilst the upper two floors of the Lower Station were built as a temperance refreshment house.

❷ Cross the road by the pedestrian crossing and walk down to the terraced area: this is one of the quays at which barges travelling the Severn used to dock to load and unload cargo. If you keep to the riverside edge of the this area you'll come to the start of the path you'll need to take to follow this walk, but first you may want to head back across the road to have a look at some of the caves on its far side.

CAVES

A 1989 survey identified 35 caves in the town and concluded that they could be divided into four classes: those that provided sole habitation; those that formed part of a house; those used for storage or some other separate domestic function; and those used for industrial or commercial activities. Only two caves were positively identified as primary dwellings due to the presence of a fireplace, whilst those used for commercial or industrial purposes were concentrated along the medieval waterfront. Some of these lacked putlog holes which would have indicated fittings for shelves, suggesting that these caves were used for the storage of bulk goods. Some had fittings and alcoves which suggested they might have formed part of brewery complexes. The survey found it difficult to establish whether individual caves had natural or artificial origins and if it seemed it might be the latter, at what date they were constructed. The caves were owned by Bridgnorth Corporation, who rented them out, the rent often being part payable in money and part in chickens, often two of them!

One of the caves under the castle is known as Lavington's Hole after the Parliamentarian colonel who, during the Civil War in April 1646, organised the digging of a tunnel to reach under St Mary's Church, intending to blow it up as he knew that that was where the Royalists stored their gunpowder. Learning of the tunnel, and fearing the widespread destruction that would happen if it was blown up, the Royalists surrendered.

DANIEL'S MILL

There has been a mill here from the late 15th century when it was part of the Pitchford estate. At that time there would have been no resident miller, and it was probably only when the mill was extended and an upper millpool was built in the early 1600s that a resident miller took up the reins. Much of the current building dates to 1854-55 when the present mill wheel was installed, though a steam engine to use in conjunction with it had already been acquired. This beam-shot 38-ft wheel made in Coalbrookdale drives two pairs of stones. The mill ceased operating commercially in 1957 when the then miller died but it has subsequently been restored and still grinds a little flour.

The Mill is open to visitors for a small charge from 11am to 4pm on Thursday to Sunday between April and the end of October, and also has a tea room if you're ready for a break.

Having looked, or not looked, at the caves, follow the Severn Valley Path along the banks of the river, soon passing through a kissing gate into more open ground. The path goes under the bypass and then enters woodland via a kissing gate and after a while leaves the river bank and heads uphill to meet the B4555 on which you turn left on the pavement. You may want to visit Daniel's Mill and tea room on the right-hand side.

❸ The path continues along the B4555, passing to the right of a new redbrick house. Immediately past its driveway entrance with its pillars, the path heads back down to the river alongside a tall wooden fence. From here it keeps to the river's edge on a pleasant grassy track, then through a piece of woodland, and then out onto a wide grassy track once more. Follow this along the edge of the

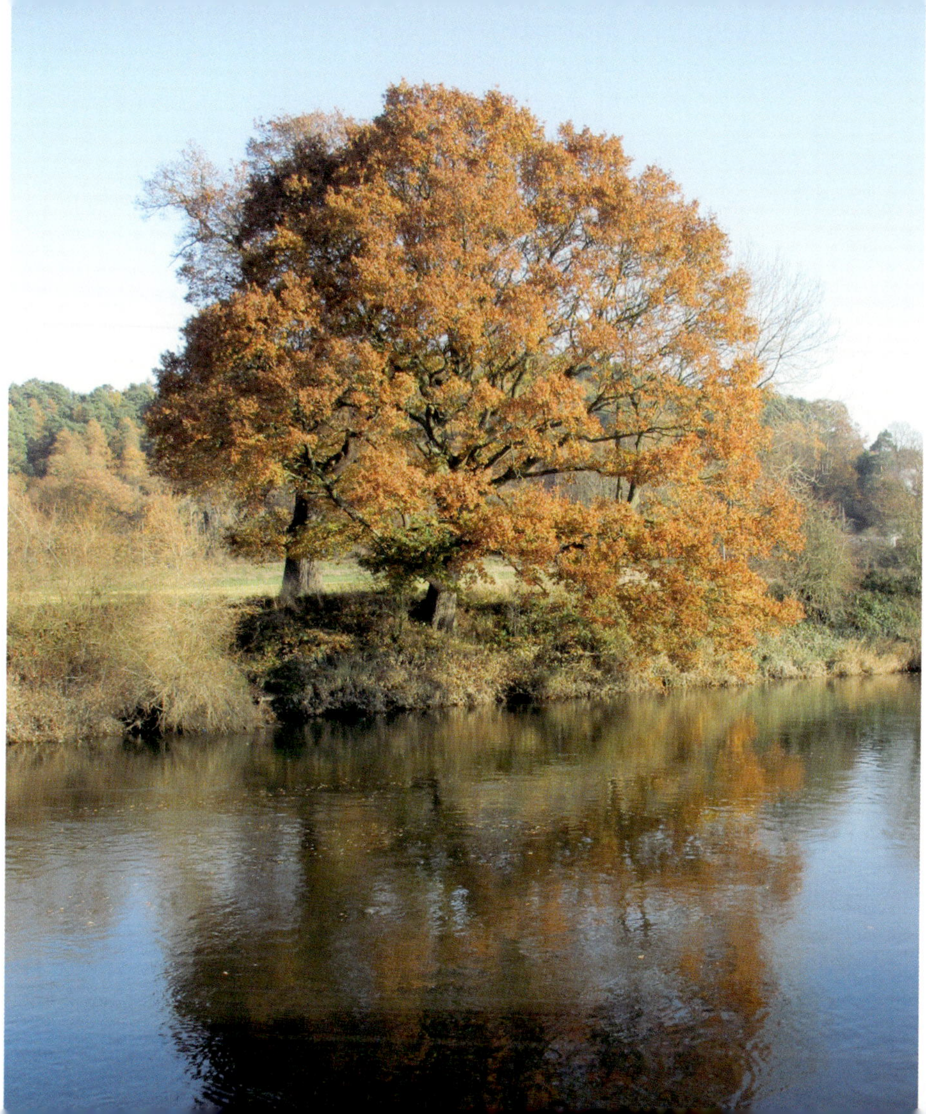
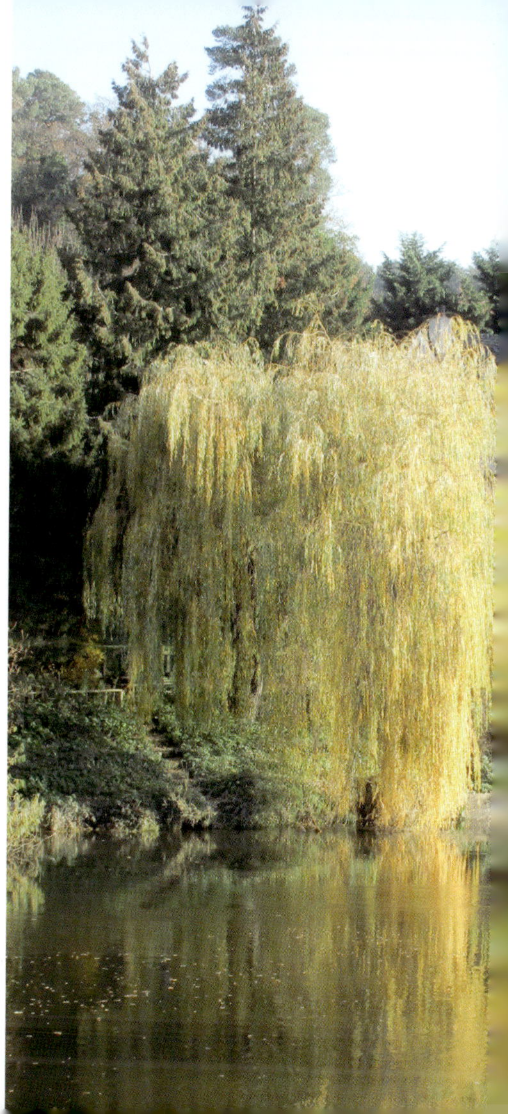

river till you reach the rocky escarpment on the far side of the river at Quatford.

④ Just past this outcrop, you want to take the path to the right that follows a grassy track alongside a tall hedge on its left and that leads towards a small escarpment. Ignore one path that you cross, but at the foot of the escarpment, turn left at a bend in a tarmacked lane onto the grassy track that runs along its foot. In due course this turns into a 're-entrant' in the escarpment and leads to a metal kissing gate into a field. Go through this and once in the field the path follows the valley bottom across

QUATFORD CASTLE

The castle was built by Roger de Montgomery, Earl of Shrewsbury, before 1086, possibly on the site of a Saxon *burh* itself constructed on the site of a Danish encampment of 895-96 when a Danish army overwintered at this spot. The castle was abandoned *c.*1101 when Roger's son, Roger de Bellême, began construction of a new castle at Bridgnorth (see page 160). In 1960 excavation in the bailey for the Ministry of Works in advance of the widening of the A442 found post holes but nothing that indicated the presence of a Danish encampment, the layout of the *burh*, or evidence of buildings related to the castle. The remains consist of a motte some 30 feet high and a small bailey covering about an acre.

QUATFORD BRIDGE AND FERRY

A bridge crossed the river here in 1086 and might have been on the site of bridges mentioned in 896 and 910. It is not subsequently mentioned and was therefore probably destroyed when a royal army besieged Bridgnorth in 1102 (see page 149). Proof that the bridge existed was found in 1780 when a large piece of squared oak was pulled out of the river bed and a second was recorded as being visible on the eastern bank. Two bridge piers were also recorded in the early 1800s. The bridge, meanwhile, had been replaced by a ferry. The path that leads away from the river at this point (and forms part of the walk) is probably on the site of the old road that led to the bridge and then the ferry.

the field to a bank at the far side which you go up to leave the field by another kissing gate.

Turn left on the track you find yourself on and almost immediately turn right onto a small path that leads through the wood (filled with the blue of bluebells at the apposite time of year), close to a field boundary, before bending to the right to soon follow a small ditch-cum-stream (that may be dry or running with water) which you then have to follow through a culvert under the railway line!

Out in the field on the far side, the path technically slants up and across the hillside to the far right-hand corner of the field, but a fence has been erected across the line of the path, meaning you might need to aim for the top of this fence where you can pass through an opening and then walk along the top of the field to a kissing gate out on to the B4555.

❺ Cross the B4555 and take the small road downhill. As you near the bottom (and before you would reach the Mor Brook and the Astbury Falls – you may want to continue down the road a little way to have a look at them), turn right through a kissing gate onto a path through woodland. After a while the path winds uphill, crosses an old track and then slants across and up the hillside to head out into a field through a kissing gate. Turn left in the field and follow the edge of the woodland to a pair of kissing gates that lead you into the next field, where you keep following the edge of the woodland on your left.

The next kissing gate you reach will lead you back into the woodland. Don't go through the kissing gate immediately reached on the right, but follow the path ahead and downhill to the disused Eardington Mill. You can walk down the side of the mill to the footbridge to get a good view of the buildings of the water mill of unknown date.

❻ Having done so, head back up the side of the building and turn left through a metal gate that leads onto a brick path and then up some brick steps, passing a house on your left. In the yard at the top of the steps, head to the left of the brick building on the other side of the yard and go through the large wooden gate onto a grassy path. This will quickly lead you back into woodland. After a while you'll pass through a metal gate after which the path is – briefly – rather awkward and boggy before it drops down closer to the riverbank. Soon it rises a short way back up the hillside onto an old track and is in better condition. You go through another gate and soon after follow the edge of a field on your right. Adjacent to the end of the field you pass through another gate and then reach a crossroads of tracks. Go straight ahead, heading slightly uphill and into the wood. This will lead you uphill to another edge of the wood.

Immediately past the edge of the wood you turn left on another path, going through a kissing gate into a field. Follow the edge of the woodland on your left and when you reach a corner of the wood, the path swings slightly right and heads for a metal kissing gate on the far side, to the right of a group of buildings and a length of hedgerow.

Through this gate (and a secondary gate), follow the field boundary on your right to a kissing gate in the next corner of the field, going through this to follow a path past a white-painted cottage and so into another field. Again keep to the field boundary on your right, pass through another kissing gate into another field and then curve left round a small wooded dingle and a cottage to emerge via another kissing gate onto a road.

7 Turn right on the road and follow it for a short way, soon reaching a footpath on the left. Go through the kissing gate and walk on a line at about 45 degrees to that of the road you were just following, across the field and downhill to a kissing gate that leads to a bridge across a brook. In the field on the far side, continue on the same line that you took in the previous field and head uphill, aiming for a pole carrying cables and across the field to another kissing gate. Through this, follow the line of old trees to a kissing gate on the far side of this field. Through this, take the left-hand fork of the track and when it meets a lane, turn left and walk up to a T-junction.

8 Turn left here and walk the short way to St Nicholas' Church, which you may wish to visit (see overleaf). The walk continues through the church's car park and so on through a kissing gate into a field. Follow the field boundary on your left down to the next corner of the field where you go through another kissing gate. Turn left on the path here and then almost immediately right across a footbridge over Bridgnorth's bypass. Across the bridge turn right, and then round a corner to the left and through another kissing gate. From here the path essentially heads in a straight line down to the station buildings. It follows a boundary on your right to another kissing gate, then crosses a road and follows a track to

ST NICHOLAS' CHURCH, OLDBURY

The church was founded (in the then parish of Morville) in the 12th century, but little of the church of that date remains, it having been heavily restored if not rebuilt in the Victorian era. The bell-turret is conspicuously Victorian, but some good quality Jacobean panelling remains inside the church towards the western end.

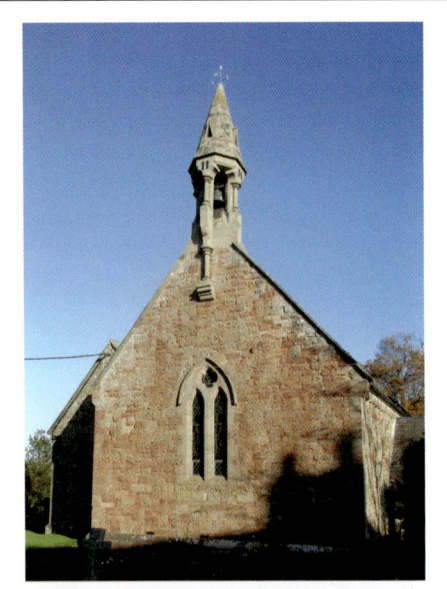

another kissing gate which leads into some sports fields. Here a line of marker posts directs you across the sports fields to another kissing gate. Beyond this the path initially follows a close-boarded fence on your left and then drops down to the railway line.

Here, turn left and follow the lane to a road on which you turn right. Just past the George pub on the left, take the road to the right which leads to the railway station. From the front of the station take the footbridge towards the town. At the far end turn right and immediately cross the road to walk up the steps and emerge by the castle grounds. Go up the steps into the park and walk past the bandstand, possibly diverting to see the slightly unusual war memorial to

WAR MEMORIAL

This is a work by the Ludlow-born Adrian Jones, most famously responsible for the great 'Angel of Peace arresting the chariot of War' that sits atop the Wellington Arch at the end of Piccadilly by Hyde Park in London. Jones was asked to design a memorial for Bridgnorth which commemorated not just those who had died in the war but also those who had returned. That ruled out a memorial 'to our glorious dead' or the use of an angel of peace, and he chose to show a soldier in action. It has often been thought to depict a Tommy having just thrown a grenade or bomb, but the stance, with his rifle slung over the throwing shoulder, is all wrong for such an action and it is more likely that Jones depicted the start of the assault on Bligny Hill by the King's Shropshire Light Infantry on 6 June 1918, a soldier calling on his comrades to advance, an action which won the regiment, then under the overall command of a French general, the Croix de Guerre avec Palme.

BRIDGNORTH CASTLE

The castle was probably commenced by Robert de Bellême c.1101-02 on the abandonment of Quatford, on a site that, according to Florence of Worcester, was a Saxon *burh* built by Ethelflaeda in 912. Certainly the original area of the bailey was extensive, measuring some 350m by 150m divided by a ditch and probably a wall into an inner and outer bailey. The inner bailey is now occupied by the public garden; the outer bailey delineated by West and East Castle streets. Presumably the *burh* had been deserted, or the Normans would have chosen to originally occupy Bridgnorth rather than Quatford.

Bellême rebelled against Henry I, whose force took the castle after a three-month siege in 1102. At the end of the Anarchy, during Stephen's reign, Hugh de Mortimer had control of the castle, perhaps through a grant of stewardship or having seized it during the troubles. In either event, when the newly crowned Henry II demanded the return of all royal castles (there were some 90 of them across the kingdom), Hugh refused. By early 1155 Hugh was almost alone in his continuing defiance and Henry II advanced with an army to bring him to order. With Bridgnorth and his other castles under siege and his lands being wasted, Hugh quickly came to terms and surrendered the castle, after which it remained in royal hands.

The remains comprise a seriously-leaning chunk of the keep probably built between 1105 and 1113 (with further work between 1166 and 1174) and a building on its south-west side that might be part of a large hall, together with a fragment of the curtain wall. A royal abode or 'King's House' was maintained in the inner bailey up to the 17th century, and documents referring to building works at the castle mention a hall with a chimney and glass windows, a King's Chamber and a Queen's Chamber with an oriel window. The documents also mention a kitchen, pantry, buttery, tilt yard and mural towers, and a barbican (added during King John's reign) that contained the constable's dwelling, dungeons and a well. In 1261 orders went out to have the houses in the castle roofed and repaired, but just 20 years later the castle was recorded as being in a poor state of repair. With Edward I's conquest of Wales in the late 1200s it was allowed to further fall into disrepair. In the unrest in the later years of Edward II's reign the castle was seized by the barons, but retaken by the Crown, and allowed to fall yet further into decay. John Leland described the castle in 1540, making mention of a 'mighty' north gate (of which remains were found in 1821 during building work) and of many newly-built timber houses in the outer bailey. In 1628, the castle was granted to Gilbert North, who promptly sold it to Sir William Whitmore. The castle was fortified by Royalist troops during the Civil War and after its capture by Parliamentary forces in 1646 was slighted, with buildings undermined and blown up. The inner bailey was purchased by the Bridgnorth Corporation in the early 20th century.

Excavations in 1995 showed that much robbing of masonry had occurred – not surprisingly given the large settlement in the vicinity of what would have been ruins after the Civil War – and also found a Roman coin and flint flakes, suggesting that the site has long been used by humans.

CHURCH OF ST MARY MAGDALENE

This church was designed in 1792 by Thomas Telford, better known as a builder of bridges, roads and canals. Its predecessors were a chapel in the castle followed by a medieval church, the latter showing signs of dilapidation by the late 1700s. Telford was asked to advise on its state and recommended starting afresh. His church is orientated north-south so as to provide a fine vista when looking down East Castle Street towards it, and he personally selected the creamy-grey sandstone of which it is built from a quarry at Eardington, south of the town. The interior is extremely light, not just in terms of natural light but also in terms of structure, with slender columns supporting the roof. There is a west gallery, and the apsidal south end was added by Sir Arthur Blomfield in 1876.

the left, and then to the right of the leaning remnant of the castle.

Keep ahead and then turn right to reach the Church of St Mary Magdalene. From the front of the church, you can either turn right and then left to walk past the upper end of the cliff railway and so back into the centre of town or head along East Castle Street laid out in the castle's outer bailey with its fine Georgian and Victorian buildings (including, on the right, the Governor's House built in red brick *c.*1633 and another that was the home of Thomas Telford for a while). At the end of Castle Street turn right to return to the High Street.

Walk 18
Worfield

4 miles in rolling countryside, largely on tracks and minor roads with some sections of footpath that are well maintained. There are a handful of stiles. This walk is perhaps of particular interest as an old painting shows the parkland that you walk through near Davenport House as it once was. And there's a pub to end the walk at!

Park near the Dog and Davenport Arms pub in Worfield.

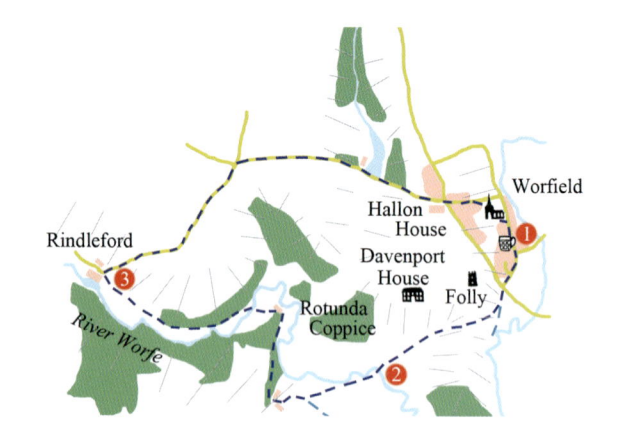

❶ With the pub to your right, walk along the road (passing Chestnut Drive to the right) until you reach a T-junction where there is a war memorial in a small green to your right. Cross the road to a field gate on its far side, where you will also find a kissing gate initially hidden from view. Go through this and follow the short length of field boundary on your right to where it makes a right-angled turn. Now take the right-hand of the two paths waymarked, heading across the parkland and quickly passing, to your right, a chestnut tree and then an oak (and keeping an eye out for a brick tower dovecote or folly built in the mid 18th century on top of the hill to your right), and so across to a stile at the bottom of a high 'bank'. Cross this stile and head up the bank following waymarking posts, and so across a ridge, keeping an eye out for Davenport House to your right, though this is partially obscured by trees.

DAVENPORT HOUSE

Davenport House was designed and built in brick with stone dressings in 1726 by Francis Smith of Warwick for Henry Davenport, who is said to have made his fortune in India. From the corners of the house four curving walls fanned out, at the end of which were 'pavilions'. Two of these were designed as stables, one as a laundry and one as the kitchen and servants' rooms. The gardens and landscaping were probably the work of Sharington Davenport, who succeeded to the property in 1731 and received advice and support from his friend, the poet and landscape gardener William Shenstone. Paintings by Thomas Robins the Elder *c.*1750 (see overleaf) show a framework of formal avenues running north-south on each side of the house, with two more distant avenues leading away to the north-west (aligned on Worfield Church) and north-north-west. The avenue running towards the church survives in part on the ridge above the pigeon house as seen from the walk, which passes through the remains of the north-south avenue as it crosses the ridge before descending to the River Worfe. A ruined temple and a gothic building (remembered in the name Rotunda Coppice) built on the slopes above the Worfe as part of the landscaping were destroyed in the 1940s. A grotto also constructed on this slope is now ruinous and stands in a fenced-off enclosure backed by two tall yew trees. Other features recorded in 1759 included a witches' temple, a Shepherd's Seat and urn, a root house, an urn to Milton, a Doric seat with two pillars, a Gothic Seat, Flora's Seat, Shenstone's Seat and a Gothic Pigeon House. The house remained with the Davenports for many generations, though in the later 1800s and early 1900s it was usually let.

Davenport House, Shropshire, by Thomas Robins the Elder

PUMPING HOUSE
Near the footbridge across the Worfe is the remains of a waterwheel and pumping house, together with brick-lined leat, which provided the power to pump water up to the grotto on the hillside above. The grotto contained a statue of Venus concealed in a recess.

On the far side of this 'ridge', cross a tarmacked lane and join a track which descends the far side and enters a field by a stile. Over this, the path turns slightly to the left and heads downhill to reach a footbridge across the River Worfe. Here it is worth turning around to look back to Davenport House so that you can see where the remains of the grotto lie, backed by two yew trees (see photograph opposite) and compare what is left of the landscaping with Robins' painting (opposite below). As you cross the bridge, look out for the remains of the pumping house.

❷ Over the bridge, the path shadows the line of the river to reach a stile across the fence on your left. Cross this, the path probably having been reinstated by the farmer after any agricultural operation, and then head to the far right-hand corner of the field, where a gate will lead you out onto a track. Turn right on the track and follow it round the hillside towards a barn and a cottage, leaving the track to go through the gate that's just to the left of the cottage's garden and so leave the field. Cross a small patch of ground to reach a stile which you cross and then turn right on the path on its far side. This will lead you through a wood and above the River Worfe to a kissing gate into a field. The path now keeps close to the rockface that forms the left-hand boundary of this field and will bring you round to a stile next to a gate that leads into a yard by a cottage. Cross the stile and then follow the track to the left of the cottage out of the yard (or take the alternative route indicated if you wish, which brings you onto the track on the far side of the houses). Keep on this track back across the Worfe and eventually it will lead you out onto a minor road near Rindleford Mill.

❸ Turn right on the road, and right again when you reach a crossroads at the top of the rise. This will lead

RINDLEFORD MILL

The site of a medieval fulling mill, then an oil mill, the sandstone part was built in the 18th century and the majority brick part in the 19th century, when the building was used to mill corn. In the late 19th century its use changed again and it was used to pump water. In 1936 it was estimated that 30,000 gallons a day were being pumped up to Bromley reservoir.

you back to the edge of Worfield, first passing a lake on the right, then with another opportunity to see Davenport House on your right, and then past Hallon House to a T-junction. Turn right here and almost immediately left to follow a minor road 'unsuitable for HGVs'. This will lead you past the old Smithy on your left and then down to Worfield Church (see overleaf for information).

Leaving the churchyard by its main entrance, you will see Lower Hall (see page 169 for information) on the far side of the road. Turn right on the road to reach the pub.

HALLON HOUSE
Felling dates of 1739-41 have been ascertained for timber used in the timber-framing that lurks behind the more recent stucco work. This was originally a longhouse, with the farm animals housed in part of the lower storey.

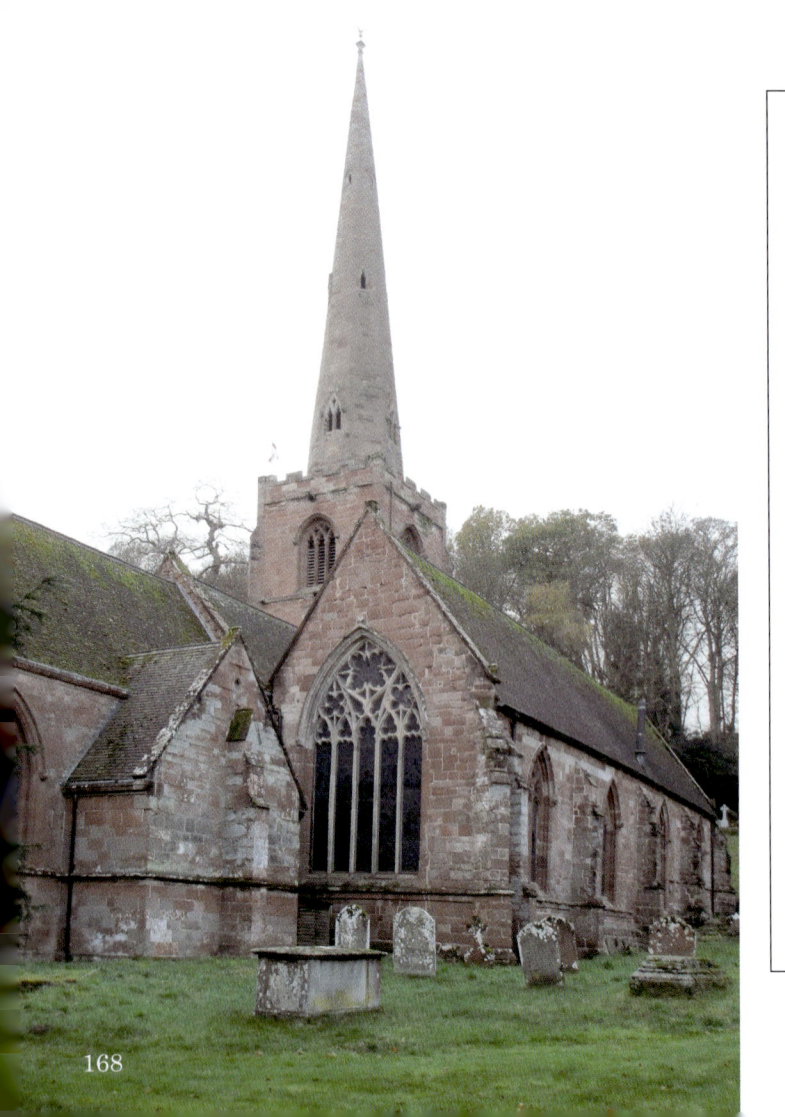

WORFIELD CHURCH

The red sandstone church consists of a south-western tower and spire (one of the finest in Shropshire), a nave with north and south aisles, and a chancel. The present church was largely constructed in the Decorated style in the early 1300s. This must have replaced an earlier church, for in the north wall of the tower (that which looks into the nave) there is a redundant lancet window opening internally, whilst externally, between porch and tower, is a small pointed window, and there are other disjointed or odd features if you explore carefully, all best explained by the existence of an earlier church on the site. In 1861-62 the chancel was heavily restored when the porch was also built. The chancel screen of 1894 incorporates some medieval pieces.

At the west end of the north aisle is a tomb to Sir George Bromley (d.1588) and his wife with their alabaster effigies; near them is a monument to Sir Edward Bromley (d.1626) and his wife, again with alabaster effigies. The alabaster reredos was made in 1887. The church is also full of stained glass which creates the dark interior experienced when you first enter.

Recent work in the church has seen the creation of a new gallery at the western end which allows for an unusual view of the interior. As you ascend the stairs to the gallery look out for the squint on the left-hand side: before the church was rebuilt this would have allowed lepers to look from the outside into the church during services.

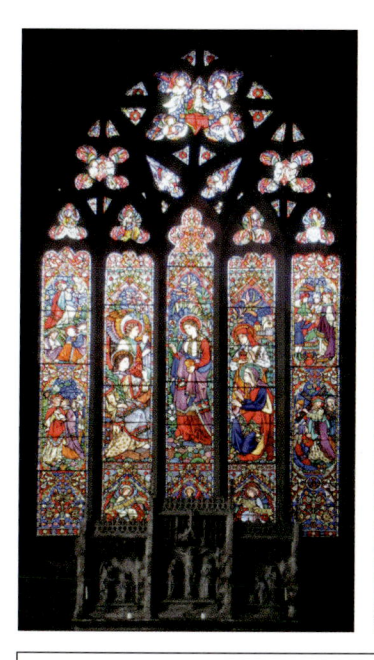

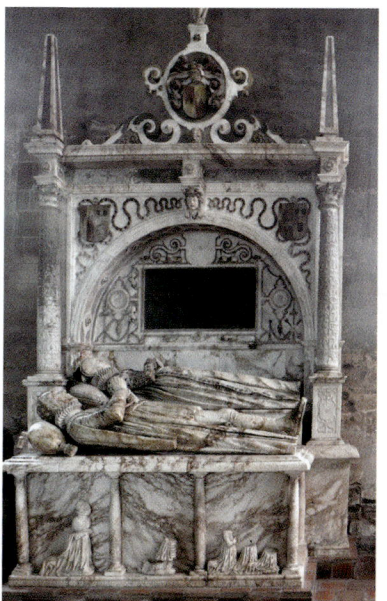

LOWER HALL

Probably built in the later 1600s, the timberwork is close studded and the house is fully jettied for two storeys with projecting stone stacks with tall brick chimneys. The main part of the house includes a parallel wing at the rear (which is possibly earlier) and is square in plan, whilst at the side and back are long timber-framed two-storeyed office wings. It was roughcast in the 1700s, but this has since been removed. The house served as the parsonage for some two centuries and was bought after the First World War by Oliver Leese, who had been wounded in the Battle of the Somme. He was still serving in the army at the start of the Second World War, being evacuated at Dunkirk, and was in due course promoted by Field Marshal Montgomery to command the 8th Army, which he led at the Battle of Monte Casino in Italy. He was knighted in 1944. He retired from the army in 1947, created the gardens at Worfield and became a noted horticulturist. From 1963, the four-acre gardens were further developed by Mr and Mrs Christopher Dumbell.

Walk 19
Claverley

4.5 miles in rolling countryside on a mixture of tracks, minor roads and paths, virtually all of which are kept in good condition (the odd part can be trampled into mud by cattle). There is one short section of B road, but this has a wide grass verge (and a pub on its far side!) The rises and descents are all extremely gentle. However, be aware that there are some stiles designed with very tall people in mind: they can have just one step set about two feet off the ground! The church at Claverley is particularly interesting due to its wall paintings, and there are a clutch of interesting buildings to be seen along the route.

Park near the church, which you can visit at the start or end of your walk. Note the ancient cross near the entrance to the churchyard.

CLAVERLEY CHURCH

The present building (there was probably an earlier Saxon church) was begun in the early 1100s, commencing with the nave, the north arcade and at least the base of the present tower. The south aisle was added in the 1200s and a chapel to the west of the tower in the 1400s, each of which necessitated new openings being made in the tower's base. The chancel was rebuilt in the 1300s in the Decorated style, and further embellishments to the church were carried out in the following Perpendicular style including the building of the south chapel and the rebuilding of the south aisle, which was given classic Perpendicular crenellations.

Above the Norman arches on the north wall of the nave is a large painting that has been dated to *c*.1200. For a long time it was thought to depict the Battle of Hastings, but now the favoured view is that it shows the conflict between seven Christian virtues and seven pagan vices using the medium of mounted knights. Over the chancel arch is part of a Doom painting of the 15th century, and other 15th-century painting survives between the windows of the clerestory (of pairs of saints or apostles) and the spandrels of the arches (the latter showing the martyrdom of St Margaret of Antioch).

In the north aisle is an incised slab memorial to Richard Spycer (d.1448) and his wife Alice, and in the south (Gatacre) chapel is found the tomb of Sir Robert Broke (d.1558), Speaker of the House of Commons, and his two wives, all three figures commemorated in alabaster. Incised slabs on the east wall of the chapel commemorate other members of the Gatacre family who also died in the 1500s. There is a Norman tub font with carved arcading and foliage, a Jacobean pulpit and an Arts and Crafts altar rail.

A 14th-century stone cross has been removed from the roadway where it once stood and now stands at the entrance to the churchyard. Just inside the churchyard on the left is a timber-framed old vicarage, its oriel window and jettied gable facing the church. Its timberwork is decorated with carved human heads and foliage.

171

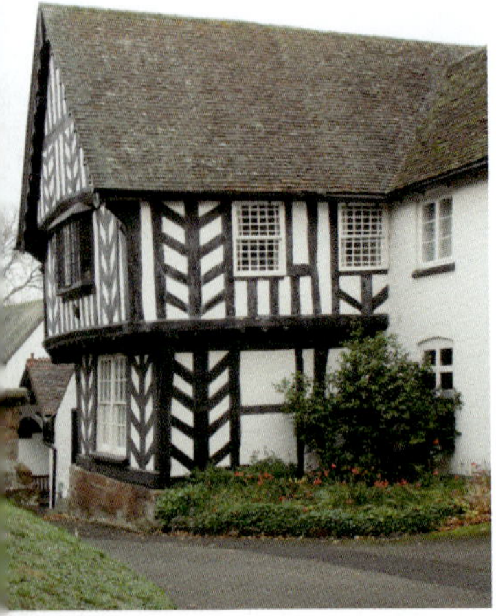
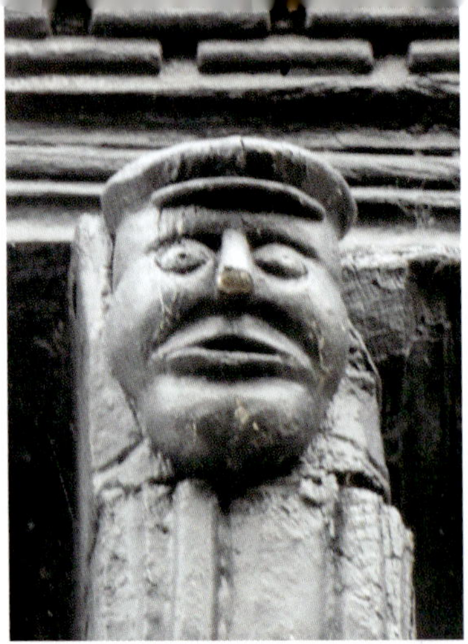
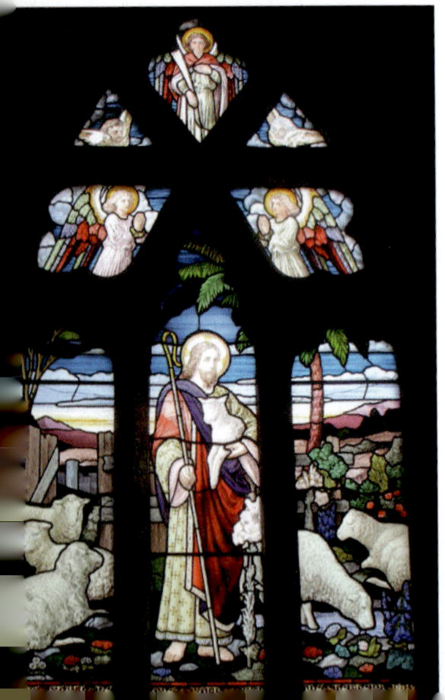
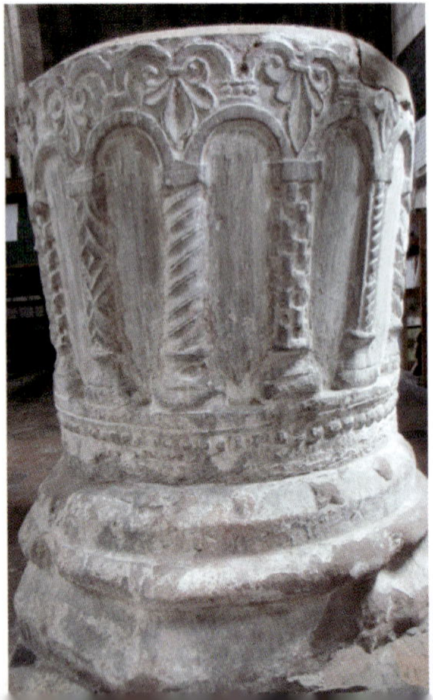
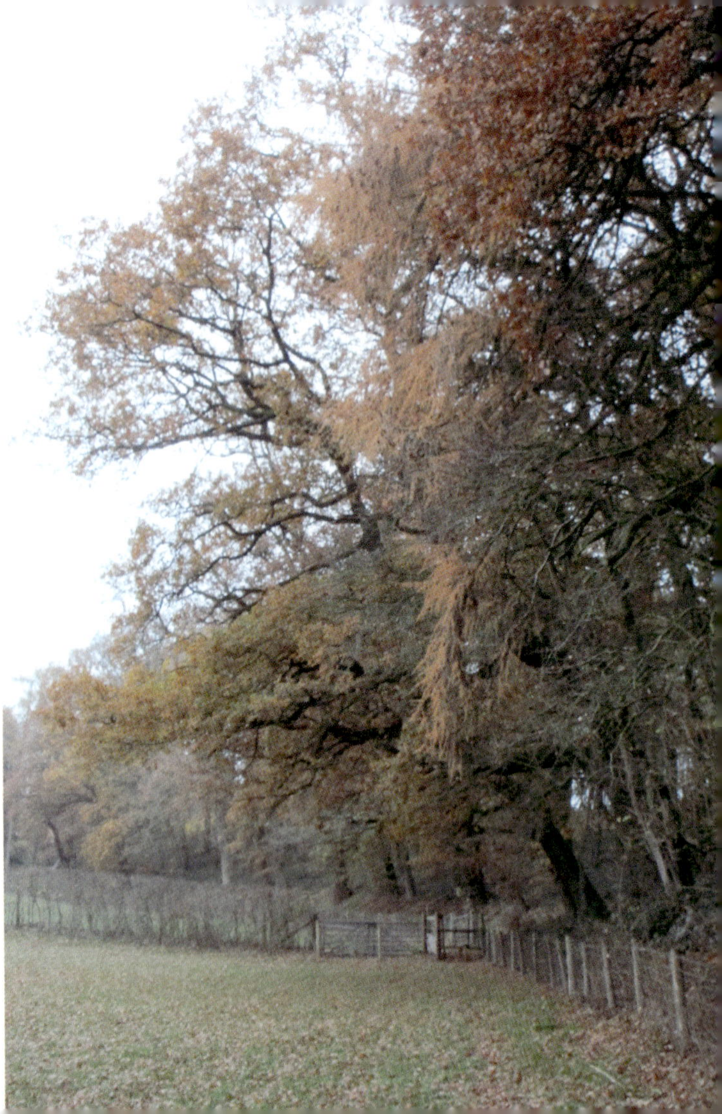

❶ With your back to the main entrance to the churchyard, turn left and walk downhill past a row of terraced cottages on your right and the church on your left and then passing Spicer's Close off to the left. Just after a spot where two 30 mph signs are painted on the road surface in white circles (and before you would reach two bungalows on your left near the edge of the village, themselves just before a road off to the left which is signposted to Hopstone and Worfield), take the gravelled track off to the right.

Keep on the track and you'll soon reach the village sewage works on the right. Beyond this, the track ends and a path turns slightly left, crosses the first of a number of high-stepped stiles and follows a fence on your right and open ground down to a brook on your left. After a while the path forks and you take the main path which swings left and crosses the brook by an old bridge and then passes through an alder grove to reach a track. Cross the track to find a stile slightly to your left, which you go over into a field. Follow the field boundary on your right to another stile, and then again follow the field boundary on your right. This will lead you to a stile which you cross to then follow a footpath between a field on your left and the landscaped gardens of the Dairy House on your right.

❷ The path will lead you to a gate out onto a road, which you cross and take another stile to then follow a stone wall on your right. This is the wall of Ludstone Hall. The

173

LUDSTONE HALL

From the 12th or early 13th century the moated manor site belonged to the College of St Mary Magdalen, Bridgnorth, whose deans used the timber-framed manor house as a residence. In 1391-1403 it was described as comprising a hall, chamber, 'frerechamber' (friar's chamber), kitchen and bakehouse, together with a well stocked fishpond and a gatehouse built partly of stone. Dean Thomas of Tutbury had intended to rebuild the house in stone, but instead between the years 1403 and 1410 his successor resold the materials that had been gathered for this purpose, had much of the house pulled down and allowed the remainder to fall into ruin. Following the Dissolution of the College, the manor was bought first by John Jones of Ludstone in 1557, and then by the Whitmore family. The present hall was built of brick with stone dressings by Sir John Whitmore *c*.1607 on a site that involved partial infilling of the moat. A court case in 1735 concerning the water supply to the remaining part of the moat shows that it had become a fishpond of some importance, for the case concerned the potential loss of 1,000 carp, 1,000 tench and 1,000 perch. In 1870 the hall was purchased by John Round Cartwright, a recently widowed fire-brick manufacturer, who then extensively restored it and lived there until his death in 1910. He also arranged for the garden walls to be built, together with a brick and stone lodge in Jacobean style, and commissioned the landscaping, which included a knot garden and a topiary garden designed in a 17th-century style.

house is visible over the wall and through a wrought iron gate; the original moated site further on is more difficult to see, but possible for a tall person in winter!

When you reach the end of the wall, the path crosses the end of a track and goes through a gate into a field. The path continues ahead, immediately passing a new barn to your right and aiming for the far right-hand corner of the field. Here you will find a small gate into the next field across which the path continues, to reach a kissing gate on the far side just to the left of a pair of electricity poles. Through the gate, turn left on the wide verge of the B4176 and walk along a short way to take the minor road off to the left signposted to Claverley. Depending upon the time of day you may wish to call in at the Boycott Arms on the other side of the B road for refreshments.

3 Having turned down the Claverley Road, take the first right, reached after about a hundred yards, signposted to Hopstone. Walk along this road, bearing left at the junction fairly soon reached. You might wish to keep an eye out for the unusual hedgerow trees, which include a sumach and a walnut (with more walnuts later on). In due course the road crosses a brook where there are some houses, then rises uphill alongside a rock face to reach Hopstone House, a black and white house on the right.

HOPSTONE HOUSE

This house has been much modified over the years. The earliest part is the 16th-century timber-framed west wing, which contains decorated plasterwork and a painted ceiling. In the 1640s or '50s the central part with its inglenook fireplace and tall chimney was added, probably closely followed by the sandstone stable block that forms the east wing. In the late 18th and early 19th centuries, a number of additions were made, including the addition of a kitchen to the north side and the raising of the east wing to two storeys in height. The front porch was added later still.

The road then passes Old House on the left (a 17th-century and later house that has been well restored – see photograph above) and The Mount on the right (a stone and brick house dating to the 17th and 19th centuries) before then dropping downhill and swinging right to meet another road.

④ Cross this road and take the narrow lane on the far side, to then pass down a shallow 'gorge' with houses to right and left. At the end of the lane a path keeps on ahead, and you follow this along. Just past a small wood on the right, look out for a glimpse of Chyknell Hall up the valley on your right. The path continues to head uphill to a junction of tracks, in the middle of which is a small hedged enclosure containing a war memorial to the 1914-18 war.

CHYKNELL HALL

Chyknell, with its two-storeyed stucco front, was built in 1814 on the site of an earlier house to the design of John Haycock of Shrewsbury and set in a wooded park created at the same time. In 1858 the house was remodelled and extended by Edward Haycock. In 1949 it was inherited by Major Gage, who commissioned Russell Page to lay out some formal gardens around the house, the same year that Page was asked to design gardens in Battersea for the Festival of Britain. North of the house and kitchen gardens is a substantial brick stables complex dated to 1792.

With your back to the entrance to the war memorial enclosure, walk ahead on the tarmacked lane (ignoring a track off to the left) down to a junction with a minor road at the edge of Claverley. Turn left on this, and walk past Powk Hall.

> ### POWK HALL
> This was built in the 17th century as an L-shaped house with a stair turret on the inner corner. The hipped-roofed western range (that on the right as you look at the building from the road) was probably the original front until farm buildings came too close.

Then walk past the village pound (marked by iron gates erected across a rock-cut holding pen) back to the church. You may want to visit the Crown Inn, run by the 'Two Crafty Brewers'.

Walk 20
Highley

4 miles. One of the shorter walks in this book, it is unusual in passing through recent industrial history involving navigation on the Severn, the Severn Valley Railway and coal mining that only ended in the late 1960s, and also includes a church and a visitor centre. The walk is on a mixture of roads, tracks and a path along the banks of the Severn – be aware that parts of this can be very slippery in or after wet weather. Being set in a river valley, the walk does involve descents into it and ascents out of it, but none are steep.

Park in the Highley Countryside Visitor Centre car park on Station Road. There is an all-day parking charge for using this car park; if you want to avoid that you could park near the church and start the walk from there, point number 2 on the walk. This walk largely follows the route of the Highley Way, so you can also use the red and white circular waymarkers for that route as guides.

❶ Walk out of the car park and turn left on the road. Where it widens and just before houses on each side of the road, take the footpath off to the right. Follow this along and up the lane it joins at its far end to come out onto the B4555. Turn right, and just past the mini roundabout, turn left up Church Lane. The church is soon reached on your left.

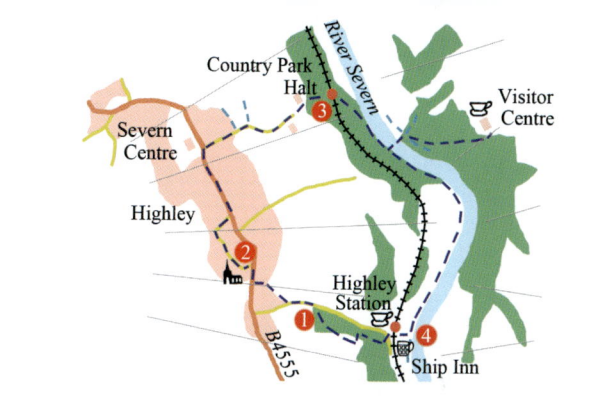

HIGHLEY CHURCH

The church consists of a nave, chancel, west tower and south porch. It was built in the Norman period but has later Early English doorways. Some rebuilding occurred in the Perpendicular period as evidenced by the windows high up in the south wall of the nave and the battlemented top to the tower. The chancel was also shortened and given a new east wall. The church was restored in 1880-81 when a new wide and high chancel arch was built. There is a medieval cross with intriguing carvings (including a crocketed niche) near the porch.

❷ From the church, continue along Church Lane, which turns into Church Street, thus walking parallel to the B4555. The street is home to the villas built for colliery officials. Turn with it to the right and around a set of well-tended allotments down Silverdale Terrace with its houses built for the miners themselves and walk back to the B road, on which you turn left. Continue along this road till you reach the wavy-roofed Severn Centre on your left. At this point, turn down the no through road on the right. When this bends to the left, keep right and walk on down the track. This passes through a passageway between two gates, marked 'The Highley Trail', and through a kissing gate. From here take the path through woodland, and cross the Severn Valley Railway at what is now named Country Park Halt.

SEVERN VALLEY RAILWAY

Work on the line was started in 1858 and completed in 1862, and it ran from Hartlebury to Shrewsbury via Stourport-on-Severn, Bewdley, Arley, Highley, Hampton Loade, Bridgnorth, Coalport, Ironbridge, Buildwas, Cressage and Berrington. In 1963, as part of the Beeching cuts, the line was closed to passenger traffic. In 1965 the Severn Valley Railway Society was formed with the intention of buying a 5½ mile section of line between Bridgnorth and Alveley Colliery sidings (now Country Park Halt). A share issue was launched and was so successful that an additional nine miles was bought south from Alveley sidings through Bewdley to Foley Park, near Kidderminster. When the British Sugar Corporation sidings at Foley Park fell into disuse in 1982, the 1½ mile section of line through to Kidderminster was purchased and a new station was built as the southern terminus of the line to the design of the station that had stood in Ross-on-Wye in Herefordshire. Some 70 staff and countless volunteers now operate the railway, money being constantly needed for maintaining track and equipment, and for carrying out major repairs such as when storms and floods in 2007 caused damage to the line in 45 places, ten of which required major engineering work to rectify.

COUNTRY PARK HALT

The Country Park Halt on the Severn Valley railway was originally the halt or station for Alveley Colliery and known as Alveley Halt, and comprised a single platform with an iron shelter. It opened in 1939 and closed in 1969, the new station being built in 1996.

❸ Over the railway line you enter an area which was a coal preparation yard, the coal being brought from mines across the Severn by an aerial ropeway; it is now a picnic area. Take the second track on the right, which follows the hillside down to a bridge across the Severn which was erected in 2006, replacing an earlier colliery bridge built on the line of the aerial ropeway. Cross this and bear right at the first fork in the path and left at the second, following the signs to the visitor centre, to follow a tarmacked track up to the centre, which at the time of writing was closed for renovation but may have reopened by the time of your walk.

Return to the bridge across the Severn and once over it, turn left along the path that follows the river bank. This will lead you to Highley and the Ship Inn, where refreshments may be had at the right time of day.

SEVERN NAVIGATION

In 1756 some 20 vessels are recorded as working from wharves along the part of the river between Bewdley and Bridgnorth. The opening of the railway alongside the river in 1862 led to a rapid decline in barge traffic to the extent that by 1869 only 45 vessels are recorded working the entirety of the Shropshire Severn.

SHIP INN

The Ship Inn was built *c*.1740 by Edward Wilcox, a barge owner, as a house. When he died in 1764 he left two cottages to his son, Samuel, who turned one into the Ship Inn, licensed from *c*.1770, the other property being known, at least from 1784, as Ship Cottage. The inn initially served the bargees working the river and those quarrying limestone on the hillside behind the inn. A modern single-storey extension has been built on the front, but otherwise the building looks unchanged from photos taken *c*.1900.

HIGHLEY STATION

Highley Station opened in 1862 and closed in 1963. It had just one platform, along with sidings for local collieries, notably Lansdale and Highley, the latter reached from the station by a rope-worked incline tramway. Most Severn Valley station buildings were built in yellow brick, but this one was built in stone and was restored to its 1930s condition by the Severn Valley Railway after it took over the line. When the railway is operating, the Engine House Visitor Centre is open, where, on payment of an entrance fee, you can see many of the line's reserve engines and some exhibitions; there is also a café.

STANLEY AND HIGHLEY COLLIERIES

Stanley Colliery, which lay close to where the present Highley Station stands, was worked between 1804 and 1823 in an area that had previously been quarried for limestone that was used for building, the stone often being sent downriver by barge for use in Worcester. Remains of lime kilns have also been found here, suggesting that some of the stone was converted to lime for spreading on farmland.

With the arrival of the railway at Highley in 1862, coal-mining in the area was once again considered and Highley Colliery began production in 1878, continuing to 1969. The offices survive (being the building on the left as you leave the car park at the Severn Valley Country Park, now converted into houses) together with the remains of shafts, spoil heaps and the line of a *c.*350m tramway that connected the mine to the railway.

A winding wheel erected in 1994 as a tribute to local miners came from Bagworth Colliery, Leicestershire.

4 To continue the walk, take the lane off to the right just before you reach the Ship Inn (signposted for Highley Station) and walk up to the station, crossing the railway line by the footbridge. Leave the station yard by its access road and cross the road at its end to enter the Severn Valley Country Park. A short distance along the path there's a crossroads of paths. Turn right and walk to the cutting that once formed the incline for Highley Colliery.

Through the cutting, turn sharp left at the next junction of paths, and then turn right (following the sign to toilets and car park) to walk up to the miners' memorial. Behind the memorial you'll see the path to the car park. (Continue through the car park if you parked near the church, and then follow the walk from point 1.)

Walk 21
Cleobury Mortimer, Mawley Hall & Reaside Manor

5.5 miles. A large part of this walk goes through the lands of Mawley Hall, which have been undergoing restoration in recent times, making for well maintained tracks that are a great pleasure to walk. Elsewhere it is largely on a mixture of minor roads and footpaths, some of the latter being muddy in or after wet weather, and one short section can be relatively closely packed with nettles and brambles in late summer and early autumn. The walk is set in rolling countryside with many river and stream crossings and meetings, so is quite up and down but with no steep ascents. Apart from passing Mawley Hall, you also pass by Reaside Manor and the site of an early forge with its associated waterworks, and there is the church in Cleobury Mortimer.

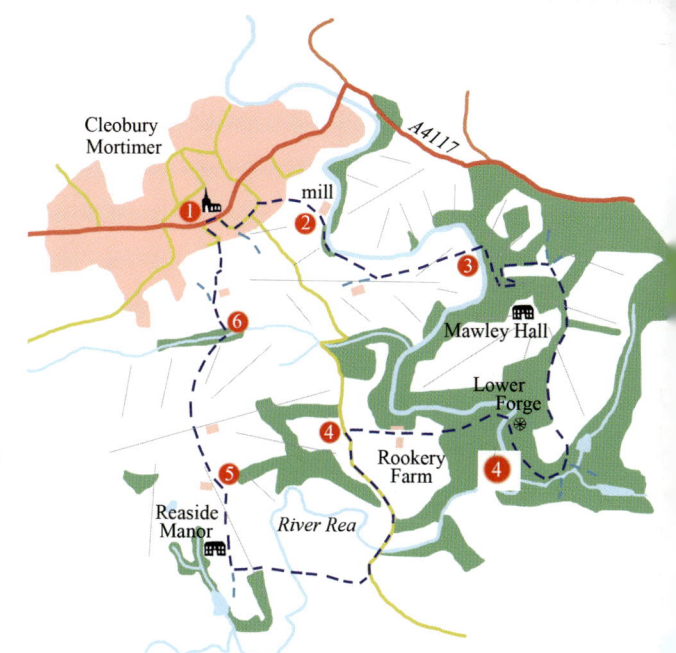

CLEOBURY MORTIMER

The name derives from the contraction of the Old English *clifu*, meaning a steep place (from which our word 'cliff' derives) and *burh* or *bury*, meaning fortified settlement. To this was added Mortimer, the manor being granted to that family after the Norman Conquest. The Mortimers built a castle north-west of the church, but this was destroyed in 1155 when a short-lived Mortimer rebellion was put down by Henry II (see page 160); its site now lies underneath housing. During subsequent years the town acted as a local market centre, a role boosted during the 1500s by the ironworks established alongside the River Rea (see page 191). It retained its status as an important urban centre for a rural hinterland in the following centuries but recently, despite an expanding population, has lost many of its civic amenities (railway station, magistrates' court, police station, even an agricultural college) in common with many equivalent-sized towns.

ST MARY'S CHURCH AND CHURCHYARD

The church began life as a Saxon minster church and now comprises a nave with aisles, a south porch (of which the felling dates for timbers in the roof of 1212-42 are some of the earliest in the county), a chancel with a north chapel and a west tower and spire (with a noticeable twist due to the warping of some timbers and rot in others). The carved stoup now in the porch was found in a garden and probably dates to the 1300s. The church was started in the Norman style, but building continued through the 1200s and early 1300s in the Early English and then Decorated styles. The north chapel was probably founded by the Roger Mortimer who was responsible for the overthrow of Edward II and who was executed in 1330. In the 1700s, the church's walls were bulging outwards; Thomas Telford was called in and stabilised them, with buttresses added later. Some Victorian stained glass in the chancel's east window commemorates William Langland, author of *Piers Plowman*, who may have been born in the town in 1332, though it is more likely that he was born near Ledbury. The Victorian restoration of 1874-75 overseen by Sir Gilbert Scott was a work of restraint.

The churchyard was originally roughly circular, but additional land was acquired to the north-east of the church in 1853. There is a lack of obvious signs of burials taking place in the churchyard, with inscriptions on surviving gravestones dating from 1748, but earlier burials must have taken place here. In 1893 a new burial ground was opened at the western end of the town.

The base of a medieval churchyard cross remains to the right of the porch as you enter the church, remodelled in the mid 1800s to form the base for a sundial.

Park in central Cleobury Mortimer and then walk to the church.

❶ After having had a look (or you can leave it till after the walk!), walk down Lion Lane on the other side of the High Street opposite the church, and follow it round to the left (ignoring a footpath that heads off from this corner). Keep on the lane past a turning off to the right and then, opposite a turning off to the left, turn right onto the signposted bridleway (though it's more like a footpath) and walk uphill between houses to emerge onto another lane by the appropriately named Mortimers Cottage on your left.

Turn left on the lane and follow it to its end, soon reached, to then take the path to the right of a red brick bungalow. This will lead you to a tunnel of vegetation, beyond which a track will lead you downhill, passing Cleobury Mill. The track leads downhill past a house and through a gate into a yard at the end of a lane.

CLEOBURY MILL
Cleobury is recorded as having a mill at the time of the Domesday Survey, but this was probably located close to the town. This mill does not appear on the tithe map of 1846 but does appear as a corn mill on the Ordnance Survey map of 1884, suggesting it was built between those two dates.

❷ Cross this yard to a gate on the far side which leads onto a footpath which follows the right bank of the river. Keep on this path as it follows the river as it makes a bend to the left. After going through a gate into a field, the path turns away from the river and slants uphill across the hillside: the line of the path can just about be made out on the ground. At the top of the hillside you reach a hedge and you bear left to follow it along, keeping it to your immediate right. At the end of the field you reach a gate through which you go to enter the next field. Again follow the hedge line on the right and it will lead you down to a footbridge across the Rea.

❸ Cross the bridge (there used to be an ironworks alongside the river to your left) and turn right on the earthen track at the far side. This quickly meets a bend in a stony track. Take the left fork. The track winds up the hillside, heading back on itself in due course to pass the walled garden of Mawley Hall and the area where the greenhouses stood, and then the track rises to meet a tarmacked lane. Turn right on this and, passing a new 'car park' on the left, made for all the workmen due to start restoring Mawley Hall in 2019, walk up to the junction of tracks in front of a gateway. Here you turn left on the wide tarmac track. This you now follow for about a

REA IRONWORKS

Two forges were founded on the River Rea below what is now the site of Mawley Hall by the future Earl of Leicester, Robert Dudley, c.1563. Lower Forge, the site which you pass on the walk, was first known as the Cleobury Iron Works, whilst Upper Forge, first known as Cleobury Dale, lay upstream of the footbridge you crossed before ascending to walk round the walled garden. The forges would have been some of the first ironworks outside the Weald and Lower Forge had two charcoal burning furnaces by 1584, the charcoal coming from locally managed coppices and the ironstone from Clee Hill just a few miles to the west. Over time, relatively low quality pig iron may have been produced on Clee Hill and then brought to the two forges to be refined into wrought iron, the water power driving large hammers, bellows and rollers. It's possible that before they built Mawley Hall on the hill above, the Blounts built a house for themselves at Lower Forge in the late 1600s, for later the ironmaster is recorded as living in a house of four storeys built in brick, which would seem excessive for a man of that status at the time.

The sites were to become of national importance in the history of iron-making. By 1743 Upper Forge had a blade mill with water-powered grinding stones, and the two forges were later producing ironwork for clients as far afield as Cornwall. By the end of the 18th century the two forges were owned by different people, with Sir Walter Blount of Mawley Hall owning Lower Forge and Upper Forge being owned by the owner of Kinlet Hall. The forges had ceased production by 1844, the ironmaster's house being then converted to a Roman Catholic school by the then Lady Blount. The school was demolished c.1950 and the workers' houses in 1961. In 2015 the upper part of the weir was rebuilt and was found to have been made from 19th-century coping bricks. Landscaping of both sites since the closure of the ironworks has left few traces of the buildings connected with the works, but features of the associated water management system remain at Lower Forge.

MAWLEY HALL

This house was built on a new site *c.*1728-33 by Francis Smith of Warwick for Sir Edward Blount, baronet, who also had a hand in the design. It is built of red brick with stone dressings and the glimpses that can be gained from the footpaths on the walk give the appearance of a rather plain house, but the interior is awash with ornamentation: inlaid floors, plaster columns, heavy pediments above doorways, plaster ceilings and plasterwork on the walls, presumably reflecting the lively Baroque taste of Edward Blount. The house was restored in 1962 and now the grounds and house are undergoing considerable further restoration.

MAWLEY HALL PARK

A deer park existed here prior to 1552 when it is known that the park pale was either repaired or removed. In the mid to late 18th century surviving plans show that the Blounts considered plans to enhance the grounds around the Hall, but it is not known to what extent these were acted upon. It is clear, however, that the park still contained deer, for *c.*100 fallow deer were recorded in 1892. The hall was requisitioned during the Second World War, with American troops billeted between December 1943 and July 1944 in the run up to D-Day. The hall was derequistioned in 1951. In 1961 Mawley Hall was sold to Mr and Mrs Anthony Galliers-Pratt, who set about redesigning the gardens to include a parterre by the west front, a temple, an octagonal folly, an obelisk and a rhododendron avenue. Further restoration of the hall and grounds began in 2015 under new ownership.

mile: it leads first through a thin slice of woodland then, losing its tarmac surface, gains a line of trees on its left (and sometimes on its right, though this is often a strip of woodland). Keep an eye out for views of Mawley Hall off to the right – it's hard to see except in autumn/winter (as seen in the photograph on the opposite page; the one on this page is the hall as seen later in the walk). The track then bends left and drops downhill to enter woodland. Keep right at all junctions of tracks and the track you are on will lead you in a curving route to the site of a forge on the River Rea marked by a weir and various bridges.

Cross the stone bridge and then the pedestrian bridge to the left of the ford. Keep on the track, which will lead you uphill, bending to the left and following the line of an old wall on your right. Ignore a track off to the left and just keep ahead to eventually pass by the house and stables of The Rookery, and thence to meet a minor road.

④ Turn left on the road and follow it along to a bridge across the River Rea once more. The road will then head uphill and bend to the left. Past the bend look out for the footpath off to the right, itself just past a track that leads off to the right. Take this footpath, which initially passes between two hedges to join a track. Turn right on the track and this will quickly lead you into a field. Here the path (which may or may not have been reinstated after farming cultivation) crosses this field, heading towards a point just to the right of the main buildings of Reaside Farm on the other side of the valley (as in the photograph above). On the far side of the field you will find a footbridge back across the Rea (for the last time!)

The path crosses the next field, aiming to a point just to the right of the wood on the far side. Here you will find a gate and a stile into the next field. Once in this field, follow the edge of the wood uphill and at the top of the rise, bear right to a stile in the fence on the right. This will lead you into the gardens of Reaside Farm. Walk along the track towards the large 'farmhouse', which you

REASIDE MANOR

This is an early 17th-century manor house, but apparently only three-quarters of what was planned was actually built, with the service rooms ending up in the basement rather than as a separate wing. It is not known who had it built (the initials I T T R were apparently once visible on a plaque in the porch), but built it was, of local shaley stone. The porch opens into a large oak-panelled hall, whilst the most elaborately decorated room is what was the ground-floor parlour in the west wing, which is also panelled but also has rich plasterwork. An even richer scheme seems to have been intended for the room above this, but perhaps the money was running out, for only roundels featuring mythical beasts were completed within the frieze.

pass to its right, and then follow its driveway past 'castellated' yew topiary. The track then gains a tarmac surface and rises uphill.

❺ Just over a cattle grid the tarmacked lane reaches a modern storage 'barn' on the left. Here the path turns right off the lane and goes through a gate into a field. The path then heads directly uphill, passing to the left of a timber-clad house on the crest of the ridge, heading in due course to a stile in the far field boundary situated just to the left of what appears to be a shallow, circular man-made pond (which might be dry in summer). This actually originated as a limestone quarry.

Once you are over the stile the path follows the field boundary on your right to a stile in the next corner of the field. Across this, the path bears slightly right to follow the bottom of the indent in the hillside and wind its way down towards the far right-hand corner of the field, to join a track on which you turn right, to follow it out of the field and across a small stream.

❻ Across the stream you reach a stile/gate on your left and cross into another field. Once in the field you follow the field boundary on your left uphill, but once adjacent to the remains of some buildings on the other side of the field (and just past a large tree), turn half right to head towards the far corner of the field. As you near this you'll see a stile in the right-hand hedge, which you cross. Cross the corner of the field and follow the field boundary for a few yards to reach a small gate on your left. Go through this, and then head diagonally down and right across the next field towards its far corner. Here you will find a kissing gate, through which you go. Then follow the field boundary on your left to another gate which leads out onto a lane. Go straight up this lane, passing between houses, and it will lead you out into the High Street opposite the Talbot Hotel. At first glance this looks to be a pukka black and white building, but though the core may date to the 17th century, the frontage dates to the 19th century and is fake half timbering.

Walk 22
Stottesdon & Sidbury

6 miles largely on paths across and along field edges with some lengths of minor road. Some stiles were in poor condition in the summer of 2021, and one footbridge was missing several planks and needs great care to cross. We have written to Shropshire County Council (as the highway authority and so with responsibility for maintaining paths) to point out these problems so they may have been resolved by the time you come to do the walk. There are two churches, an old manor and the site of another, and a good pub at which to end the walk if you wish.

❶ Park somewhere in the village. With your back to the pub, the Fighting Cocks, turn left and walk along the road to soon reach a pair of footpath signs off to the right, where the edge of the road contains a strip of light green tarmac and there is a sign pointing to Station Street one way and the High Street the other. The first footpath sign is marked 'Bromley Way' and the second 'Bridleway' and it is the second that you want, to take a track that quickly leads into the farmyard of Hall Farm. Keep on through the farmyard, leaving it by the gate just to the left of the farmhouse.

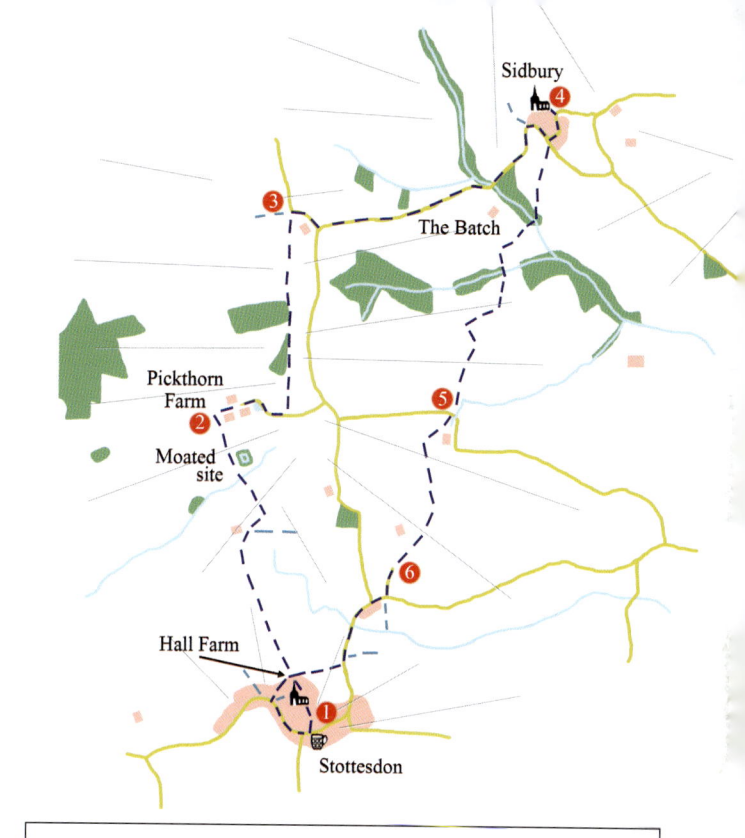

STOTTESDON
There is documentary evidence for a market here from 1243, though most of the buildings in the village date to the 19th century.

HALL FARM

The rectangular stone range of the farmhouse contains an upper-floor hall, of which the timbers forming the roof have been tree-ring dated to 1452-54, with no smoke-blackening, suggesting there was never an open hearth in the middle of the floor. It has been suggested that it was built to serve the community as some kind of church or court house, Stottesdon being the centre of a Hundred. A chimneystack was inserted in the mid 1500s when the building was converted for residential use.

Once through the gate, turn left and walk down across the large field to its far left-hand corner. Here you will find a stile out onto a farm track on which you turn right and then immediately cross another stile on your right into the next field. The path now follows the long field boundary on your left up to a gate and a stile into the field beyond. Once in this field, ahead you will see a house nestling amongst a group of trees, and your path turns to head for the right-hand end of this group, aiming for a stile you should be able to see in the fence. Cross this, and turn right on the track on its far side.

Now, look along the track and you'll see that in a few hundred yards it passes between hedges that run away to its left and right; about halfway between where you joined the track and that crossing point, you want to cross a stile in the fence over to your left. Once you are over the stile the path heads to the far side of the field, aiming to the left of a small wood, where it crosses a pair of stiles and a footbridge into the field beyond. Here the path aims for a gate at the furthest right-hand corner of the field, to the left of all the farm buildings. As you cross the field you pass a clump of tightly packed trees on your right; a moated house once stood on this site and you will also be crossing the site of a deserted medieval village.

🔴 **2** Leave the field by the gate or stile at its corner, turn right on the wide track and walk along it through the farmyard and past Pickthorn Farm with its duckpond and then a bungalow on the right. About 150 yards beyond the bungalow look out for the stile in the hedge on your left which you want to cross. Follow the field boundary on your left across the field to a stile into the next field. Again follow the field boundary on your left, passing by

PICKTHORN MOATED SITE & DESERTED MEDIEVAL VILLAGE

It is known that a house once stood on this low-lying moated site, the central island of which has been raised by material dug from the now dry moat, but the house was demolished in 1760. The site is now split between two fields and part has been planted with trees, whilst drainage works have damaged areas of the site. These did, however, unearth some pottery dating to between the 13th and 15th centuries, assorted pottery of the 17th and 18th centuries, and a fragment of glazed medieval floor tile, the latter suggesting that at least one room in the house was expensively decorated. The original house was probably built by the Baskervilles, who held the manor in the 13th and 14th centuries.

To the north-west of the moated site (and south-west of Pickthorn Farm) once stood a medieval settlement which probably started life as a township of the Saxon manor of Stottesdon. There were still eight tenements in 1571, but it gradually reduced in size until only the single farm was left. The site was bulldozed in 1971, destroying most of the surviving features above ground level.

clumps of woodland, to reach a stile into the next field. At the end of this field you cross another stile to enter a grassy farmyard. Keep following the field boundary on your left, as much as parked farm machinery will allow, and leave the yard via a gate onto a track. Turn right on the track and within yards you'll reach a road.

SIDBURY CHURCH

The church consists of a nave, a chancel, a chapel on the north added in 1734 (which is now a vestry), a Victorian porch and timber-framed belfry. Herringbone masonry in all the walls of the nave suggest an early Norman foundation, and a blocked Norman doorway survives in the west wall of the nave. In the vestry are comparatively imposing memorials to Anne and Richard Cre(s)swell, that to Richard noting his service to Charles I during the Civil War. The church was restored in 1881 when the porch was added (don't be fooled by the herringbone masonry used in its construction), and again after a fire in 1911.

❸ Turn right on the road and you'll soon reach a junction where you want to turn left on the road signposted to Sidbury, Deuxhill and Bridgnorth. Follow this road into Sidbury and turn left at the first road junction you reach in the village, signposted to Bridgnorth. Follow this along till you reach a semi-circular length of track on the left (and opposite a red Royal Mail post box) which serves the metal gates (with crosses in the ironwork) for the grounds of Sidbury Church. Go through the gates and up into the churchyard.

④ Having looked at the church, return to the road, turn right and walk back to the road junction. As you approach this, you should see a stile to the right of the signpost straight ahead of you, and this you want to cross into a large field. The path here may not be that evident, but it slants across the field downhill heading to a point into the woodland in the valley bottom about 100 yards to the right of the field's bottom left-hand corner. Keep some 60 yards to the right of the two trees that stand on their own in the field as you descend. At the edge of the woodland reached on the far side of the field you should find the entrance (possibly obscured by vegetation in summer) to a path slanting down through the woods to a footbridge across a stream. Cross the bridge and follow the path which then enters a field. Once in the field you want to head across it, the path now paralleling the hedge on your right, behind which lies The Batch.

> **THE BATCH**
> An early 17th-century timber-framed farmhouse with much herringbone brickwork in the panels. It contains a notable 17th-century 'well' staircase, and one room on the first floor has a painted panel of Abraham offering Isaac as a sacrifice, dated c.1600-25. Some other wall paintings probably of this date have since been lost.

At the far side of the field, cross a pair of stiles into the next field, where you turn three-quarters left to cross a corner of it to find a stile into the next piece of woodland. Over this stile you cross a dilapidated (in summer 2021) footbridge and then cross another stile into another field. Here you turn right and follow the hedgerow along till you reach a gate in it near the crest of the field. Go through the gate and you want to cross this next field aiming for a gate on the far side where the hedge makes a zig-zag, the angle of which is pointing almost directly at you: as an additional guide the single large tree in the opposite hedgerow is some 100 yards to the left of the gate. Once across the field, go through the gate and follow the hedge on your left for about 50 yards to then turn left through another gate that leads onto a track hedged on both sides. Follow this track and it will in due course lead through a gate into another field, where you follow the hedge on your left to a gate that leads out onto a road.

🔴 **5** Cross the road and go over the stile on the far side into a field, the path now passing to the left of an old Nissen hut but staying to the right of all the other farm-buildings, aiming in due course for a telegraph pole that stands some three yards into the field near a corner in the adjacent hedgerow. Turn left around the telegraph pole to follow the hedgerow on your left down to a stile in the corner of the field. In the next field follow the hedgerow on your left and it will take you to a double stile in its far left-hand corner, the second of which is in poor repair. Cross this and then follow the hedgerow on your right uphill till you reach a large gap on your right near the crest of the ridge. Turn right through this and follow the field boundary on your left downhill.

When you reach a large gap on your left in the corner of the field, go through it and turn right. Ahead of you, across a corner of this next large field, you'll see a length of metalled lane running directly away from you. It is the gate in front of this that you want to head for across the corner of the field, though depending upon the state of the field you may choose to follow the headland round to the gate. Leave the field through the gate.

🔴 **6** Turn left on the lane and walk up it to meet a road, on which you turn right. You pass one road off to the right then cross over a small stream. As you rise up beyond the stream you come to the word 'Slow' painted on the road surface; about 50 yards past this there is a gate into a field on your right. You want to head through this, to then follow the hedgerow on your left to a broken stile and gate into the next field. Once in the next field follow the track ahead and go through the gate at the end of the field by the farmhouse and into a farmyard – hopefully you'll recognize this as the gate and the farmyard near the start of your walk! As you pass through the farmyard, retracing your steps, look out for the stile soon reached on your left opposite the ends of a couple of Dutch barns. Cross this stile and almost immediately go over another one, to then walk along a path that will lead you into the church-yard of Stottesdon Church. Leave the churchyard by the tarmacked lane that serves it to return to the village.

STOTTESDON CHURCH

In Saxon times the church was the centre of a widespread parish and the west wall of the nave is thought to retain part of the Saxon building. The church now comprises a nave with aisles to both north and south, a chancel, a porch and a west tower. The west wall of the Saxon church therefore now faces into the tower, and you need to go into the tower to see the Saxon doorway with its remarkable, albeit not beautiful, tympanum that originally led into the church. The doorway may well have been rearranged at some point, for the stones that form the roughly triangular frame to the tympanum look as if they have been rearranged, whilst the lintel carries images both the right way up and upside down, suggesting it may have originally been designed to lie flat, as a tombstone for instance. Apart from the Saxon work, there is Norman, Early English and Decorated (the chancel with its sedilia), along with a Victorian screen, which separates the nave from the chancel. The south aisle was much rebuilt in a major restoration of 1867-9. The font is Norman and the carving belongs to the Herefordshire School of Romanesque Sculpture and dates from *c.*1140. It includes interlace and images of a large bird pecking the head of a smaller bird (often a feature of the Herefordshire School), a griffin, a lion turning his head to bite his tail, and an Agnus Dei. There are also some fragments of medieval stained glass in the windows.

Walk 23 Bitterley & Titterstone Clee

7 miles (more if you extensively explore Titterstone Clee) mainly on footpaths, most of which are in good condition. It also includes walking along a length of the old incline used to lower carts full of stone, so making the ascent of Titterstone Clee comparatively gentle; the descent is steeper. There are a few stiles. Apart from the extensive remains of quarry buildings and associated workings on the hill along with a hillfort and cairns, the walk includes passing Bitterley Church and Court, and following part of the route of the incline in addition to the section on which you walk.

The church in Bitterley is usually locked, but the churchwarden's phone number is posted in the church porch, so you could phone him to see if you can gain access.

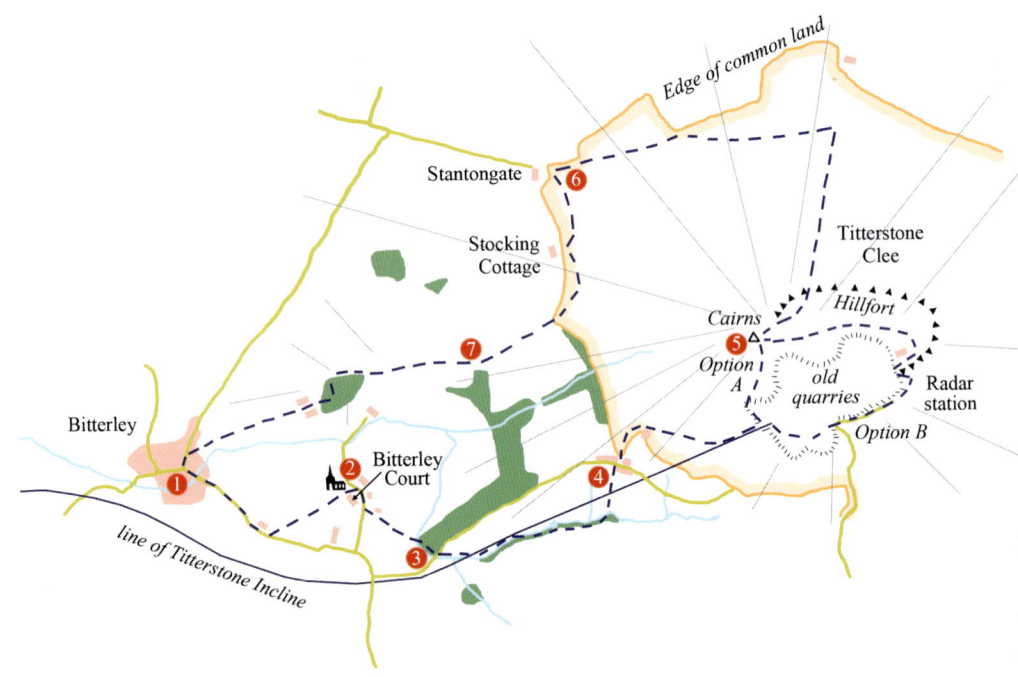

① Park near the school in Bitterley. Outside the school there's a signpost pointing towards many international landmarks. With your back to the school, take the road that is most closely in the direction of Mount Fuji! (The other two roads are signposted, but this one is not; a red telephone box should be on your left as you start up the road, if it hasn't been removed.) You will soon reach a track off to the right, which has an information board about 'Bitterley cockpit and moat'.

BITTERLEY COCKPIT AND MOAT

The sign by the road states 'The site of a former Elizabethan manor allegedly occupied by Katherine Parr, last wife of Henry VIII' and invites you to take a wander round the site and see if you can spot the moat (only the southern part remains and is water-filled) and the site of the cockpit. If you can spot the latter (it is an oval mound, measuring c.10m by 9m and under a metre high with a depression in its centre, all as suggested by the illustration on the sign), then you will have found one of only two surviving cockfighting pits so far identified in Shropshire. It was built of stone and brick, and thus probably at the same time as the now almost vanished Park Hall. This was built of brick c.1620-30 to a T-plan with an octagonal stair turret in the north-west angle of the T. The house collapsed in the mid 1900s and is now in the last stages of decay. As for it ever having been home to Katherine Parr, this would seem unlikely. To start with, it would have had to have been an earlier house on the site as she died in 1548, and although her life and previous two marriages took her around the country, the nearest to here that she is known to have lived is briefly at Wick Manor in Worcestershire with her second husband, and at Sudeley Castle in Gloucestershire in her final few months with her fourth husband.

Don't take the track, but keep on the road until you reach a pair of cottages on your left. Just past these, go through the small gate to the left of a pillared gateway into the parkland of Bitterley Court. Bitterley Church stands before you on the other side of this parkland, and the footpath heads directly towards it, aiming for the right-hand side of the tower. Go through a gate in the wall into the churchyard. (For information on the Court and the church, see overleaf.)

❷ Walk through the churchyard and turn right on the road at its far side, and follow the road round as it bends to the right. Just past a green barn on the left you'll see some bungalows, also on the left. Turn up the stoned track that serves as their drive, and when this bends to the left after some tens of yards, go ahead through the

BITTERLEY COURT AND PARK

The core of the Court dates to the mid 17th century. This was remodelled in 1768-69 by the architect Thomas Farnolls Pritchard for Charles Walcot, the son of John Walcot of Walcot Hall near Bishop's Castle. John ran up huge debts and the estate was sold to the Clives, Charles acquiring Bitterley Court with the balance due to him. Bitterley was to remain the family seat till 1899. Pritchard gave the Court a Georgian interior, notably an entrance hall bisected by Doric columns, the house being further altered the following century. It has an H-shaped plan, with the external walls rendered at the time of the Pritchard remodelling so as to hide some of the disjunctures between the old and new work. Nearly half the windows on the south front are 'blind' but glazed to give the impression of being actual windows. The clustered brick stack built on a star plan survives from the earlier building.

A park was created in 1827 but now only remains in ghostly form in the field you cross to reach the church, though extensive grounds still adjoin the house itself. A possible deserted medieval village site is evidenced in what appear to be house platforms and sunken lanes seen in the field that you cross, but when the Time Team carried out some excavations in 2012 they only found evidence of agricultural management of the land, including post-medieval farm buildings and enclosures.

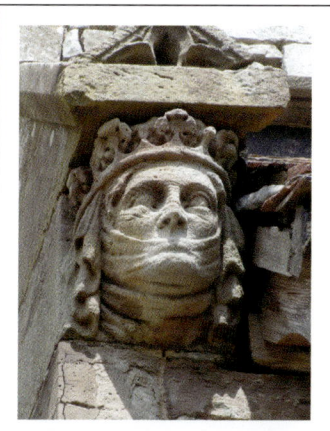

BITTERLEY CHURCH

The church dates largely from the late 1200s, is in the Early English style and comprises a nave, chancel and western tower. The timber-framed top to the tower and its spire were added during restoration in 1880-81. There is a Norman font carved with arcades and foliage; a 13th-century iron-bound chest; a Jacobean pulpit, lectern and reading-desk; a Jacobean tomb to Timothy Lucye, who is shown kneeling and wearing armour; and a screen dating from 1924.

To the right of the church as you walk past it there is a particularly well-preserved example of a 14th-century churchyard cross (possibly erected during the reign of Edward II) with a stepped base and lantern head (albeit somewhat mutilated) depicting the Crucifixion on one face and possibly the Virgin and Child on the opposite. It is considered to be one of the finest medieval churchyard crosses in the country and was carefully restored in 1899.

field gate. The path now follows the left-hand side of the line of an old field boundary/sunken track, to the far end of the field. Here you will find a pair of gates into woodland. Go through these, and turn right on the track on the far side, immediately going through another gate. After not many yards, a small path diverges to the right from the track. Take this and follow it out to a minor road.

③ Cross the road and go through the gate on the far side. Follow the path along the edge of the field and this will soon go through an opening under a pipeline. This opening crosses the line of the Inclined Plane that led down from Titterstone Clee, which will be your friend for much of the upward journey.

Having passed through the line of the Inclined Plane, the path swings left and takes a route between it and the stream, to head back out into the field after a short while. Keep to the edge of the field and follow it up to a stile. Cross this stile, and then go over the footbridge you immediately find to your right. Ascend the bank on the other side and pick up the path which is close to the field boundary on your right. In due course you will reach a dam wall across the little valley, the footpath crossing it at its right-hand end via a rather makeshift gate. Soon another gate is reached, and after passing through it, you need to cross the stream, then ascend the

TITTERSTONE INCLINE

A narrow gauge (three-foot wide) incline was built in 1881 when substantial investment was made in the quarries on Titterstone Clee in response to the demand for dhustone required in the building of Cardiff Docks. The 1.5 mile long incline carried up to 600 tons of stone a day and linked the quarry with the Ludlow and Clee Hill Railway at Bitterley Junction, 200 yards south of Bitterley Court. The trucks that carried the stone were attached by heavy wire cables to a drum house near the stone crushing plant by the quarry, which paid out the cable to control the rate of the descent of the filled truck. At Bitterley Junction the stone was loaded into wagons that were pulled by train to Ludlow. A second standard gauge incline ran from Bitterley Junction up to Clee Hill village and served a network of lines that ran around three sides of the hill serving quarries and coal mines. The narrow gauge incline closed in the 1950s and the standard one in 1962.

grassy bank on the other side into a field. A little way up into the field, you'll find a marker post.

As indicated on the marker post, the path now shadows the edge of the woodland on your left. Just past a point where the woodland protrudes into the field you will reach another marker post. This points you down a steep slope where you will find a footbridge back across the stream. Cross this and then a stile to head up a grassy bank with its scattering of young trees. Shadow the field boundary on your left and you will reach a stile into the next field. Keep shadowing the field boundary on your left and the path will lead you back through the line of the inclined plane into another field. Follow the field boundary on your left to a small gate at the left-hand end of a terrace of cottages. Go through this gate, head up some steps and cross a stile, then pass through the garden of this cottage, leaving by more steps and a gate out onto a lane.

🔴 **4** Turn right on the lane and after a few yards take the wide stoned track off to the left. This will lead you round to a gate and cattle grid onto the open hillside that surrounds Titterstone Clee. Keep on the track as it bends to the right and ends in front of a house. Here you turn left, away from the house, following a grassy track which will

TITTERSTONE CLEE

The hill is formed by a basalt intrusion in Carboniferous rock, and thus mined for coal and quarried for rock. Coal, basalt (known locally as dhustone [Welsh *dhu* means 'black'], which naturally breaks into ashlar blocks suitable for building and was later used for road building) and ironstone (from which iron could be smelted) were mined from medieval times. Coal was mined in bell pits, a shallow pit which 'bells' out at the bottom as as much coal is extracted from the seam for as little effort in digging tunnels and propping roofs as possible before risk of collapse, flooding or problems with ventilation would mean the miners would start the process over again further along the seam. There is still evidence for some 2,000 of these pits on the eastern side of the hill, often now filled with water. (You stand a chance of seeing some if you follow option B and take the tracks and road that lead to the radar station.) The quality of Titterstone Clee ironstone was high, with the ore being taken to forges for smelting at Bringewood on the Teme, at Downton west of Ludlow or to other forges in the vicinity of Ludlow. Quarrying for dhustone intensified in the 19th century, with a western quarry opening in May 1881 and an eastern one in 1910. Where you emerge from the footpath along the incline you are faced with a litter of concrete buildings largely dating from 1912-13 which replaced buildings made from the quarried dhustone. These buildings would have included sidings at the head of the incline, a drum house, a stone crusher, tanks and an engine house. At its height, quarrying employed around 2,000 people. In the mid 20th century the Magpie Quarry opened on the south-east of the hill. The quarries near the top of the hill ceased production by 1953 but a new quarry was opened on the south of the hill and still operates, well screened from the passing A4117. In 2005 it employed 18 people producing about 80% as much stone a year as 2,000 had produced earlier and has planning permission lasting to 2048.

bend to the right and lead you onto the inclined plane. Turn left on this and follow it up to the old workings.

Here you have two options: you can head left and clamber round the side of one of the quarries, (option A on the map), keeping the quarry to your right, and head for the trig point at the top, or you can take a more gentle way and see more of the workings (option B on the map). To do this, turn right, keeping the concrete ruins on your left, and past the last structure, bear left up the hill. When you come to a meeting of paths, take the left hand one, which heads steeply uphill. Cross a road and continue up the path on the other side through a wide gateway, along a stretch of tarmac, then bear left on a track back onto the road. Follow the road up to the radar station; as you pass between the two quarries you might be able to see, below to your right, the tops of some of the old bell mining pits. Just to the right of the station's gate, you'll see a kissing gate. Go through this and along a path that skirts the edge of the station (and is quite close to the hillfort rampart – see the photograph on the right), then meets the service road beyond it. Follow this past the 'golf ball' radar installations and in due course you'll see a trig point ahead of you, on top of what is called the Giant's Chair; head across to this.

TITTERSTONE CLEE HILLFORT AND TWO CAIRNS

Human occupation of the summit appears to have begun in the Bronze Age, when it was used for ritual activities. By the early Iron Age people had started to build a rampart that would encompass some 70 acres, one of the largest hillforts by area to be built in Shropshire. Excavations in 1934 revealed that the rampart was initially built as a timber-revetted earth embankment but parts were later rebuilt as a drystone wall covered in turf – an unusual form of construction for hillfort embankments, but reflecting the available materials. There is evidence that the wall was modified over time, with elaborate entrance gateways being constructed in a final phase, the main entrance at the south-east being flanked by two stone and timber guard chambers. Quarrying in the early 20th century has badly damaged its southern side and the wall can now be best seen on the northern and eastern sides.

The path that goes from the trig point to the next cairn to the north-east then follows the course of the hillfort ramparts to its left as it continues ahead to join the Shropshire Way. Much of this section of rampart is, now at least, a tumbled mix of angular dolerite blocks. Just beyond where a post stands to mark the route of the Shropshire Way the line of the rampart can be made out (see photograph overleaf).

If you were to follow this line further round to the east (instead of following the route of the walk) you would find the most prominent surviving sections of the rampart, standing up to 1m high in places on the hillfort's northern side and up to 2.4m on its exterior face on its eastern side.

In 1991 excavations in advance of building a new radar installation in the interior of the hillfort revealed a collapsed drystone wall, presumably either of a hut or stock enclosure, some post holes and laid stone surfaces. (The radar installation was built in 1964 and is

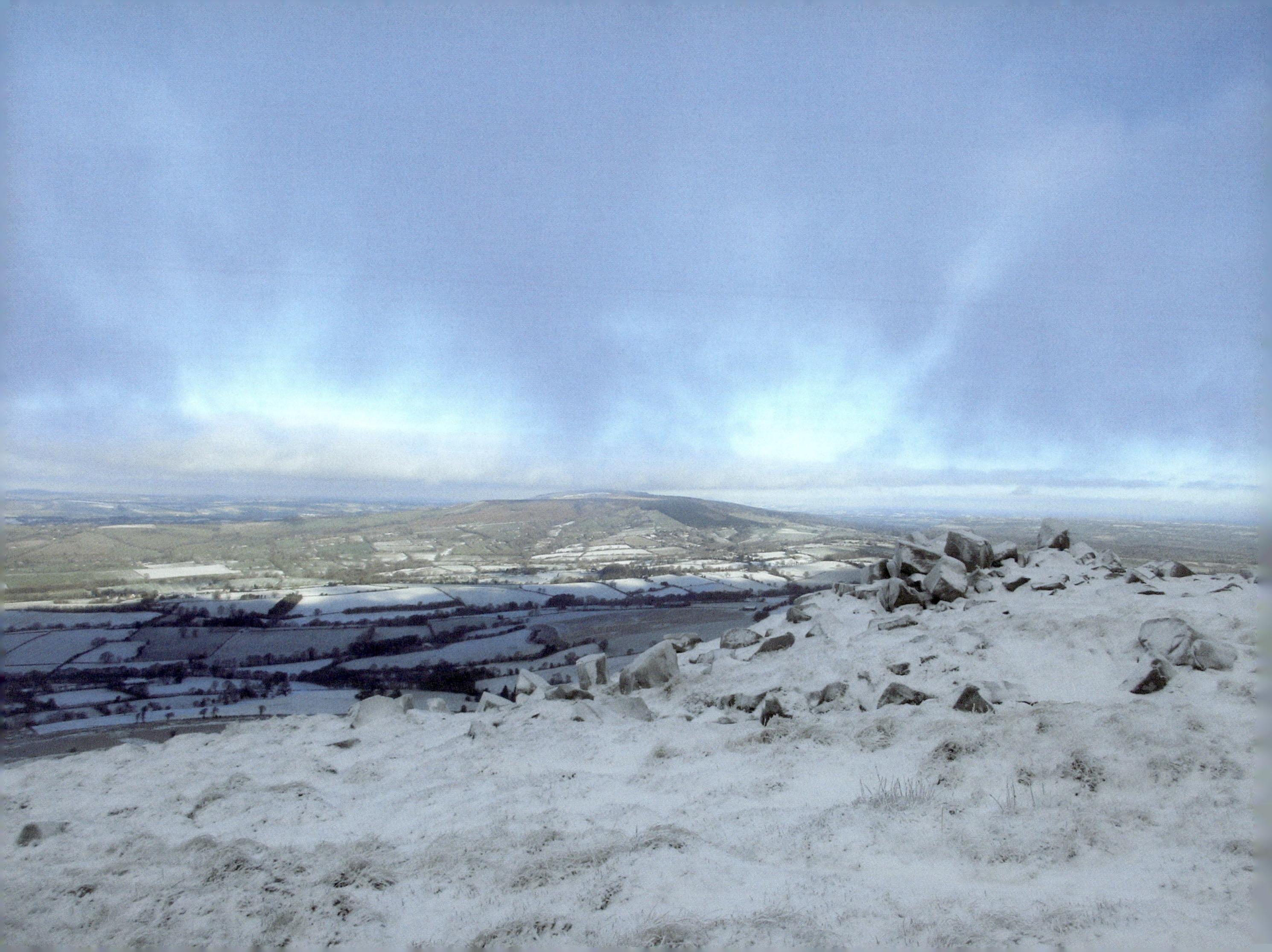

TITTERSTONE CLEE HILLFORT AND TWO CAIRNS (cont) now part of the country's air traffic control system. The white spheres protect the radar scanners from high winds as well as making repairs possible in all weathers.) The lack of finds and relatively low embankment suggest that the site may have been the focus of ritual activity during the Iron Age, rather than designed for defence.

The remains of one or possibly two cairns lie in the western part of the hillfort. The possible cairn surmounted by the trig point is now a rather jumbled mess. Some construe it as a mound 10m in diameter with a portion of stony bank 3.5m wide and 0.5m high curving around its western side. Others think that the bank, some 2m wide, only survives on its eastern side and may be the remains of a cross dyke, rather than a cairn, that symbolically separated the highest point of the hill from the rest of the summit. A small roughly circular enclosure built into the southern end of the bank may be recent in origin, possibly being an observation foxhole dug during the Second World War.

The second cairn lies some 80m to the south-east of the trig point, part of it now missing due to surface quarrying. What survives is a flat-topped and well-defined mound 23m in diameter and 0.8m high. Blocks of stone that now protrude through the turf form a continuous stone kerb around the mound. Excavations in 1932 revealed a circular pit 1.3m in diameter under the centre of the mound that had been dug 2.3m into the original ground surface. (The excavation trenches themselves survive as shallow depressions 1m wide, one at right angles to the other.) The cairn is believed to date to the early Bronze Age. (Two bronze palstaves were found between two blocks of basalt on the north side of the hill in 1889, and a Saxon spearhead from the 7th to 9th century was found during quarrying on the west side.)

❺ From the trig point you can either head round to the next cairn, known as the Giant's Chair, to the north and thence to a marker post signing the Shropshire Way, or make your way to the post by heading a short way towards the radar golfballs and then turning left to follow the Shropshire Way. From this post you follow the Shropshire Way down the hillside, further marker posts helping identify the route. The photograph on the opposite page shows one of the marker posts with the wall of the hillfort running from left to right just behind it. Initially you will be heading for a point to the right of Brown Clee, the next large hill, but gradually the path will swing you more directly towards Brown Clee. As you descend you'll see that the path is heading for a V-shaped junction of field boundaries at the edge of the open hillside.

A few hundred yards before you would reach this junction you want to turn left off the Shropshire Way and head towards the field boundary on your left (so as to cut off a chunk of distance), so keep an eye out for a suitable sheep path that allows you to do this. Try to find a path that eventually leads you close to this field boundary (a number of sheep tracks gradually coalesce into a more major path). All being well, you'll be quite close to the boundary when it makes a sharp turn to the right and heads downhill. To make sure you're finding your way, walk down to this point, and then continue along a track (formed by a vehicle) which broadly follows the contour round the hillside, though descending slightly. In due course the field boundary will rise back up the hillside to meet the track, from which point you stay on the track and follow it along the boundary on your right to meet a stony track that emerges onto the open hillside (near to a house called Stantongate).

❻ Turn left on this track and it will lead you along to the boundary of a house called Stocking Cottage (not that its name is displayed). Just before the gate to the cottage, turn left on a smaller track and follow it along for about 100 yards or so, to then take a smaller path that bears right: you're aiming for the bottom of the commonland to the right of a stretch of woodland ahead of you. Once you are following the fenceline on your right, ignore a 'bridge' in the fence should you spot this, and you will soon find yourself in a corner of fences near the woodland. Here, cross one stile, then another, to cross into a field below the woodland. Diagonally cross this field to its far corner, the path passing to the left of a large single tree that stands clearly in the field (the base of a second lone tree is initially obscured by the lie of the land). Go through the gate at the bottom of the field onto a track.

❼ Turn left onto the track and follow it as it bends right to continue descending the hillside. Where the track bends to the left, keep ahead over a stile into a field. Cross this field, aiming for a gateway just to the right of the wood on the far side of the field. Go through the gateway and then follow the track, which runs parallel to the wood, (the photograph alongside looks back the way you've come), across this next field to its far side. Here, turn left and follow the track into the wood, and keep on it as it turns to the right and leads down to some farm buildings.

Turn right through the farmyard, with barns to left and right, to leave the farmyard on a track. When the track turns to the right, go through the gate ahead into a field and continue walking down the hillside following the field boundary on your left. In the bottom corner of the field you will find a stile into the next field. Once in this next field, follow the field boundary on your right and walk down to a gate at the far end which will lead you out onto a track. Follow it down to a minor road.

Turn left on the road to return to Bitterley School.

Walk 24
Burwarton, Aston Botterell & Brown Clee

9.5 miles. One of the longer walks in the book, the climb up to Brown Clee is steady rather than vigorous, though part of the descent is quite steep in places and can be slippery. The walk includes one of the greatest ranges of countryside of any of the walks in this book, from fields to woodland to moorland to parkland, with wide views in most directions. Much of it is on tracks or minor roads with some lengths of path, most in reasonable condition. There are a handful of stiles between Burwarton and Aston Botterell, and the occasional other one. The walk includes remains of the old workings on Brown Clee; the church, manor house and castle site at Aston Botterell; the church at Loughton; a Second World War memorial to aircraft and their crews lost on the hill – and more.

You can either start the walk in Burwarton if you wish to end the walk at the Boyne Arms (built *c.*1840), using the inn's car park, or at Aston Botterell, where you can park near the church. The walk as detailed below starts at the

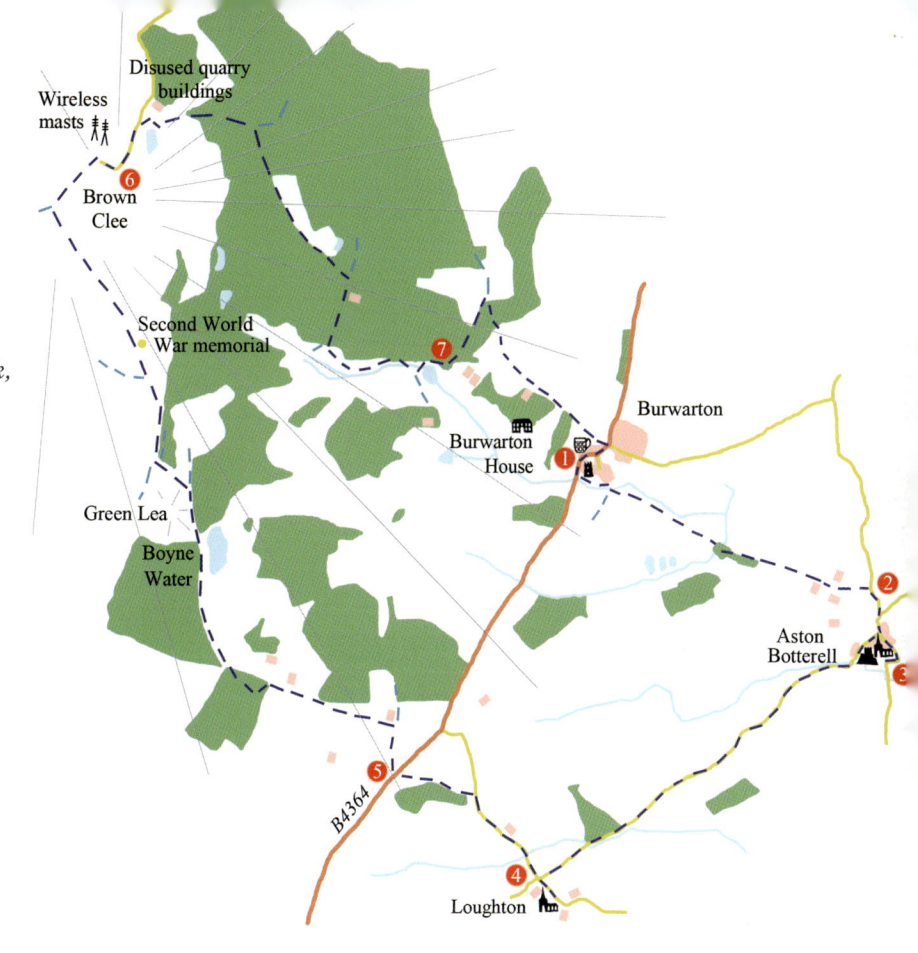

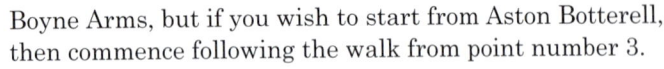

Boyne Arms, but if you wish to start from Aston Botterell, then commence following the walk from point number 3.

❶ Turn right out of the inn car park and follow the pavement and you will soon reach on the right-hand side the pillars to a gateway and a small white-painted Italianate lodge built *c.*1839, one of the entrances to Burwarton House. Opposite this, on the other side of the road, you will see a footpath sign and a small gate. Cross the road and go through the gate, to then cross the bottom of a long lawn below the Dower House. The path then leads through a gate into what was part of the churchyard, the chancel arch of the original church still standing but hidden under a mass of ivy. A bridge, not available for use by the public, leads off to the right to the later church, now a private house. Cross this old, but still used, churchyard following the boundary on your right to a gate which leads to a short length of path to the left of a stream, which in turn leads to a lane that serves a small timber-framed and red brick farmhouse on your left.

Cross this lane and go over a stile to then follow on your right a boundary to the grounds of another house and a stream on your left to reach another lane. Turn right on this and immediately go through a gate into a field, where you turn left to follow the field boundary on your

BURWARTON OLD AND NEW CHURCHES

The two-cell Norman church, of nave and chancel, with no tower or aisle, was unroofed by 1876. Its north and south walls have since collapsed, but the chancel arch remains and stands overgrown in the midst of the church's graveyard. The site was cleared and the building recorded in detail in 1983.

A new church was built in 1875-76 in yellow sandstone quarried from Burf Hill in the Gothic style to the design of Anthony Salvin, who had built Burwarton House in the 1830s, and included a south porch and west tower. After its closure in 1972 it was converted into a house, its interior spaces respected but divided by partitions, but fittings such as a reredos and most of the stained glass have been removed.

left to the far end of the field. Here you cross a stile into the next field, which the path crosses diagonally, heading for a point about 50 yards to the right of the far left-hand corner, in so doing passing to the left of a large tree that stands in the field. On the far side you reach another stile which you cross, the path then winding through a small copse to cross a small ditch-cum-stream by a bridge to enter a small plantation of Christmas trees. Here the path offers alternatives, one wending its way down through the trees but we suggest the alternative, which turns left just before you reach the trees to enter a field, then turns right down the field edge, keeping the plantation of Christmas trees to your right. Just beyond the end of the plantation and shortly before the end of the field, the path turns right into a patch of vegetation and then left to reach the true corner of the field, where you will find a bridge across a stream, followed by, on your left, a double stile with bridge between which you cross to enter another field.

Head straight across this field to a gateway to the right of a large oak on the far side, and then head to the immediate left of a house built of stone and red brick. Here you will find a small gate that will lead you onto a short length of track which you follow to meet a concreted track on which you turn left. Follow this down to a minor road.

❷ Turn right on the road and keep ahead at the first junction, and then bear left at the second and follow the road round to head into the village of Aston Botterell with its church, manor farm and castle site.

ASTON BOTTERELL CHURCH

The nave and chancel date from the late 1100s and early 1200s, the south aisle from the mid 1200s, the porch was built in 1639 (a date carved into it) and the tower was rebuilt in 1884, much of the church also being heavily restored. The church is most notable for its memorials: the north wall of the chancel holds a large slab commemorating John Botterell (d.1479) and his wife, whose figure is best preserved, and in the south aisle stands an impressive monument to an Elizabethan, John Botterell, and his wife, their children depicted kneeling against the tomb chest, a common motif of the time.

ASTON MANOR FARM

Some features of the house (notably an internal doorway and part of a large fireplace with a particular style of moulding) suggest that the original building was constructed during the 1200s. To this was attached a late medieval hall range. The building was altered in 1576, a plasterwork ceiling containing the date and the Botterell coat of arms, the earliest plaster decoration to survive in Shropshire. The plasterwork also includes faces, said to be those of family members, possibly the A.B. and W.B. of the initials written in the plasterwork.

ASTON BOTTERELL VILLAGE AND CASTLE SITE

At Domesday the manor is recorded simply as Estone, 'eastern settlement'. By 1203 it was held by William Botterell and by 1263 the settlement was recorded as Estin Boterel when a charter was granted for a weekly market and a three-day annual fair.

The moated castle site measures some 40m by 32m inside the moat and appears to have been constructed as a ringwork, i.e. with a wall surrounding an inner ward or bailey, rather than as a keep. The remains are most prominent on the north and west, whilst the south side has been raised to provide a level platform on which to build. It is probable that the ringwork was replaced by what is now Aston Manor Farm as the seat of the manor. Adjoining the castle site to the south and west are banks denoting former field boundaries which appear to be later in date than the ringwork, one running up to its western edge.

The village appears to have shrunk in size around the time of the Black Death, it having initially also encompassed land in what is now a field north of the lane that runs round the castle site, as evidenced by earthworks.

❸ Having visited the church, walk down the path from the church doorway and turn right to look at the information board about the castle by the field gate. The board indicates that you can enter the field to have a closer look at the earthworks if you wish.

Having seen what you want to see of the earthworks, keeping the church to your left, walk along the road around the church and Aston Manor Farm, bearing left at the road junction soon met, so taking the road signposted to Loughton. Past the last house on the right in the village of Aston Botterell, look out for the humps and bumps in the next field on the right which indicate the site of part of what had been a larger medieval settlement, and then follow the road along till you reach a crossroads.

❹ Turn left at the crossroads and walk along for a couple of hundred yards till you reach the pathway into the churchyard of Loughton Church.

Having visited the church, return along the road and then keep ahead at the crossroads. Pass the Old School on the right and just after the road has bent to the right and all but reached its highest point, take the wide track off to the left and follow it up to the B4364.

❺ Cross this road onto a wide gravelled track, keeping right at the first split quickly reached and then turning

LOUGHTON CHURCH

There was once a medieval church here, but that has vanished to be replaced by the present building dating to 1622, built at the expense of Bonham Norton. It is a simple building consisting of just nave and chancel with a western bellcote, and probably stands on or near the site of the earlier church as the south doorway and chancel arch both appear to reuse earlier cut stone. The porch and north vestry were added in 1904. Aerial photographs suggest that several building platforms might exist in neighbouring fields, indicating that the settlement was once larger than it is today.

left at the second, to immediately pass a cottage (2 Banbury Lane) on your right.

> ### 2 BANBURY LANE
> This is probably a former squatter's home that began life as a single-bayed, single-storey cottage before the enclosure of Loughton Common. Built mainly of dhustone, it is now a two-storeyed, two-bayed house.

This wide gravelled track will then lead you steadily uphill to reach, just after another track leads off to the right to head to a house, a field gate and a footpath gate into some recently felled and replanted woodland.

Go through the gate and keep on the track. This swings first left and then right to slant across the hillside, later passing above a ruined building and associated enclosure and then a lake called Boyne Water. Towards the end of this lake the track passes through a gate and you keep ahead on the track, ignoring a path off to the right. The track will lead you just below the summit of a small hill called Green Lea to your left, and you can see the remains of miners' bell pits on both sides of the track, as you can further on along the walk (see the box on Brown Clee on page 226). Shortly after the point where the track starts to drop downhill, take the footpath off to the left that leads across a short patch of boggy ground and alongside a fence and then a beech wood, at the far end of which is a choice of stiles: one ahead and one to the right. Cross the one ahead and then turn right to follow the wall alongside the beech wood down into a dip. Here you depart slightly from the line of the wall to head for a wooden fieldgate which is marked with a circular waymarking sign for the Shropshire Way; you do not want the metal gate to the left of this wooden gate which leads onto a path of clear grass sward. Go through the wooden gate and follow the rough track, but look out for the small memorial soon reached just off the track to the right.

WAR MEMORIAL

The memorial tells of 23 allied and German airmen killed on Brown Clee during the Second World War. On 1 April 1941 a German Junkers 88A bomber aiming to target Birmingham lost its way in thick fog and crashed into the hill; its four crew members all died. The other aircraft were two Wellington bombers (at least one airman survived one crash), a Hawker Typhoon and two Avro Ansons.

Keep following the track, which will lead you to meet another track which passes through a gate in the fenceline you have now reached to your left. Here you turn right on the track which leads away from the fenceline and initially heads towards the radio masts on the summit of Brown Clee, the track then gradually swinging to the left. At a point somewhat adjacent to the radio masts on your right, the track meets another on which you turn right and head up to the summit of Brown Clee to a toposcope just to the right of the radio masts.

BROWN CLEE HILL

The hill was both mined for coal and quarried for ironstone from medieval days, and later for ironstone, dolerite and dhustone. The coal mining was probably largely carried out by the use of bell pits (for which see page 210), the prior of Much Wenlock granting a licence to dig coal on the hill as early as the 14th century. The initial stone quarried was ironstone, but demand for this fell in the later 18th century with the decline of nearby iron furnaces. Even so, in 1793 nearly half of the 31 households at Abdon included miners, though most were probably also smallholders. In 1851 the parish had four self-employed pit owners, four miners and a coal haulier. But coal mining was then on the decline too, with just one miner recorded at Abdon in the 1881 census. Dolerite was quarried in the late 19th and early 20th centuries and then, in 1907, the Abdon Clee Stone Company began quarrying dhustone to be used in road building, an operation that continued till 1937. The buildings that remain on the hill were largely used for the crushing and grading of the stone. There are tales of workers at the quarry coming from Ludlow and Bridgnorth and living rough for the week, returning home at the weekends; having been blasted out of the hillside, the stone was initially broken by manual wielding of 28lb sledgehammers and then loaded into trucks on light railways to be taken to the crusher. Some of the workers cut the dhustone into blocks for paving or building. Of the two masts on the hill, one is owned by BT, the other by the government.

6 From the toposcope, head down the steps on the east side of the hill to join a metalled lane, on which you turn right. Follow this along till you are above a small lake on your right, with ruined mine buildings to your left further along the road. Here you take the waymarked path off to the right, to walk above the lake for a few yards and then drop steeply downhill into some scattered woodland. The path will swing right and then, after a while, left to reach a gate in a line of fencing.

WOODS ON THE SOUTH SIDE OF THE HILL
These slopes have been wooded for many years, but it was not till after the Second World War that many of the older stands of broadleaved trees were incorporated into a larger 'forest'. Pools were made in the woods and near Burwarton House (see page 229) connected by channels to serve as reservoirs in the event of a fire at the house. Boyne Water, the large pool you passed on the right as you approached the top of the hill, is also known as the Odessa Pool as it was created in the 1850s during the Crimean War. It is believed to contain the remains of one of the Wellington bombers that crashed on the hill during the Second World War. Management of the woodland involves clear-felling an area each year and thinning other parts.

Don't go through this gate, but turn right along the track and follow it along to soon reach another gate through which the track gains a harder stony surface. Follow this down to its junction with a more major track, on which you turn right, passing above a house. Soon afterwards the track passes through another gate, once through which you want to take the grassy path that heads down the hillside through a landscape of scattered large trees. This path curls round a group of three large beech trees to keep the valley's main stream to your right and continues dropping down the hillside, becoming a more prominent track as it does so. In due course it crosses the stream, then rises to a gate through which you turn left on a track and then go through another gate to meet a lane.

7 Turn left on the lane and this will lead you above a set of farm buildings, beyond which you may be able to see (especially in winter) the quadrangular brick stable block of Burwarton House marked out by the white cupola on one of the buildings, one feature of its simple Italianate detailing.

BURWARTON HOUSE

The house was built between 1833 and 1839 to an Italianate villa design by Anthony Salvin for the 7th Viscount Boyne, whose father had married the local heiress Harriet Baugh. The house was extended by Salvin in 1876-7 for the 8th Viscount, further enlarged c.1900 and again in 1922, before being much reduced in size in 1956. The surrounding estate was further added to and even when 8,500 acres were subsequently sold in 1919 it still essentially owned the land in the parishes of Burwarton, Cleobury North and Aston Botterell. The 'home' estate still comprises some 1,000 acres.

When you reach a junction with another lane, turn right and this will lead you past the well-hidden buildings of Burwarton House. Past the entrances to the house, keep following the fence on your right rather than the lane and this will lead you to a stile out onto the B4364. Turn right on the road and this will lead you round the corner to the Boyne Arms. (If you started out from Aston Botterell, then return to the instructions at the start of the walk to find your way back to that village.)

Walk 25
Bouldon, Clee St Margaret, Nordy Bank, Tugford & Broncroft

8.5 miles. This is probably the walk with the greatest variation of sites in this book (if you exclude those that also feature a larger town) with a variety of churches, a mill, a hillfort, mining remains and a castle. You may well need to visit the pub in Bouldon for refreshment at the end! Set in rolling countryside, the only relatively major ascent is that to Nordy Bank hillfort. The walk is on a mixture of minor roads, tracks and paths, all in good condition, though short sections can be muddy in winter or fairly tightly packed with vegetation at the end of summer. There are some stiles and one ford, but we have given an alternative route to avoid the latter if you feel unable to make it across.

Park somewhere in Bouldon. If you plan to start or finish the walk with a visit to the Tally Ho pub, you could park in their car park, and we will describe the walk as starting from there.

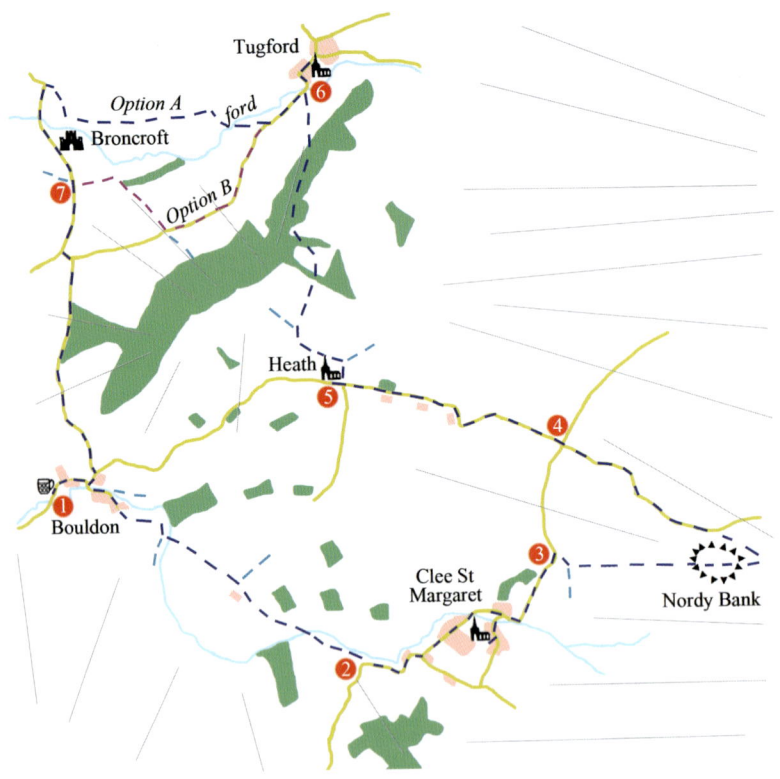

❶ Turn left out of the pub car park and walk along the road through the village until you reach a no through road off to the right. Turn down this road and walk along it past the farm, staying on the road as it turns into a track and rises up between some houses and past Bouldon Mill on the left, which retains many of its mill workings. Beyond these houses the track will bend to the right, whereafter you need to keep an eye out for a stile soon reached in the fence on your left. Cross this and head down the slope to a footbridge across a stream.

Once you've crossed the bridge, the path turns up the bank and follows the field boundary on your left. At the end of this field you will come to two adjacent farm gates. The one on the left leads onto a track which is your route up into the farmyard at the top of the rise. The track may be overgrown with nettles depending upon the time of year; if it's impassable, you could instead take the right-hand gate and keep shadowing the track through two fields and so enter the farmyard. Once you're in the farmyard, keep straight ahead between the various buildings to join a major track at its elbow. Keep ahead to pass a house and then a bungalow on your right. Cross a stile, walk through a small orchard, then go through the left of two field gates and follow the track downhill. At the bottom you'll reach a lengthy ford, but you cross the stream by the footbridge on the right and enter a field. Keep to the left-hand side of the field and near its far end drop down to a gate which leads back onto the track, on which you turn right and follow it up to a minor road.

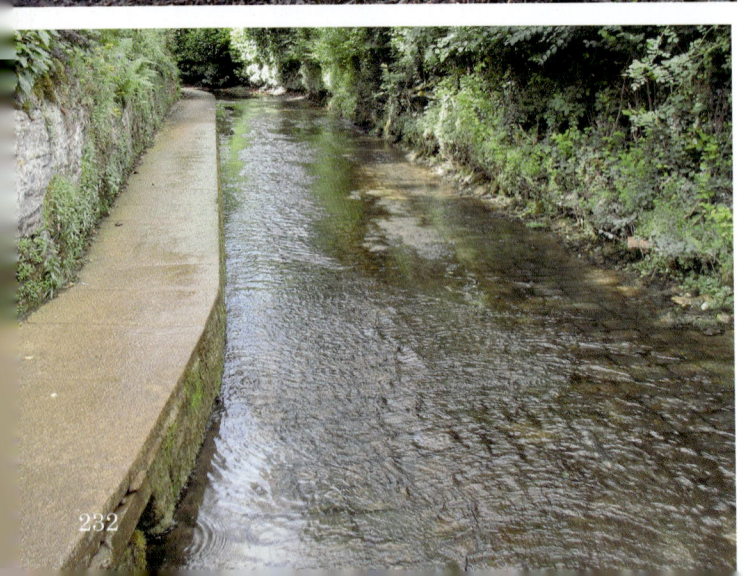

❷ Turn left on the road and follow it along, ignoring a turning to the right, to reach a ford into Clee St Margaret – there is a footpath alongside the ford. Turn right at the junction reached at the end of the ford and walk up to the church.

Return down the hill into the village and go past the ford, now on your left. After about a quarter of a mile, where the road makes a sharp turn to the left, take the track off to the right called Marsh Gate. You'll soon reach a car parking space, to the left of which is a gate that leads onto the common known as Clee Liberty, a sign telling you a little about it.

❸ Go through the gate and walk ahead up the narrow strip of common and the ramparts of Nordy Bank will soon come into view. Walk up the hillside into the hillfort for widespread views, notably north-westwards.

CLEE ST MARGARET CHURCH

The earliest parts of the church include the herringbone masonry in the north and east walls of the chancel and the slightly crude priest's door in the south wall of the chancel. They could be Saxon in date, but are more likely the work of Saxon masons working on an early Norman church. One would expect the narrow chancel arch to also be early, but confusingly it has a pointed arch. Large squints have been cut through the walls to either side at some stage to improve the view of the chancel from the nave. The church was restored in 1872.

NORDY BANK

This is a univallate hillfort, roughly oval in shape, and is unusual in being positioned below the summit of the hill on which it sits. On its south-eastern side the rampart is close to an area that has been quarried and mined as evidenced by the various pits, linear open-cast mines and spoil heaps that stretch away towards Titterstone Clee. An original entrance through the rampart was at its north-east corner and was in-turned, broadening and flattening of the adjacent banks suggesting that a guardhouse was sited here. A second entrance may lie in the middle of the southern side where the ramparts curve very slightly inwards – but this entrance may be modern, as certainly are all the other breaks in the rampart. Within the hillfort slight irregularities in the surface level might suggest the survival of buried remains of structures, these being most clear in the north-west part of the site, where there is a rectangular building platform 8m square and two low mounds which are thought to represent material cleared from sites in preparation for building work. A small square ditched enclosure might mark the site of a Second World War Home Guard hut. Part of a flint arrowhead and another of a flint blade have been found on the site.

You can either walk back down from the hillfort the way you came up and take the track that turns right and leads to a wooden gate onto the lane that passes alongside the hillfort's northern flank, or cross the fort and go through the area that has been quarried and mined beyond it and join a wide grassy track that is marked with waymarking posts every now and then. Turn left on this and follow it to join the lane which then descends to the gate just mentioned. Through this gate walk downhill along the lane and keep going until you reach a crossroads.

❹ Go straight over the crossroads and follow the road for a further three-quarters of a mile until, just beyond

HEATH CHAPEL

Consisting of just a nave and chancel, the chapel was built c.1140, in mauve rubble sandstone with yellow sandstone dressings. It has been left largely unaltered since that date, with the exception of an enlargement of the window in the north wall some 300 years ago. The south doorway has chevron decoration; the font is a Norman tub with a frieze around the top; medieval wall paintings survive in a poor state (one of St George adorns the south wall and there is one of the Last Judgement above the chancel arch) along with remains of 17th-century texts; the pulpit and box pews date from the 17th century (parts of a medieval rood screen have been reused to frame benches and pews against the north wall). The chapel was restored sympathetically in 1912.

another crossroads, you reach Heath Chapel in a field on your right.

5 Having visited Heath Chapel, turn left on the road (so as to retrace your steps for a few yards), then immediately turn left on a tarmacked lane. Follow this alongside the field in which the chapel stands and at the end of the next field, take the gate into this field, to then follow the hedgeline on your right. Over to your left are the humps and bumps that represent the deserted medieval village (see overleaf).

Keep following the hedgeline on the right to the far right-hand corner of the field, and take the gate into the next field. Turn right here (two paths meet at this point) and follow the field boundary a short way to a gate into the next field. Go through this and then follow the field boundary on your right to the corner of woodland on the far side of the field. Again go through the gate here into the next field. Here the path turns slightly left, away from the line of the wood on your right, and crosses the field to a gate on the far side. Through this gate follow the clear track downhill for about 20 yards, then turn right across the corner of the field (there's a way-marking sign to indicate the path) to a gate into a wood. Through the gate keep straight ahead on the woodland path, ignoring all side turnings, and eventually you'll come to a gate at the far edge of the wood. Go through this and walk down the field following the hedgeline on your right. Go through the gate at the bottom.

🔴 **6** Turn right along the road to visit Tugford Church. To find the church, look for the church notice board on the right near the road junction: the church is reached by crossing the small field behind this board.

Having visited the church, return to the road and turn left back along it, following it out of the village. Keep an eye out for a pair of metal footpath gates, one a kissing gate, on your right. When we have walked this route both early and late in 2018, the footbridge to which the left-hand gate leads has been closed, ruling that out as an option. So, there are two other alternatives.

HEATH DESERTED MEDIEVAL VILLAGE

The field to the north of the chapel contains the remains of the medieval settlement, including what was still shown on a map of 1771 as a moat-like rectangular feature, surrounded on three sides by water. Four tenements still existed in 1770 (there were only seven taxable families in 1327), the map of 1771 still showing roads, fishponds and earthworks relating to the settlement. There was also a deer park, now only defined by modern field boundaries. The present remains include five possible platforms for houses or barns, hollow-ways, a circular stone-lined well, and a 'flat-topped pond bay measuring 40m in length, 14m in width and up to 1.6m in height'.

TUGFORD CHURCH

The single-cell church with its plastered barrel ceiling is largely Norman with an Early English tower. The priest's door in the south wall of the chancel has a badly weathered floriated tympanum, possibly brought from elsewhere, and there are tomb recesses in the external north and south walls of the chancel. Just above the inside of the south doorway are two small and damaged stone sheila-na-gigs. There is a west gallery. Some very small fragments of medieval glass have been included in the east window. A survey of the timbers suggests that the 13th-century tower was originally surmounted by an earlier timber spire which was taken down and some of the timbers reused in the tower itself. In 1720 the upper two stages of the tower were rebuilt, perhaps due to the weaknesses caused by the spire.

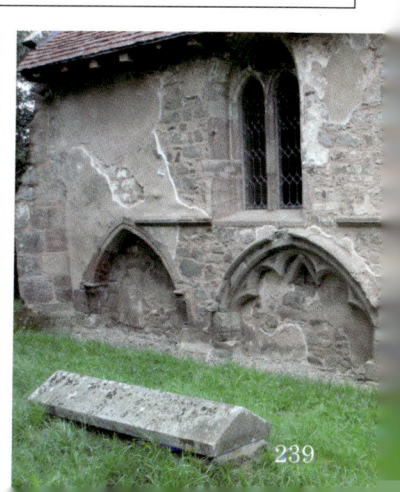

A) The advantage of this route is that it gives you good views of Broncroft Castle; the disadvantage is that you will need to cross a stream which doesn't have a bridge and only some stepping stones, so (depending on season) wellies might be advisable. But you reach the crossing quite quickly, so you could investigate and take option B if you don't fancy the crossing. To follow route A, go through the right-hand gate, the path bearing left through a narrow field at the end of which is the stream and its ford, reached through a gate. Once across the stream, go through the gate on the far bank and walk up the field, keeping the hedge on your left. When you reach a track, turn left and follow it between hedgerows. When the track ends at a field gate, keep ahead down a sunken path and follow this to meet a road, on which you turn left and walk up to Broncroft Castle.

B) If you don't fancy the stream crossing, continue along the road until, after about half a mile, you come to a stile on each side. Cross the stile on your right and follow the field boundary downhill, crossing the field near the bottom to reach a stile in the opposite field boundary just above a small piece of woodland. Once over the stile, turn right and follow the field boundary to another stile and so out onto a gravelled lane. Turn left on this and walk up to a road. Turn right to see Broncroft Castle just ahead of you, and then turn about to head back up the road.

7 Both routes have rejoined at this point. Keep walking up the road until you reach a T-junction where you turn left and then immediately right. Follow this road into Bouldon, turning right at the T-junction on the edge of the village, then following the road through the village back to your car or the pub.

BRONCROFT CASTLE

The original castle was built round a courtyard with a great hall on its south side flanked by towers at each end, with a projecting wing on the north-west side. The manor was acquired by the Burleys c.1361 and the castle might have been built by a Sir Roger Burley during the reign of Richard II. Some consider that the castle might have been built by Sir Simon Burley, tutor to Richard II, but he came from Herefordshire, where he held Lyonshall Castle, and in any event by 1386 had fallen foul of the nobles opposed to Richard II and been unjustly executed. John Burley, another contender for the builder of the castle, who was six times knight of the shire between 1399 and 1411, and William Burley, who succeeded him, were both described as 'of Broncroft' and served the Fitzalans – who were opposed to Richard II, again making it unlikely that it was Sir Simon who built the castle – and later the Talbots. The castle was held by the Royalists at the start of the Civil War but captured by Parliamentary forces in 1645 and slighted in 1648. It nevertheless continued to be occupied and was restored between 1663 and 1685. It was completely transformed c.1868 by the architect J.P. Seddon. The square south-western tower (that to the right of the current entrance) from the earlier castle was retained and given a new machiolated entrance, and a new north-west wing was added with a large bay window. The base of the south-east tower also dates from the earlier castle, whilst a third battlemented tower was built above service quarters.

Walk 26
Diddlebury

7.25 miles on a mixture of minor roads, paths and tracks in undulating countryside. There are several stiles and one ford – in summer or dry periods this is manageable in walking boots, but in winter or wet periods Wellingtons may be advisable, as they could be for the track that leads into Diddlebury. We have started the walk from Diddlebury, but you may wish to start and end at either the Corvedale Brewery, or at the White Swan in Aston Munslow, in which case start the walk at points 3 or 7 respectively. It includes an interesting church in Diddlebury and passes a number of other historical features, though much of the pleasure of this walk is simply the largely gently rolling countryside through which you pass.

Park near the church in Diddlebury, perhaps near where the stream flows through the village. You can visit the church at either the beginning or end of the walk of course, but that's where the walk starts.

1 Standing on the road with your back to the church turn left and walk down to the concrete footbridge with a single white rail that crosses the stream, but don't go

DIDDLEBURY CHURCH

The church dates back to Saxon times, and Saxon work remains in the north wall of the nave, which includes a Saxon window set high in the wall and a doorway, and part of the base of the tower. Extensive herringbone masonry survives in the north wall inside the church. A window in this wall contains the fragments of a Saxon cross, one with interlace and one with scrolls, birds and two human demi-figures. Seen from the outside, the west wall of the tower contains a tall blocked Norman arch which presumably led from the tower to a forebuilding since demolished, the inserted doorway dating to the late 1100s when the tower was also raised in height. The chancel also dates to the 1100s (with some remodelling in the early 14th century), its north window containing some restored medieval glass depicting the Crucifixion. A south aisle was added in the 1200s, its walls rebuilt in 1862. The porch was added in 1883.

over it! Immediately before it, turn left through a gate (the post carries a sign for the Three Castles Walk) which leads onto a path which keeps to the stream's left bank. Follow this across a driveway and a stile to another footbridge on which you then cross the stream. Beyond the bridge, cross a patch of ground to a stile into a field. Once you are over the stile, the path rises up the bank in the field to a kissing gate in the hedgerow at the crest of the rise; as you ascend look over your left shoulder for views of Delbury Hall.

Through the kissing gate you enter an old parkland landscape dotted with old oak trees, and might even spot the even earlier remains of ridge and furrow ploughing crossing the ground in front of you (as seen in the photograph on the right). You want to cross this parkland by aiming at the left-hand end of the wood that lies on its far side and largely to your right. About one-third of the way across you will cross a tarmacked lane. At the corner of

DELBURY HALL AND PARK

Delbury Hall is a large mansion built of brick in 1753-56 by William and David Hiorne of Warwick for Frederick Cornewall. Cornewall had served in the Navy, losing an arm at the Battle of Toulon in 1744, and after the Battle of Minorca in 1755 his evidence was largely responsible for the conviction and execution of Admiral John Byng. He bought Delbury Hall in 1752 and was MP for Montgomery Boroughs for three years from 1771, but hardly ever appeared and never spoke in the House, citing ill health. The stables are contemporary with the hall. In 1827 it had a park that ran from the hall grounds south-west to what in 1883 was Corfton Plantation. By 1883, however, the park had been done away with, though the walk passes through its remnants as you leave the environs of Diddlebury.

the wood you will find a kissing gate into the next field, the path then turning right along the edge of the wood to quickly enter another field. Here the path turns half left to diagonally cross the field to its far corner; the path may or may not be evident on the ground (we have walked the route at times when the farmer has clearly reinstated it after an agricultural operation, and at times when he hasn't).

❷ At the far corner of the field head for a stile out onto a track on which you turn right and then immediately left to cross two stiles and a bridge across a stream and so enter another field. Here, follow the field boundary on your left. Ahead of you, and above the roofs of a property called The Mount, you will see the remains of a motte and bailey castle. The path will lead you out through a kissing

MOUNT MOTTE AND BAILEY, AND CHAPEL

This castle site comprises an oval motte with a roughly rectangular bailey measuring 120m by 100m to its east which would have contained most of the household buildings and is surrounded by perimeter earthworks. The motte stands some 6m above the base of the surrounding ditch where this survives, and a bank around the southern side of its summit suggests that it might once have supported a stone ringwork. At Domesday the manor was held from Roger de Lacy by Robert de Furches, who also held several other manors for which he owed two or three knights' fees. It may be, therefore, that Corfton was the centre or caput of his holding and that he built a castle and home here.

    The Ordnance Survey maps also mark an old chapel here, but there seems to be much confusion about this. Some consider it to be the original chapel to the castle, though there is apparently little to suggest this; others think it was not built until the 18th century (a marriage is recorded here in the late 1700s), and yet others doubt it was ever a chapel. All that remains are the stone-built rubble walls of a rectangular building measuring some 9m by 6m recently used as a grain store by the farm that now abuts the castle motte.

gate onto a lane on which you turn right. Follow the lane along to the B4368 which you cross. Here you will find the Corvedale Brewery.

❸ Take the minor road next to the Corvedale Brewery marked with a no through road sign and signposted Corfton Bache and follow this along the bache. The lane will later turn into a track, pass through a field gate and later become a path as it winds its way along the foot of the grassy bache, almost immediately passing an old quarry on the left. The rock here is calcerous siltstone; other quarries you'll pass are dug in Wenlock limestone (as you approach Wenlock Edge) and Aymestrey limestone in quarries by the side of the road as you return.

As the path nears a house it regains the form of a track, and just before you reach the house the track zig-zags up the slope, to turn left in front of a hedge above the bache and so pass above the house (and another beyond it) to drop down and join a lane.

❹ Turn right on the lane and almost immediately left through the second of two field gates. The path now heads uphill, with farm buildings off to your right, to another field gate some 30 yards to the right of the top left-hand corner of the field. Once through this gate, the path bears slightly left and aims for the far top corner of this next field where there is another gate. Go through this gate and continue through the next field – the path will

SUN INN AND CORVEDALE BREWERY
The Sun Inn was first licensed in 1613 and the Corvedale Brewery was established in an old chicken and lumber shed behind the pub in 1997 and now brews several different ales. It is open seven days a week and serves food both lunchtimes and evenings.

hopefully have been reinstated here after any agricultural operation, but if not, initially aim for the top of the strip of woodland on the right-hand side of the field (your eventual target is the far right top corner of the field). The path should head to a gateway into another field positioned just above the strip of woodland on the right, but don't go through this gateway, instead bear left to follow the field boundary on your right and so reach a gate into woodland at the crest of the ridge. (The photograph above shows part of this path in the summer, looking back to where you've come from.)

Once in the woodland, the path turns left and slants downhill across the hillside, eventually following the bottom edge of the wood on your right. After a few hundred yards, just before the path comes adjacent to a house across a field to your right, it forks. Take the right-hand path which leads in a few yards to a pair of stiles and gates which you cross or go through, so passing round an oak tree to enter a field. Turn left and follow the field boundary on your left downhill. This will lead you to a farm gate onto a track down which you walk, passing a house on your right, to meet a minor road.

🔴 **5** Turn right on the road. Follow the road along and when you come to a T-junction just below Wenlock Edge, turn right in the direction signposted Middlehope and Diddlebury. After about a quarter of a mile, take the signed byway off to the right, joining it by going through a gate. Follow this along, ignoring smaller tracks to left and right, and you will come to the ford of which a warning was given at the start of the walk. Once through the ford, the byway meets a minor road.

❻ Turn right on the road, and after about a third of a mile the road starts to pass between woodland on both sides. Soon after the woodland on the left comes to an end there is a track off to the left that almost doubles back on itself. You don't want this one, but the next track you come to on the left, which is opposite a stile in the fence on the right. Turn down the track, which almost immediately bears right in front of some young woodland and becomes a path passing between two hedgerows. The path soon turns to the left and then starts to curve round to the right. Where the path seems to disappear somewhat on the ground and starts to head more steeply down an old hollow-way, you want to take the stile on your left to enter a field.

The path now follows the field boundary on your right to the far side of the field, where a pair of stiles either side of a small spinney leads you into the next field. Here your path turns very slightly right and crosses the field and a

249

WHITE HOUSE, ASTON MUNSLOW
The eastern range encases a late medieval aisled hall of basecruck construction. Probably during the late 16th century, a two-storey, gabled crosswing was added. The southern half of this became part of the white rendered range with a central doorway that was added in the 18th century.

small dry valley aiming for a gate to the left of a large oak tree on the field's far side. Go through this gate and follow the field boundary on your right to a gate and stile on the far side of the field, as you do so, about half way across looking down on the roofs and black and white gable wall

of the White House to your right, and so drop down onto a lane.

7 Turn right on the lane and follow it down to a junction of lanes. Keep on the main lane if you want to go to the Swan Inn on the B4368 in Aston Munslow, or go straight ahead towards a red brick bungalow.

If you've started from the Swan, turn right out of the pub's car park up the minor road till you come to a junction with other lanes, and turn left to head towards a red brick bungalow.

Just before this bungalow, called Ashlea, turn right on the gravelled track. Follow this along to its end where it becomes a path, and then keep along the path. This will lead to a stile into a field which you cross to go over another stile and then reach the driveway to Aston Hall. Cross the driveway and a stile to enter the next field which you cross to another stile. Over this the path turns slightly right to cross the next field, aiming for a single footstep across the fence into the next field. Once across the next field and another stile on its far side you'll

ASTON HALL
Built some time between c.1620 and 1665, it has an E-shaped front of two storeys built of Corvedale stone with the earliest part of the building being a timber-framed wing at the back. A second rear wing serves to give the whole building an H-shaped plan. At the front is a garden with flanking walls and pillars. The house was owned by the Smith family from 1492 to c.1914.

reach another drive which you also cross. You then head straight across the large field ahead of you – there may be a well-worn footpath helping show the way.

On the far side of the field you'll reach the old hollow-way met with before. Once in the field on the far side of the hollow-way, the path turns slightly right to cross the field, aiming for a stile on the far side. Cross this and then walk along the field boundary on your left to return to the road on which you were walking a while ago. Turn left on this and follow it down to the B4368. Cross the B road and turn right to almost immediately go up the steps and through a gate into a field. The path now follows the field boundary on your right. Ignore a kissing gate to the right and pass through three further footpath gates to reach the grounds of Diddlebury's primary school. The path turns right here and follows the fence around three sides of the school grounds to pass through another gate into the gravelled area in front of the school. Bear left here to return to the church.

Index

Abcott Manor 29
Abdon 226
Acton Burnell 108
   Castle 110
   Church 109
      anchorhold 109
   Concord College 116
   Hall 110, 115, 116
   Home Farm dovecote 111
   Park 115
      sham castle 115
   Statute of 111
   Tithe Barn 108, 110, 111
Allcroft, John Derby 19
Alveley Colliery 181
Anarchy, the 2, 13, 160
Arlescott DMV 132
Arthur, Prince 5
Aston Botterell 221
   Aston Manor Farm 221
   Castle 221
   Church 220
Aston Eyre
   Church 144
   Hall 145
Aston Munslow

Aston Hall 251
White House 250

Baker, William 116
bargain companies 67
barytes mining 66, 74
Baugh, Harriet 229
Betchcott 90
   Hall 90
   Middle Farm 90
Bishop's Castle 46, 55
   Carriage Works 61
   Castle 55, 56
   Church 61
   Porch House 56
   Powis Institute 56
   Railway 55
   rotten borough 55
   Three Tuns Brewery 56
   Town Hall 56
Bishop's Moat 59
Bitterley
   Church 207
   Cockpit 205
   Court & Park 206
   Park Hall 205

Blakeway, Jacob 121
Bletherus 90
Blomfield, Sir Arthur 161
Blount family 191
   Sir Edward 192
   Sir Walter 191
Boat Level 66, 77
Bog mine 72, 77
   Visitor Centre 77
Bonaparte, Lucien 16
Botterell, John 220
   William 221
Bridges Inn 83
Bridgnorth 149
   Bishop Percy's House 150
   Castle 160
   Castle Hill Railway 150
   caves 151
   Church of St Mary 161
   College of St Mary Magdalene 174
   Lavington's Hole 151
   Market Hall 149
   Town Hall 148-49
   war memorial 159
Brockhampton DMV 120
Broke, Sir Robert 171

Bromfield
- Bronze Age Cemetery 8, 11
    - Robin Hood's Butt 11
- Moated Grange 14
- Priory & Church 12, 13
    - Gatehouse 12
- Railway Station 12
- Roman camp 11

Bromley, Sir Edward 168
- Sir George 168

Broncroft Castle 241
Brookes, Dr William Penny 134, 136
Brown, Lancelot 'Capability' 105
Brown Clee 224-27
- mining & quarrying 226
- war memorial 224, 225, 228

Burley family 241
Burnell, Sir Nicholas 109
- Robert 108, 109, 110, 111, 115, 119

Burwarton
- Churches 219
- House 229

Bury Ditches 49
Byng, Admiral John 245

Caer Caradoc 102
Cantilupe, Bishop 55
Caratacus 100
Carr, Revd E.D. 93
Cartwright, John Round 174

Castle Ring 79
Charlemagne 42
Church Pulverbatch Church 88
Church Stretton 98
- Battlefields 100
- Buck's Head Inn 98
- Church 98, 99
- Longmynd Hotel 98, 107
- Rectory Wood 105
- Roman Catholic Church 98, 99
- Silvester Horne Inst. 98
- Spa 98
- Square, the 98
- Tudor Cottage 98

Chyknell Hall 176
Claverley
- Church 171
- Powk Hall 177

Clee St Margaret Church 233
Cleobury Mortimer 187
- Church 188
- ironworks 187, 191
- Mawley Hall 192
    - Park 192
- Mill 189

Clive, Henry 15
- Robert, of India 15, 56

Clun
- Castle 52-53
- sheep 39

Sun Inn 45
Trinity Almshouses 46
Youth Hostel/Mill 47

Clunbury
- Church 33
- Hall 33

Clungunford
- Castle site 38, 39
- Church 39

Cockerell, Charles 14
Coleman, Revd T.B. 105
copper mining 66
Corbet, Walter 82

Corfton
- Mount Castle & Chapel 246
- Sun Inn 246

Cornewall, Frederick 245
Corvedale Brewery 246
Coston Manor 30
- moated site 30

Council in the Marches 2, 29
Craven, Dame Elizabeth 19
- William, 1st Earl 19

Craven Arms 17
- Hotel 26
- Land of Lost Content 27
- Secret Hills Discovery Centre 17, 27

Cressett family 140, 145
- Thomas 143

Cres(s)well, Richard & Anne 200

Daniel's Mill 152
Davenport, Henry 163
   Sharington 163
Davenport House 163, 164
de Bellême, Robert 149, 154, 160
de Castello, Herbert 85
de Furches, Robert 246
de Hopton family 35
de Ludlow, Laurence 19
de Say, Picot 33, 52
Diddlebury
   Church 243
   Delbury Hall & Park 245
Dudley, Robert, Earl of Leicester 191

Eardington Mill 156
East Grit mine 67, 69
Ecgfrith 43
Elizabeth I 55

Fitzalan family 52, 53
   John 55
   William 53
Forrester, Richard 150
Fortey, C. 11
Foster, F.W. 116
Fowler, Hodgson 13
Foxe, Charles 12, 13
Francis, Thomas 13

Gatacre family 171
Grit mine 67-69

Haughmond Abbey 90
Haycock, Edward 176
   John 176
   William 15
Heath
   Chapel 236, 237
   DMV 238
Helgot 119
Herbert fitz Helgot 119
Highley
   Church 180
   Colliery 185, 186
   Ship Inn 184
   Station 185
Hill, William 93
Hiorne, William & David 245
Hoarstones 65
Holdgate
   Church 118
   Castle 119
   DMV 119
Hopstone House 175
Hopton Castle 35-36
   Quarter 36
Howard, Henry, Earl of Northampton 46

Jones, Adrian 159

Kempson, F.R. 120

Ladywell mine 65, 67
Langland, William 188
Langley
   Chapel 113
   Hall & Gatehouse 114
   Park 114
lead mining 65, 66, 67, 72, 74, 77, 122
Lee, Sir Humphrey 109
   Sir Richard 109
Leese, Oliver 169
Leigh Level 67, 77
Leofric of Mercia 128
Llywelyn the Great 53, 82
Long Forest 82
Loughton Church 222
Lucye, Thomas 207
Ludlow 2
   Broad Gate 4
   Bull Inn 6
   Butter Cross 6
   Castle 2, 16
   Castle Lodge 4
   Church 2, 5
   Dinham House 16
   Feathers 7
   Great House 7

Palmers' Guild 5
Racecourse 8, 12
Raven Lane 4
Reader's House 6
town walls 2
Ludstone Hall 174
Lutwyche, Edward 122
Lydbury North estate 55

Mainwaring, Sir George 19
Prof. John 105
Marmion, Philip 85
Mawley Hall 192
Park 192
Merewalh 128
Mitchell's Fold 63
Tenement 63
More, Elinor 120, 121
Jasper 120, 121
Mary 120, 121
Richard 120, 121
Samuel (Parliamentary commander) 36
Samuel and Katherine (of Shipton) 121
More Arms pub 67
Mortimer, Hugh 160
Roger (d.1330) 2, 188
Morville
Church 137, 138

Hall 138, 145, 146
Much Wenlock 134-36
Ashfield House 136
Church 128, 134
Guildhall 135, 136
Priory 33, 122, 128-29, 226
Raynald's Mansion 136
Munslow, Richard 82
Mytton, Thomas 122

Nordy Bank 234
North, Gilbert 160
Norton, Bonham 222
Norton Camp 23

Oakly Park 15
gatehouse 14
Offa, King 41, 42
Offa's Dyke 41-43
possible watchtower 43
Old Grit mine 67, 68
Oldbury Church 158
Ovenpipe mine 72

Page, Russell 176
Parr, Katherine 205
Pemberton, Revd R.N. 105
Percy, Thomas 146
Perkins Beach mine 74
Phillips, Niall 17

Picklescott
Bottle and Glass 89
The Gate Hangs Well 96
Pickthorn moated site & DMV 198
Pope, Catherine 93
Roger 93
Portway, The 80
Pritchard, Thomas Farnolls 122, 206
Prynce, Richard 29
Pulverbatch Castle 85

Quatford 154
Castle 154

Ratlinghope Church & Priory 82, 93
Reaside Manor 195
Reinking, Lt Col 24
Reynolds, William 122
Rhys of Deheubarth 53
Rider vein 67
Rindleford Mill 166
Robins, Thomas, the Elder 163, 164

St Milburga 99, 128
Salvin, Anthony 219, 229
Scoltock, Samuel 115
Scory, Bishop 55
Seddon, J.P. 241
Severn, river 154, 183
Severn Valley Railway 155, 181

Country Halt 181
Shenstone, William 146, 163
Shipton
    Church 120, 121
    Hall 122
Shrewsbury Abbey 138
Shropshire Mines Trust 72
Sidbury Church 200
    The Batch 201
silver mining 66, 77
sin-eating 82
Smalman, Francis and Ellen 124
Smethcott
    Castle 95
    Church 95
    DMV 95
Smith, Francis, of Warwick 163, 192
    Sir Herbert 140
Smythe family 109, 110
    Sir Edward 115, 116
    Sir Joseph Edward 115
    Lady Mary 109
Spycer, Richard & Alice 171
Squilver vein 67
Stackford, Thomas 4
Stackhouse Acton, Frances 19
Stanton Lacy Church 10
Stanton Long Church 120
Stapeley Hill 67
    Cairn 64

Stiperstones 74-76
    Devil's Chair 75
Stitt 78
Stokesay
    Castle 18-20, 24
    Church 20
Stottesdon 197
    Church 203
    Hall Farm 198
    Pickthorn moated site & DMV 198
Sydney, Sir Henry 4

Tankerville mine 71-72
    Watson's Shaft 72
Tasker, John 116
Telford, Thomas 22, 26, 161, 188
Titterstone Clee 210-14
    hillfort & cairns 212, 214
    Incline 208
    mining/quarrying 208, 210
    radar installations 212, 214
Trilleck, Bishop 55
Tugford Church 239

Upton Cressett
    Church 142
    DMV 143
    Hall 140, 141

Vardy, George 75

Vernon, Henry 19

Walcot, Charles 206
    John 206
Weaver, Arthur 146
Wettleton, Battle of 24
White Grit mine 67, 68, 69
Whitmore, Sir John 174
    Sir William 160
Wigmore Abbey 82
Wilderhope Manor 124
Wilderley Castle 87
Wilding, Matthew 90
Wood Level 65, 66, 68
Woodhouse, Sir Michael 24, 36
Woolstaston
    Bowdlers House 92, 93
    Castle 92
    Church 93
    Hall 92, 93
Worfield
    Church 168
    Davenport House 163, 164
    Hallon House 167
    Lower hall 169

zinc mining 66, 77
Zouche, Lord Edward 121

Also from Logaston Press

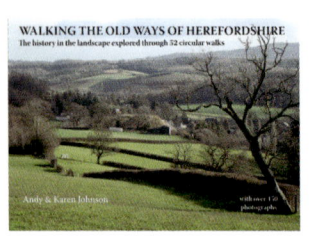

Walking the old ways of Herefordshire: the history in the landscape explored through 52 circular walks
by Andy and Karen Johnson
Paperback, 384 pages, over 450 colour photographs and 53 maps
ISBN 978-1-906663-86-5   £12.95

Each walk passes or visits historical features about which background information is given. These include churches, castle sites, deserted medieval villages, landscaping activity, quarrying, battle sites, dovecotes, hillforts, Iron Age farmsteads, Saxon dykes and ditches, individual farms and buildings, squatter settlements, almshouses, sculpture, burial sites, canals, disused railway lines – to name but a few, and including some that can only be reached on foot. The walks have also been chosen to help you explore Herefordshire from remote moorland to the historic streets of the county's towns, and of course Hereford itself. The walks range from 2½ to 9½ miles in length, with the majority being between 3½ and 6½ miles. The combination of photographs and historical information makes this more than simply a book of walks, but also a companion to and celebration of Herefordshire.

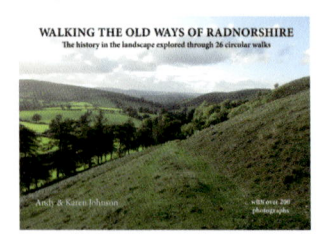

Walking the old ways of Radnorshire: the history in the landscape explored through 26 circular walks
by Andy and Karen Johnson
Paperback, 176 pages with over 200 colour photographs and 26 maps
ISBN 978-1-910839-07-2   £12.95

Each walk passes or visits historical features about which some background information is given, including churches, nonconformist chapels, castle sites, dykes, tumuli and other prehistoric remains, Roman forts, a battlefield, medieval houses, spas, upland farming systems, drovers' roads, squatter settlements, inns and a dismantled railway line. Several of these features can only be reached on foot. Some walks follow river valleys whilst many more wander Radnorshire's rolling hills and provide expansive views. Others explore the county's towns and their nearby landscape. The walks range from 3½ to 10½ miles in length, the majority being between 4 and 7½ miles.

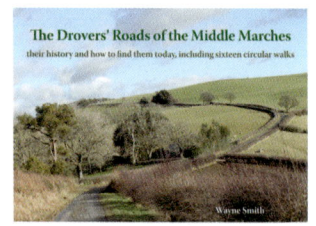

The Drovers' Roads of the Middle Marches: their history and how to find them today, including 16 circular walks
by Wayne Smith
Paperback, 176 pages, 50 colour and 12 b/w photos, 17 maps.
ISBN 978-1-906663-74-2   £10

This is the story of the men who until as recently as the 1930s used to walk with their sheep and cattle out of Wales along the ancient trackways to the markets and fairs of England. The journeys were carefully judged – too slow and the expenses of feeding and accommodating men and beasts would mount, too fast and the animals would lose condition. The drovers were often entrusted with commissions and even money to be taken to London, a practice from which the first banks developed. Wayne Smith describes the routes the drovers took, and includes sections in 16 circular walks, all illustrated with his own photographs.

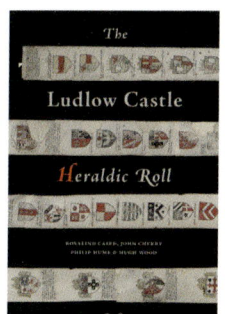

The Ludlow Castle Heraldic Roll
by Rosalind Caird, John Cherry, Philip Hume & Hugh Wood
Paperback with flaps, 256 pages, colour illustrations
ISBN 978-1-910839-37-9   £12.95

The roll provides an excellent vehicle for explaining the entire history of the castle and of the Council of the Marches ... An enjoyable and accessible guide, one which contains everything that might be wished. To round it off, the complete roll is illustrated on the fold-out front cover, inside of which is a reconstruction of the Elizabethan chapel. – **The Antiquaries Journal**

Dating from *c*.1580, the roll contains 42 coats of arms of the owners of Ludlow Castle and members of the Council in the Marches of Wales, from the eleventh century to the sixteenth century. This book tells the story of the Roll – of Sir Henry Sidney who commissioned the Roll, the context of its making, its close relationship to Ludlow Castle's Round Chapel and the people whose coats of arms it contains.

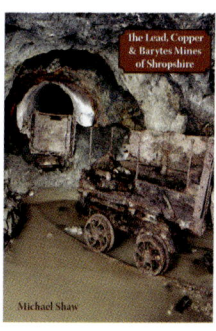

The Lead, Copper and Barytes Mines of Shropshire
by Michael Shaw
Paperback, 320 pages with over 200 b/w illustrations
ISBN 978-1-906663-09-4   £12.95

From the late 1700s to the mid-1900s Shropshire became famous for its lead mines. The first few chapters cover the early history of Shropshire's mines, then look at the products and what they were used for, and how the mines were financed and worked — tales of boom and bust are numerous. The following chapters then give an account of each mine in some detail, mines being grouped together by area. Michael Shaw has scoured the hillsides of Shropshire, spent years researching records and books, and talked to surviving miners and members of the Shropshire Caving and Mining Club who have investigated many of the shafts and levels. The result is this extensively researched book, copiously illustrated with photographs, maps and plans.

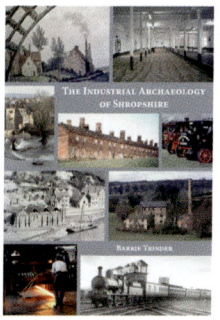

The Industrial Archaeology of Shropshire
by Barrie Trinder
Paperback, 304 pages with over 140 colour and 70 b/w illustrations, mainly photographs
ISBN 978-1-910839-05-8   £15

This is a completely revised and updated edition of that first published in 1996, and now includes over 140 colour illustrations, together with 70 in black and white. Shropshire was one of the birthplaces of Britain's Industrial Revolution, and the Ironbridge Gorge features heavily in this book, for its mines, the variety of its manufactures, for its role in the Severn Navigation and for its ingenious canals and early railways. The county's other coalfields, near Oswestry, around Shrewsbury, in the Wyre Forest and on the Clee Hills are analysed in some detail, which gives perspective to the achievements of those who worked in and around Coalbrookdale. Industry also flourished in the Shropshire countryside, with the use of water power, brick-making, and industries related to food production. Market towns housed foundries, coachbuilders and later railway engineering works, as well as such traditional industries as corn milling, tanning and malting. Then there are the imposing monuments of lead mining around the Stiperstones; textile manufacturers from humble cottages to the mighty iron-framed flax mills in Shrewsbury; and the county's roads, canals and main line railways.

Also from Logaston Press

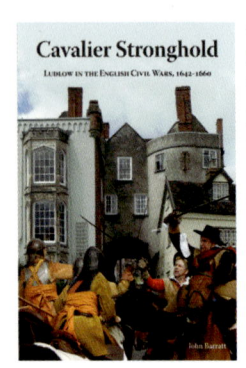

**Cavalier Stronghold:
Ludlow in the English Civil Wars, 1642-1660**
by John Barratt
Paperback, 128 pages, 40 b/w illustrations
ISBN 978-1-906663-77-3   £10

The Royalist stronghold of Ludlow lay far away from the tramp of armies, but the Royalists saw it as a source of funds and manpower, which gave rise to growing resentment. The infamous Royalist capture of the Parliamentarian Hopton Castle and then Brampton Bryan in the spring of 1644 saw them at the zenith of their powers, but their triumph was short-lived. The defeat at Marston Moor saw remnants of Royalist units operating without much central authority in the Marches, which in turn helped to bring about the Clubmen risings. Spring 1646 saw the siege of Ludlow itself.

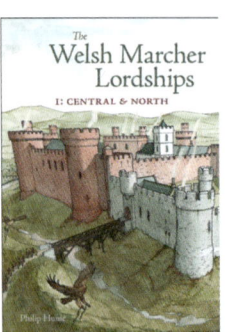

**The Welsh Marcher Lordships, Volume 1:
Central & North**
by Philip Hume
Paperback with flaps, 320 pages, *c.*200 colour illustrations
ISBN 978-1-910839-45-4   £15.99

Philip Hume has set a high standard in developing a new popular history of the lordships of the Welsh March. – **Paul Dryburgh**

This volume covers the traditional Welsh counties of Radnorshire, Montgomeryshire, Denbighshire, Flintshire, together with the adjacent lordships in Shropshire and Herefordshire, that also became Marcher lordships. The book describes the distinctive features and powers of the Marcher lordships, and how they evolved in the context of the significant events in Wales and the Marches between 1066 and 1282, that shaped their development. Richly illustrated with maps, family trees, photographs of castles, abbeys and other artefacts, the book provides a particularly rich account of the fascinating history of the Welsh borderlands during this period.

The Story of Bishop's Castle
edited by David Preshous, George Baugh, John Leonard, Gavin Watson and Andrew Wigley
Paperback, 176 pages, over 40 colour and 35 b/w illustrations, mainly photographs
ISBN 978-1-910839-08-9   £12.95

Bishop's Castle is a small market town in Shropshire, 22 miles south-west of Shrewsbury, and within two miles of the Welsh Border. It grew up around a Norman castle built by a bishop of Hereford, received a Royal Charter from Queen Elizabeth I in 1573, and enjoyed a colourful political life as a rotten or pocket borough. It maintains its historical role as an important focal point in a sparsely-populated rural area, offering a wide range of facilities and services. This book, written by a number of local authors, offers readers a broad view of the origins and historical development of a rather remarkable town.